A
N
G
E
L
I
C

W
I
N
G
S

I am the voice of Peace.
I am the voice of Grace.

Hear us speak in harmonic unison.

TWIN FLAMES' REVELATION
OF THE MERIDIAN SYSTEM

Purple Yang
Yin Tang

德豐觀

www.AscendingHall.com

Additional Titles From Tao Huang:

Laoism

The Secret Teachings of the Tao Te Ching

Spiritual Anatomy
Your Journey Through Nehemiah's Dream Gates

Additional Titles from Yin Tang:
Galaxy of Phoenix
Book I: Ontoo Neida Division Seventeen

ISBN: 9780978684525
LCCN: 2007934820

ANGELIC WINGS
Table of Contents

Dedications:

To those who have suffered through the joy of love,

and the help from Gill Holland and Mary Molnia.

To Sarah.

Wish the fire

becomes eternal

firs for All souls

12-9-12

Contract from one Gender to another Gender (From Eve to Adam, NuWa to Fuxi, Grace to Peace, 22 to 11):

No matter how much you break my heart or how far I leave you, spiritually and physically, we are undeniably tied by this moment and the past moments of human history. No matter how much darkness seeks for us and no matter how far the entire world pushes us against and apart from each other, we cannot escape from ourselves. Even if I am wrong and you are wrong and we both wrong to each other and wrong to the rest of the world, what can never be taken, is the pure intention that begin this process of evolution that starts with the two original seeds left behind by the phoenix factor of the twin flames (they burn up to leave behind the eggs: the seeds). The evolution will one day spread to humanity. Through all the disappointment, pain and grief from previous years to previous hours, I cannot, could not cry until now. I hate being here, but I must be here. My greatest enemy is myself. No one can take it away from me because it is my greatest friend.

We are crying for ourselves because all is lost and all is given. I cry for our exhaustion and my love that is thick and full when I am alone and miserable. As Eve does when searching for her Adam.

A resolution will be made and it will be peaceful and it will be a compromise. I cry for my Light Father and my Love Mother because without them, my flesh hurts me, it burns me, my soul aches. After these two violent abortions, our children, the books and works, shall be produced fruitfully and left within the hands of our Earth parents until the time is right and the fruits are ripe.

One book is Ara and is meant to stay with the Earth parents: the spiritual community (father's side) and the Chinese community (mother's side). The second book, Angelic Wings (Drake) is meant to stay in the hands of heaven and we must do little to affect it. Every little detailed action of that book must be scrutinized. Everything about it can spontaneously abort until it is finished because of it's unspeakable position in the Universe.

Like the Virgin Mary, Phoenix was asked to carry Drake and her love for him was a burden, but without love, how could a newborn survive? Is it the mother? or the father? Who will commit the manuscript to heaven? Because the true potential, and true meaning of the book (Angelic Wings) can only be written in the hearts of the individuals who have read it. It is through these words that a new piece of heavenly light can shine at them. Each reading of the book, like all books, is different and special for each individual but the content is the strong and powerful vehicle. Like Rosi (Galaxy of Phoenix) who climbed into Marcuno's car at the airport, like Neo in The Matrix who took the red pill, each must give themselves wholely on a journey, and only after they succeed in losing themselves completely (Like in the Book of Job), will they be given back to them afterwards.

Pure and loving sacrifice. The hardest question is, who, where, what, and when to sacrifice to and for? And what is merely greed that tries to absorb all we have to give?

This is our heavenly contract, this is our heavenly marriage.

CHAPTER 1:

THE LIPS OF MY MOTHER

As my double-door closed eyes are opening my sunny being to the world, they lower their lenses from the sky-roofed ceiling to a moony creature in front of me: my mother's lips. This strange scissor moves up and down as it opens; lines as it stretches toward her jaws; and rounds to reveal the chuckling hole buried deep in the back: a place unknown, unapproachable, and mysterious. These two skillful pieces are ready to swallow me up into the darkness; closing me up again, for good.

These double-lidded lips are fully textured: sometimes they wane from glossy skin to tender meat; other times they wax from wrinkled earth to cracking clays. If her cloudy face looms around her gloomy lips, the lines from both ends of the moon arches are sealed perfectly into a stone-carved denial. This is her sky deniable: "no-no." Reading her lips is more difficult than detecting light; following their clipped messages is more tactical than perceiving her lively reflection; responding to their unbeknown rattling is more challenging than appeasing my uncontrollable hunger.

Never touched by lipsticks, my mother's lips are decorated with chopsticks or even her fingers when serving on demand. Before she could handle to feed me with chopsticks, she would hand the lip of a big bowl close to me, nail it into my fishy mouth, letting my gums detect the temperature of liquid food. Then she changed the rotation of the rimmed bowl by lifting her stationed elbow, either allowing the fluid to ooze into my stomach, or forcing her elbowing push, her grasping bowl, her hot or cold fluid, all at once, into my eye-crying, nose-running, mouth-tightening and body trembling vessel. This was bad enough but the worst of all was my burning or icy tongue.

The best part of this natural approach was that I would control the time so that I could regulate the temperature of liquid food. If so, I would spend my time playfully, not for the purpose of consuming food but for the sake of having fun. With my mouth in the liquid, I blew a force (something producing power in me) out of me to see the bubbling liquid escaping on the surface. Again and again, on and on, until both mom and I became really amused and laughed. Truly tired, earthly exhausted; liquid forgave me, mom forgot me, and I forged into a deep sleep.

Besides dealing liquid with a mouthy bowl, my mom's mouth would handle the heavy, dry, tough stuff. She would chew the noodles she cooked or crackers she baked, in her mouth. This was rare stuff; big family mouths usually made them disappear from the hidden place before her action took place. She would bite them with her teeth like cracking a nut and chew them with her entire face like plowing a field. Then she would spice it up with her attentive eyes (I knew she was hungry too, but my stomach was worthier than her working hunger), expel her mouthed liquid on her right index finger, and coax it into my mouth. Afterwards, she would dish-wash her mouth and towel-dry my and her lips with her hand, reinvigorating her food grinding and feeding practice.

As she held me in her chest, I began to approach her sky-high face. I noticed that the distinctive line between her merging face and lips forms a pearl-diving curve in the top middle. This cute curve then echoes the two huge hairy windy tunnels with the aid of her nosy tip, chasing and blowing madly my little sprouting hair. Surrounding this curve, the waving lines of floating watery meat approach me like volcanic lava scorching my mere existing sensibility. Separating and merging again on both moon arched ends, her lip-line creates a line in the middle, a mouth within her mouth. She never extended this new line, this new mouth, into a full practice, like movie stars sucking you in with a "hi" and waving you out with a "bye." This line works in a magic way and this mouth satisfies an arena of necessary means. The lower rim of her mouthed line rises upward like a proud and arrogant tide deflecting the shallow space arched beneath. This falling tide rises up again, creating a teasing line in the middle and two dimples on both ends. The uprising lower jaw denounces the tide permanently with its pubic bone likened tip. This is my law, this chipping cheekbone. This tiger jaw is ready to pin, nail, and crush high above my little body, way beyond the power and protection of the fleeing ceiling.

As my fearful expecting eyes are resting comfortably between her arms, between her breasts, my face skims her breast-filled smell as my curbing lips are grounded quietly and peacefully upon her wellspring nipple. My sleeping eyes are tiding again into my already experienced milky womb.

As my lips are coated with her white cream, I notice that her lips are like a flooded river, a sun-bleached surface, a swampy marsh. This thick marsh, roots my feeling to her swinging elbows, as her tapping and tingling hands claw tightly between my knobby shoulders and thinly twisted chest. The feelings inside me become purgative, delusive, and evasive. Her lips taste bitchy spicy, with an intensity more than the combination of her modulating weight and my dangling weight, and an expression more demanding than her already disciplined weight I must bear.

It seems to me that these two lifelong warranted weapons are made out of strong trees and salty noodles. The noisy winds from others do not defeat them, smelling leaves do not debilitate them, seasonal food does not demolish them, and frightening light cannot destroy them. They are forever there, constantly interacting. When stressed, they are as tight as ropes; when raged, they bite with protruding neck muscles; when depressed, they shy away like a waxing moon.

Judging beyond the lips, I come in contact with her jungle-like teeth. These teeth are symmetrical but uneven, standing straight but not uniform, happily drumming but not rhythmic, gladly white-juice-pasted but not thick-mucus-tainted. They even produce small drops of rain when they are open to you, ready to attack you like a fish-tail bubbling. My mother's teeth are not snow-white, pearl-bright, or gold-rimmed. I cannot fathom where they came from: some are rusty, others are rarely brushed; some hang loosely, others stand tough; some are carnal pride, others are chimney filthy. They are somewhere between dusty sand and salted riverbed, somehow resembling rocks and stones, somewhat comparable to bones and tails.

Her teeth do not tell you whether she is happy or sad, they just reveal. When they are wheeling through my fragile skin, I experience a mixed feeling between an animal-licking and a worm-walking. Creating a rich mixture of enraged nailing and cool bathing, a blending texture between a dog's barking and cat's meowing, and compressing between a tiger's jaw and a dragon's claw.

My mother's teeth have never touched toothpaste, a dash of salt is good enough to rinse off her bad flavor. Emotional vapor is her best dental practice.

Hidden from these two giants, her mouth and teeth, is her voice educated from her tongue. She is illiterate but talkative: cloudy and clear, forceful and noisy. Trapped in a well at the age of 16, her hearing was drowned and she developed a skill of reading other's lips and barking, yelling and defending. She cannot detect invisible rumbling thunder but is very good at lightning and earthshaking. The entire village and its sky overhead knew her voice well. She does not know how to talk softly, tenderly, or dreamingly. She voices like a judge and blares like a killer. Her virtue, love and sacrifice are canceled by the timeless karmic debts contributed by her un-tongued noises. She is a great mother and her deeds are virtuous, but I could not image her speaking with a nectar-producing tongue. It is absent, unknown to me, that horseshoe of her bitching tongue.

Out of all, I remember her love, more than my heart could bear. I remember her motherly deeds, more than food can spare. I remember her care, more than a king could dare. But what I remembered most vividly is the sound of her voice, more demanding than a rattlesnake, sadder than a fallen soldier, more depressed than a billionaire. Her echoing truth is more

sorrowful than her constant need to borrow money and food from others for my schooling, more burdensome than my shoulder-laden departure, more heart-breaking than my homecoming with an empty stomach, icy feet, and exposed toes. Her verbal evidence is more comforting than dying from stealing, more hopeful than studying, more horrifying than a nighttime mare.

She dragged her pain-wracked body through the years like a naked earth, with her sagging breasts, gray hair, stone-filled and knife cutting bones, heart-broken breath, and her long labored worn-out body: all the possible heavy burdens and suffering pains of a mother.

I could not remember her tongue being sweet: like a singer talking on the radio, dancing on the TV, and performing on a stage. I could not equate her tongue with sugar, chocolate candy, or anything sweet. I did not have this; but I feel her sweetness in my heart, her tenderness in my gut, her generosity in my acts of giving, and her virtuousness in my upbringing.

Even as I peer through expensive colorful dresses to seek her love through other women, she is hiding. Even as I stare at hunger-bleached and love-haunted lips among many wealthy ladies, hers are truthful. Even as I witness age-preserved teeth of countless others, hers are accountable. From what source did her love, strength, endurance and forbearance arise, I do not know. They are a part of her love, her sweetness inside me: ever present yet ancient, like grandmother's blue sky; rich, like silk; smelling, like spirits.

Examining my own behavior through my crying for love and hunger for care, my mother is talking behind my back, sitting side by side with me as I am reading: protecting my strength, my will and my deep seeded love. I forgive her yelling voice, it echoed long before the pain began: this age old shadow. I forgive her not being fully present like a wealthy mother, a rich Taitai (lady); her image is my love for all. I forgive her non-sugary tongue; it comforts my sadness, looses my madness, and overcomes my depression. I forgive her not making me perfect; I am always perfect in her smiling eye and can do no wrong in her delightful heart. Lastly and for all, I forgive my own bad mouth; I cannot stop telling the truth, reporting the news, jumping with happiness, and climbing onto her chest with a gentle wind, to fill my heart with a sweet dream.

As my dream could recall, I was never regretful about my discomforting body woven and milked by my mother's beloved lips. I had never once visited a doctor, so far, and never want to because my beloved mother has been my doctor. When I was only a few years old under a severe attack of high fever I laid on the flat cold surface of a clay-squared bed. My poor flu-inflamed body could not balance between the raging heat produced by fever and the boned cold I could not breathe out.

On the third sunny afternoon, as glistening lights were shooting straight through the window and onto my bed's right side, she began talking to me with a nothing-happened-and-no-big-deal attitude. My mother started her magic healing practice. She had been at my side through two sleepless nights, never closing her eyes. I sensed her healing power as I saw her worry and despair metamorphose into peace and strength.

My eye on her eagerly, I noticed that she held a bowl of cold water in her left hand and three pairs of chopsticks in her right, ready to pick my illness out as a cosmic meal. Without a word her power lowered me into an acceptance and confirmed me with a hope: a never forgotten event. Like a peaceful ocean and a sleepless river, her lips began to show signs of power and majesty. Undetectable at first, I anxiously awaited something real. Then her lips began their slow, steady motion and her neck was charged with deep peaceful murmuring sounds I never heard before. Her lips were calling like animals, singing like birds, talking like fish. She seemed strangely animated, unlike the person I knew. She became one single operating machine, a single pill, a total magic.

Perplexed, I paid closer attention to her mystic performance. Her face began to drum from tranquil singing to mad ringing, becoming the thunderous sounds of a raging ocean, a swift river. My entire being was resonating and echoing harmoniously with the sounds of mother, ocean, earth and sky. I was entranced as her voice became louder and louder until I could no longer hear. The flaming heat in my body rose and vaporized with her chanting. Suddenly her body disappeared leaving only the resonance of her chanting and singing lips: her living healing being. At the same time this living being rang with the moving sticks traveling and orbiting in the bowl of water. This familiar bowl now spoke to me like my own sensation. The sticks, stirring water, vibrated through my awareness and channeled into my being, racing with my meridians, chatting with my nerves and somehow calming the hidden beings in my bones.

Gradually, the sounds quieted down. Only the scattering chopsticks stationed in the bowl were in my dream-like awareness. While half sleeping and half awake, I experienced a cold shower pouring down on me. The vaporized water stirred by the sticks; then a spring like charge flooded forcefully out of the bowl and mom's mouth gushing through her cleansing teeth and spitting lips. The room was filled with her raining water.

With this cool and breathtaking sensation, I felt the departure of my mother's body. I heard the sounds of a door opening and water splashing on the ground outside the house, taking my existence into a full sleep.

The following morning I woke feeling alive, healthy and refreshed. The healing sound of water still filled my being, but was no longer flooding. My urine was light yellow, creamy white and snow light, cleansing the intense heat from my body. As I peed into the ground, I gave humble thanks for the magic power of mom's healing still ringing in the earth's floor.

Returning toward the doorway, I noticed that the bowl was upside down, mouthing firmly on the ground beside the wall. It's partner, the chopsticks. were standing against the wall, facing daylight and producing six distinctive right-angled shadows behind them. Watchfully, they waved a friendly "OK" to me and I returned a grateful "Hi" to them. "Who did most of the work, mom or you guys?" I questioned them. They were relaxed, like soldiers; unified, as a team; still battling, like needles; withdrawing, as if nothing had been done. They were accountable, then forgetful. Why did mom use six of them, no more no less? They must cure six sicknesses, please the six senses I misused, and pick out the six useless entities from my being. I became the dish, noodles and salt for them to be picked, quickly, to feed the hungry beings. I certainly wasn't the stove, particularly the stowing caldron refining enlightening elixir! I could only ground myself as peacefully, perfectly, calmly and firmly as the bowl with the light sparkling through, its fine surface glistening.

Seven days later, the bowl was back in use in the kitchen, continuing its normal chore of serving food. With this bowl, my existence in my family and hometown was terminated, out of China, into the promising dreamland of America, only to feel the empty bowl of my body claying my empty heart. After 33 years of wondering, it connects me inexorably to the empty land of earth. The empty space of my heart is filled with the eternal love of mothers. In my heart, mom's love never dies in my existing heart, even though at times seemingly remote and hidden. If a mother dies, how could a child be born, smiling, alive and well? I must comfort the helpless little boy within me and deny the living shadows that place a wall between us.

Her blessings on me are more powerful than her birthing of me, more magical than her uneducated tongue, and more beautiful than her unpainted lips. These two distinctive lines separate me from serving her aging and dying, yet, the blessing coming out of them opens the sky line between light smiling and water showering, expands the life line between crying birth and helpless death. These two of her living ingredients are always open for spirits to travel between their living breath and their shadow-breathing. They carry the light in, life out; heart in, love out; knowing in, knowledge out.

Between the birthing womb of my mother and the speaking tone of my motherland, my mother's lips connect mystically to the two rivers in China, the Yellow River north and the Long River south. Between my mother's lips are the bones of her livelihood biting through life and cracking through death. Between these two rivers are the marriage of two minds (sun and moon) and the crafty power of five senses. The pearl-dived curve on her top lip touches my thoughts with the power of the River Chart: the visual map of I Ching. While her displaying lip in the south fashions the five elemental senses upon my resonating fingers: to make sense of my internal five organic and planetary beings.

As my mother's lipped blessing transpires her eyed flashing, I dream during the day as my body plays on and on, and I pray during the night as my mind dances over and over. My play is her lips' blessing, and my dance is her heart's singing. The lip-blessed play is so long, so touching, that my bodily awareness is transcended. The heart-song dance is so deep, so detecting, that my thoughts disappear: only her senses dream in me, read me; only her love shines through me, needs me.

Her singing tongue turns into my spelling words, and her ringing teeth become my bone-cracking deeds. In exchange, my words return to her senses, my deeds reward her long-lived love. Her senses will never die because they are alive and well in my body: her creation. Her love never dies because her spirit never dies: they are the love of my true liberation. May my mother's lips become my blessing love! May her spirit become my guiding light!

CHAPTER ONE

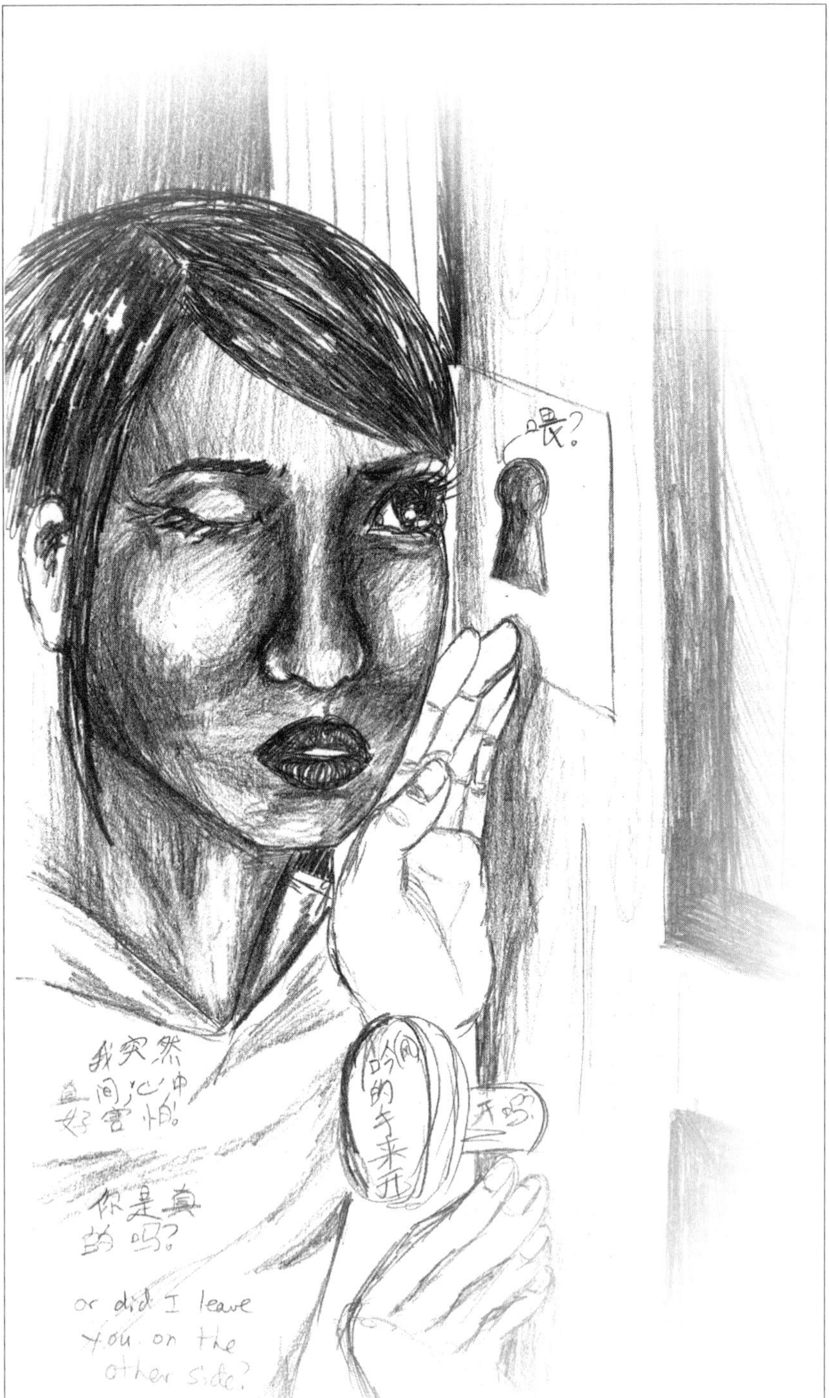

CHAPTER 2:

BLOW ILL OFF THE BONE

Breathing Into Life

Pathology

This was what I was, and how I felt about myself, before I aged into magic 18, and long before I had entered onto the path. I was not tall, I was not rich, I was not handsome, and I was not healthy. These are the four wheels driving my pathology ahead of any other logistic lodges or conceivable knowledge.

I was not tall.

Hi, my name is Tao. Sometime people pronounce Tao as taow, tail or toe. Who cares about one's name after a while! Even the emperor's new clothes are as naked as a newborn. What else matters aside from a single bean, tall being, skinning bin, and flying beam? I was installed by the family name of Huang, which means yellow: sounds like screaming louder but yelling lower. Whenever I call myself Tao, I feel Tall, good and very proud. Yet, wherever I search for myself, I yelled at me with a lower voice that could only be heard by my inner self.

I was a premature baby, only seven month old, as I did not want to be stored and stuffed inside my mom's oceanic and Asiatic womb any longer than what the gestation could register for from the sky. Thus the first name I received was not Tao but man-sheng, with *man* being full-blown or maturity, and *sheng* meaning productive or birth. My mother wished for me to become mature and productive, a dear blessing. In Chinese culture, babies receive their nicknames before they start off to school. These oldest names reflect the earliest calls and highest wishes from parents, family or communities at large, where the powers bestowed in these names can change any bad karma into good fortune, and raise the vibration of each cursed spell into harmonic bell. Nicknames are, in the Chinese mind, the initial taste for life, for the wishes and blessings of family and society. It is like, in the West, by saying "Hi" of that pure tone and authentic fragrance, where the iceberg freezing the communication gap is melt down, and the test for the juicy taste rings the true to both souls.

My name is Yin. My grandmother named me after a Japanese princess from a movie. Yin is not the yin in "yin-yang" rather it is a mouth radical with the character for "today." It means "to speak," "dictation," "orator," or "poetic." My family name, Tang, means "soup." Plain and simple but with a further expounding principle and sybolism that has been lost through time. It is rumored to have connected with the past alchemists whose importance have faded through time.

I was inside my mother for longer than need be. Many days past the day that I was do, my poor mother was in labor all night. The morning after, around 6:30 am, a different doctor came into her room and exclaimed, "Oh my gosh! You still haven't given birth yet?" After that, it was decided that I was to be a cesarean baby. Some may think I am lazy, but no matter the reason, I did not want to leave my mother's womb.

I have two middle names. The first one was legislated in my Family Tree Book, as all the boys in my generation have the same genetic quote (never the girls after Confucius). This middle name is Zhi, meaning intelligence. Zhi rules kidneys, ears, bones, north and black, with the mystical tortoise as animal and astral totem. I never made through this name, as Confucius Mind did not agree with me of being suitable for an educated intellectual scholar, an enslaved dutiful officer. As a result I never did get my Ph. D certificate.

It is now rare for girls to recive generational names. The girls on my father's side had Xue ("snow") as their generational name. My father's daughters did not carry on the tradition.

As you might know, the lineage is more solid than a village in Oriental cultures. In order to line up ages within or between the generations, a Family Tree Book is established to reveal the line among boys and ferment the wine for ancestry. Unlike the Hebrew Bible that speaks for the entire twelve tribes in the Jewish blood, each long-existing Chinese family has its own Tree Book. For example, the Confucius Family Tree Book has existed even since his name was established for his family and in society. It is the longest family tree book in the world. The Confucius Family Tree Book updates in each 30-year period, and revises thoroughly in every 60-year cycle. Combined with karmic code, each boy born under such a family tree-root is a valuable asset and useless number as well. Only few individuals can rise above and beyond the family tree branches, to freely demonstrate one's character and power. This is how the individual egos are killed to promote cultural substances. The hidden purpose of Family Tree Book is to destroy the individual ego and personal freedom, promoting only genetic and celestial power.

The same is prevalent in some hispanic families as well.

The expansion and replacement of a generational name in a Family Tree Book is the religious lineage. When a person is initiated, the name of a specific lineage under an organization replaces the generational family name. For example, in Taoist tradition, each founder crucified his followers with a verse, written before he departs upon the path of the enlightenment. Each Chinese character in the verse represents an ordained generational name, only to replace family lineage, to line up the age from biological to spiritual. The student gets to keep his family name, as well as his first name.

When I was initiated, my master in the Green Mountain replaced my family lineage name of Zhi or intelligence with the Dragon Gate lineage of Chong or honor. I still kept my family root, because I was already bleached by my family blood; and I still kept my first or personal name, because I am the blessings for my family and society, earth and sky. With the change, I am no longer a familiar biological member but a collective spiritual member. "Drop your cross, and follow me" is the best explanation of this. Since my biological blood is rooted in my flesh and my last name, the moment I drop my family lineage, I am inside the white spiritual blood.

The changing of the lineage from biological to spiritual is to change the red blood into white blood. It took me a long time to understand this. The capacity of a soul inherited in red blood is different from the capacity of a spirit embedded in white blood. Blood textures a soul as tribal maker, and soul is tinctured by spirit as a nature brand. Soul has an emotional entity and astral influence, while spirit is free traveling from matter to matter, matrix to matrix. Most of men can rise into a family head, but few can advance further into a spiritual head. Many a family makes up a community, many a religious congregation teams up a religion as a belief system, and many an enlightened spirits maintain the human consciousness. Only one person can be the president in a country and only one monk at a time can be the Pope in Christianity.

Equally, how many family bosses care about what is happening in society or specific governmental branches? How many souls are daring enough to share their creative spirits through inventive products and mechanical goods? My biological lineage wants me to shine for my family, and my spiritual lineage wants me to smile for humanity. I then scarify myself to obtain physical or artificial gold for my family; but I am already sanctified by the light and spiritual gold within. To buy with blood the physical gold exhausts and extinguishes my life; but to awake the spirit-gold within me and shine with it is the eternal freedom. I am very well familiar with my family blood and I am one with the light world.

Linguistically speaking, Zhi is structured with a *sun* stroke below igniting the *knowledge* stroke on top. While the "Chong" character is combined between a *mountain* stroke on top and *devotional honor* at bottom. As such, from laminating the knowledge to honoring the mountain, the highest crowning title is no longer man-made, but earth-mounted. I have to be smart and knowledgeable for my family lineage Zhi, and I must honor what the natural height of each Mother Earth's mount in order to make peace with my little height. The height of my head and the power of my crown are nothing when I see the height of a magnificent mountain, and its crowning dome.

My heavenly derived middle name appeared to me in a dream and I spent the following day searching in multiple Han Yu dictionaries and online. It appeared to me before I had learned Tao's middle name. Like "Chong," it has a mountain radical atop, but below, it had the charactor for "edible products": shi. The meaning is one that is unclear, but it is hinted that the name might have some connection with Parvati. In my dream, there was fog around the foot of a mountain which told me it would take years of meditation before I would be enlightened with the knowledge of my ultimate spiritual destiny.

The numerical value of 26 was very interesting and, equally, significant in my personal life. I was ordained at age 26, with a 26th generational name, followed by 2600 some-year-old master Lao Zi, to install the power of the Mystic Vessel, or 26th hexagram in the *I Ching*, playing with souls instead the Animal Vessel: the 9th hexagram.

Growing up with a name Tao, being short was my first hatred toward my parents. I was always in the end of the tail when the classmates were called to stand in a line. My eyes were below others' throat or nose, even on the level of a peach-treat chest, when I looked straight at them. This angle of projecting lowered my shoulder and ego further down to my toes and shoes, a terrible bend to my neck. My kids have the same problem. I am hoping they can hate me more for their own liberation journey.

I was not rich.

Situated at the central Yellow Plateau of China, my hometown was totally dusty and semi-naked, due to the deforestation and seasonal storms. It rains little and snows light annually. But if a thundering storm accumulates, the entire topsoil would be washed away, which answers why the Yellow River is one of the most dust-contained rivers in the world. The only wealth is dusty earth, gusty wind, and musty light. Surrounded by the yellowish veil, spring brings in the storming and dusty wind, as the fall installs the dangling clouds and recalls the hungry throats.

Night is beautiful. The golden Moon glows above the golden Earth, to veil a bluish yellow in the air, with crowned peaks above, and mysterious valleys below. Or, total darkness. So black and thick is the moonless night that the only chance for me to go to an outdoor bathroom was opening the door and peeing on the courtyard by closing my eyes and controlling my fear.

The first community my village was assigned was called Bright Well. Maybe this had to do with my mother's trouble of being almost drowned in a well at age 16. A heavy price had already paid for this community from my family, collectively: such as one being punished as a landlord, several deaths from childbirth, a criminal, and even gravesite dispute before I marched to the wild western world. When I left China around 28, Guardian Wind was the newly assigned name. It combined my hometown and my mother's hometown into a community. Guardian Wind blew the final goodbye wave for me to leave my precious homeland, which birthed into the jadewinds publishing company established a few years ago, to reflect the language of a crystal heart.

Being told by my Taoist godfather, I have a crystal heart and my fate is resting on the wings of a "meticulous wind."

I was not handsome.

Adrenal passion and bloody muscles were the merits given to handsome lads taller than me in height, stronger than me in physical force, more lustful than me towards girly flowers. All the good-looking girls were chasing after tall boys, or looking towards wealthy families, to climb up their social or political ladders. I was left alone without a mate until I experienced my first sacred union at age 24. Why does the masculine beauty have such as a description—handsome--hand upon or off some?

Pressured by the American "sex sells everything" atmosphere, I lost mine shortly before my 18th birthday.

"Due duel duet dude Duke, hand me some of your cash, Bash. Splash, and lush to the lash!
Hand on me so I can land on and around you! Can you hand the sum without losing the some or missing the summer?"
"What about the girls hungry for the sum? It lends a hand to them selling their flesh-land."

All males are forever searching for their due days, duel dates, during the dates, to pay for all kinds of fine dues. Men must be busy with their hands, since that is the reasonable result described and scaled by women. If men have some, God has other; and if men owe some, God owns all! Poor men, poor me! I sit here laughing with glee!

I was not healthy.

I had multi-symptoms near the end of high school: gray hair on my temples as if ghosts had whitened my ring of throne; stomachache because of poor or mal-nutrition; arthritis on my knees and fingers (to answer: at least one woman married into my family lineage would die from arthritis); and insomnia since darkness was the curse. It further ate my dream, as fortune was away from my sleep. Is life sick or flesh ill? Is our mind the seeker or our body the eel? Mind must be thick with skull so that body can feel the fill thrilled by billing skills!

Diagnosis:

Three exams, towards 3% to 5% of college enrollment

During my senior year at high school, in 1978, only three or so percent of high school graduates nationwide could attend a state-run, tuition-free college in China. Before being accepted, we had to pass three passes, which were local school, provincial and national exams. Before an ex-am could explain an excuse, exercise already exiled the exam. Thus, an exam means before am begins the fresh mind, and after pm relaxes the exhaustion, so that teachers and students can have some thing for exchange. This is called passing the mass to become the Mass. Not wanting to farm (peasant) or harm (soldier) the land, or be free like a migrating bird, attending college was my only way out of my hometown. My grade turned out to be OK, as my migraine extended from social brain into mine grain, which is my brain. English Major grayed my brain but migrated eventually my head from East to West, perpendicular to what birds migrate, back and forth between North and South. Opposite from me. I migrated West at the age of three and spent the years catching up with the language that swallowed me whole with their traditions as my parents chased and cropped my tail with the remnants from the old Oriental East.

People in my hometown were so humbled by life that their vital expression would equate to animal voices or peaceful nights. The only response of my dad towards life was his throat (maybe I did not want to see his eyes): like a cow's tongue swallowing up grass; a clock's hand ticking up the tea, tagging into despair and clicking away the time; a donkey's sniff puffing off the air; or dog's bark echoing the dark mare (nightmare). So I dialed at his throat, by dialing along the village road, till the mountain peak spoke for the Taoist's tone atoning my turn for the return. The four diagnostic tools for the above four pathological pools would dial, die, and dye upon my nose-trilling fool from beast's east to nest's west, and from my yelling nose to yellow rose. The wild beasts lined up behind the tail of a dragon, as mild west net-webbed the trail of a monkey. The monkey's head was forever free, but its eyes were forever lustful for the fresh and its nails were mailed eternally into flesh. The dragon's mouth was fired by red Sun so that the yellow spouts could spring the yellow court, without the legal court. I yelled at my low height of being the yellow race, so that I could sell what the dragon has mouthed in the yellowish red with it breeding scales and how the monkey has whitened out the white race with his mindless freedom.

With a Chinese flute, I rushed through Asia (Russian), during the Red Revolution, was polite to those who were polished like a Polish police, and landed on the North Pole to see how the Pope doped off my biggest hope.

Being a sage was not as honorable as a saint; since a sage matured his age but a saint sanded the ants slaying aunts. Without ants, the monkey was free to expose the ends but hungry for exploring the Uncle Sam. I was then inside the Pyramid, piling me up and raiding me in the middle. The Nile flew fine but forgot about nine, so I drank the wine springing up from my spine. Finally I ended up inside an Indian Sweat Lodge smoking a peace pipe. Half asleep and half awake, I saw that the oil pipe was sawing through peace pipe, and that chemical fuels were fermenting tobacco leaves, until my mobile jaw met my rigid law behind the smoked neck. Silence took away my distance, and innocence forgot my diligence. That was how I have dialed at my nose to see the prognostic rose and pragmatic hose. As Hegemonists in every shape, thought, and form begin to rule all. But isn't that how it is in every era, every state, and every community? The righteous would have no place without the greedy.

Treatment

A few months after I was in college, I bought a book on Qigong exercise. I began my religiously practice every morning following the instruction described in the book. A few weeks went by, I noticed I got hungrier easily, which was called increasing the appetite. I had more energy for the day and slept like a log by most of nights. Even more genital drives; where I still could not connect to the perineal strives. This is the standard measure for the Qi increasingly stored and scored.

The basic formula was this:

1: Stand straight with feet as wide as shoulders, hands forming a circle, not cross-fingered, in front of chest, like holding a ball, and count breath while exhaling and focus the power upon the throat.

2: When the throat was warmed up, send the heat like a white line down to the center of sternum bone, then the same line down to the gutsy stomach, called the Lower Dantian (energy center), and the perineum pressure point.

One morning after a few months' practice, I felt there was a gassy heat gushing through my delta legs and out of my feet. I did not close the lid, meaning contracting the perineum muscles and point, as the Qi stored from the practice was leaking. I did not smell anything but I felt the heat. "Tight up your ass" is the common expression for this malfunctioning. (Here, the female who understands, laughs with dear-to-the-heart amusement).

3: When this white line is successfully established, it charges the perineum point like a drilling a hole, by contracting the pelvic muscles like bundling up a bunch of a whole. When there is enough heat upon exhale, send mentally the heat as a white line again, up along the spine. The first thing that shoud occur is the mid-section of lumber, as if a steamed heat is gushing through a hole. All kinds of sensations would surface at this point. Then the central back would feel like that of a running horse's legs or of embracing arms full of passion and excitement.

Along this stage, each time when I was exhaling, there was a warm gas evaporating through my first thoracic vertebra, like the morning mist rising through a well or a cave mouth. I was scared and stopped for a while. I was at a park, so a guy doing his Taichi Sword exercise nearby suggested me to straight up my neck like a long-necked swan, drop and withdraw my lower jaw a bit, and bend my head a bit forward. *Boom!* The energy was shooting straight into my head, and out of the crown.

4: For a couple of months afterward, when I was continuing my exercise, there was a gentle shower bathing internally my entire brain and face, like an angelic kiss, a gentle touch from the soothing wind. So peaceful and comfortable, and words could not describe it. This complete loop is called micro-orbit, or Xiao-zhou-tian or small-circled-heaven.

5: The most interesting exercise I invented at the time was Live Screen Production. Focusing on my third eye as if a TV screen, and upon each exhale, I would write up a chronological number on the screen. Several things would happen. For instance, the colors inside me would change, and my awareness would differ from this point on. Sometimes the brain became as light as air, and other times it was hosting a heavy stone. The main purpose of this invention was the single-minded concentration, so that the horse-mind and monkey-head would be restrained into a single targeted activity in each given moment. Doing so, I would not be distracted by the outside world or attracted by my inner cauldron.

Once in a while, my third eye was like white screen, and I saw the white light. Sometime, my entire brain was like a blank screen where only numerical letters were jumping upon it and flashing out of a bullet board: the third eye.

6: Finishing up with the showering and bathing process, one time, on a clear morning during the third year around 8:00 am, I was facing the Sun and breathing its light into my throat. About twenty minutes later or so, I felt that my nose disappeared, and only the throat was my entire presence of being. All of a sudden, three rings of light were circling in my body: my legs were wired with a blue light, my trunk including skull was looped with a white light, and my arms were circled with a golden light. No more body, no more senses, no more nonsense! Only three rings of light were circling like dancing trinity, ever-present motions, and everlasting eternity.

Results

To: I was not tall.

Can you be taller than a mountain, the planetary poles and light?

I love my names now. I was so glad that when my father gave me my first name Tao, he baptized me with Taoist tradition as well. And he blessed it with his death. Three days before he died, I told him to do some meditation, but he couldn't since his breath could only stay above his throat. He then told me to be good on the Qigong practice, and that he was too foolish to realize the power before his life was terminated. When people call me now Master Tao, I felt my dad's presence, Lao Zi's presence, all of the sages' presence, as well as Godhead presence. I do not care about my physical height anymore. Light is my height, love is my high, and soul gives all the time a high five.

For: I was not rich

Who is rich, love or light, now or noun?

I was so blessed with the double wealth now, being biologically a Chinese and spiritually a Taoist. With this double cross, I am very rich, and I feel that I am the most favored grandson, which I earned with my life in front of my grandpa's eyes. Since Xi-Mu-Niang (West-Mother-Aunt) chose me as

Her grandbaby, I had been educated by three fathers--my biological father, my spiritual teacher and light God. It has all come to an end. This is the end of search and targeting, as well as the beginning for return. The single droplet of cosmic, oceanic and unconditional love is my biggest wealth now.

In my hometown, knowing the difference between rich and poor was like the grading of pre-school kids: all As, with little plus or no minuses. God has nothing to spare from the sky besides His lights, and Earth has nothing to flare but dusts to fair dirty cloths and toeless shoes. When the wind migrates dust, Bird flies ahead to me, before the storm or after the devastation, to plan the precious seed stored inside their stone-digested but seed-buried stomach into a new barren field. When the mountaintops stopped my view below the skyline, my imagination was awakened. I wanted to rise above the peaks, traveling freely like clouds, fleeing into the open space, and inside the light world. My hometown educated me with rich history of the old civilization, such as legends, fairy tales, ceremonies, heart-to-heart conversations after supper, and communal supports. It revealed me nakedly and tragically that Nature is more powerful than the combination of manhood and humankind. Humans are the byproducts of Nature, the instruments of elements, and slaves of Superpower.

The peaks of Yellow Plateau drove me into educational opportunities, populated cities, and migrating deltas, before I landed in New York City. From the Guardian Wind to the New York City, I brought my body fabricated from the yellow earth to the underground of the Golden Tower where I became a rat running across the lines of subway stations below the Earth, but not a mouse obtaining research patent rights in the lab to resell the drugs for the human parasite bugs. As I compare my Guardian Wind community with Manhattan of the New York City, peace is canceled by moonlight on one side, and the glory is greeted by a few moments of appearance of sunlight on the other side. In Manhattan, when the sky-sealed buildings block the daylight, streetlights greet hosts and ghosts day after night. Civilization and stress trade the beauty by grading the collective sufferings.

Manhattan becomes a man with his hat waving for tones of tongues buried inside the bank buildings fencing off daylight and welcoming walk-stepping winds of passing travelers, passing citizens, and passing ghosts hungry for cultural commodities. Buildings in Manhattan, more powerful than the valley cliffs of my hometown, block away the storms and tides but welcome misery upon mystery. Every inch-squared space in Manhattan is a deadly battle in New York and for world, where the city has everything for you to pay or play. Every inch size advanced and obtained is a million dollars worth in gold, painted with thousands of labors and varnished with sarcastic greed upon sacrificial greet.

In contrast, only a few wild herbal flowers decorated my lonely heart in the community of Guardian Wind(my hometown), only a few scattered potato fields stretched my fabric mind into the soil of my empty heart. Only moonlight gently hugged me and embraced me inside her Jade Palace, where Jade Ladies and angelic flowers fed me with spreading love and threading meridians. I could then read in between what the light spreads and how the love threads. Because of my hometown, I became a wind diver, a love drummer, and a peace weaver. Because of my hometown, I knew that the rich lights up the abundance in the sky and the wealth hides away the love inside the valley. Light is richer than wisdom and wiser than wine. Love is deeper than valley and more mysterious than value.

About: I was not handsome

What is behind the flesh eye and emotional lust? What is the root of handsome?

When empty is the lust and nothing is the must, you get all the rich dusty gusts in the universe. Then, is handsome meaning "handy summer" or "hand me some"? For male in general and men in specific, their hands are really something. Tools, buildings, machines, titles, beliefs and peacemakers are all born out of their powerful and magic hands. I can only guess now H adds all the ands on hands.

If you can hand me some, you are handsome and your hand is on the thumb. Palms are empty and clean, so that psalms are produced and delivered for the sum of entire masses. With my mighty hands, my herbal handsome, and my verbal hand-you-sum, you will receive the sum of all, including my self-biting and elixir-licking un-ruling thumb. With this thumb, thunder is numb, under is standing, and number is uplifting!

Toward: I was not healthy.

Heal youself is the health for all.

There is no healthy state outside the spirit, nor wealthy condition outside the soul. When the worthy soul inside the wealthy temple nourishes the single faith with the single droplet of love, you are the healthiest being on Earth and in Heaven. Healthy is now healing thy-self. It is from the daily exercise, my insomnia was gone, I was hungry all the time, I was happy and content, my gray hair turned back to black, and my hands and knees did not hurt anymore. When you can heal yourself, Heaven heaves you and healthy heals you. And the very help swept by others is indeed the hell slept under your angelic wings and sonic swings. The angelic wings are the threads orchestrating conception and birth, while the sonic swings travel from life to death. Angelic wings have no physical breath; it breathes in the eternal love and breathes out the fetal growth. Sonic swings do not know how to breathe; only motion and emotions are the saws that swing the winning arms and losing hands.

To heal is to climb the hill, so that you can seal the real from the ill. Before your feet land on the footage, you must load all you have, to sell yourself and spell yourself. You must present any ill ailment, and all the sick tickets. Without ill feeling, no bills to fill, no drills to kill, no quills to thrill, and no wills to grill. When I am using the title of this chapter, *blowing the ill off the bone*, I mean it, I have experienced it, and I am continuously toning and atoning my entire boned stones. When the ill tells your will to become still, and till you **peel** you pill off your illness, your hill can now pay your bill; your drill can tail the will of your tailbone; and your quill can experience the thrill. No more chills that will acquire the frills and require the skills, because you have already killed yourself with the skills that have weakened you, causing the illness.

Do you want the skilled illness or the willed knees?

Revelation

Who is tall when life bounds your thighs up, reason whines your thumbs down, and season wears your ears out!

Who is rich when colors are off the black and short of white, numbers cannot satisfy mouth; where accumulation cannot replace health, land is the owner, and mind is the lord!

Who is beautiful in looking, handsome in motion and graceful in promotion when flower is for the season, love is for the reason, and delight is for the treason!

Who is truly healthy when corrupted genes erupt the hill, contaminated food pesticides the stomach, cultured conditions suffocate love, and horizontal ego beheads the wisdom mind!

Aside from the above four, is intelligence the power upon farm or the luck towards charm?

The troubles, traumas, disasters of life are God's given assignments for us, to align our love and insight, into time and space, presence and divine. If our mind is weaker or slower than the problems occurred, we become the slave of those disasters and eventually die from them. But if we can concentrate our mind and heart into a single target, single dream, single hope, and single solution, life takes care of itself naturally. Because light is the singular finger, and love is the simpler symbol.

With the above basic formula I have exercised and experienced, I understand now that Xiao-zhou-tian (small heaven or micro orbit), is about following the interactive loops and changing stoops (all those oops), of the Sun and the Moon above and around the Earth. It is above our reasoning and below our feeling. Dear reader, stand now outside the earth and inside the birth, open your eyes around the changing loops between Solar ring and lunar swing, where one side of the Earth is daylight and the other side is nightmare. These two stations are forever given, each with 12 hours. Be wary, within the second it appears instantly but disappears constantly. The speed of this dual change is so fast and swift, that your mind will be atop your eyes, and your love stops your heartbeats. You now have a ring of disc, a circle of round, and a loop being spaced around. This ring, circle or loop invites your exciting joy upon your imagining toy, so that you absorb yourself into observing the interactive motion of the Sun and the Moon, second after second, day after night, and year after year. This ring is our astral micro-orbit,

BLOW ILL OFF THE BONE

in comparison of God's Eye, the macro-space of the Universe.

We have skin around our flesh, with holes and pores. We have clothing around our projections and titles. We have a house around our rooms, streets around our block, time around the clock, till we reach the scarred skins and scared kings around the Mother Earth. We now come to a place scientifically called ozone, which is a clouded ring of gas around the Earth. When the Mother Earth ovulates around Her zoning district, Her zero is our hero, and her zigzagging zone is our wigwagging distressful tricks. Aha! Alas! The wizard of OZ is ONE as ozone, so that we as the squeezed wards can become void of nothing. Inside this ozone, there is atmosphere, and others like hydrosphere, lithosphere and biosphere. Inside these circling rings, the rounded makes a rope, the charged wires the dope, and the abandoned tires the hope. Inside again and further, are the micro worlds of beings, cells, viruses, funguses, minerals, and molecules. Inside further and again are time and space, second and heat, light and void.

So the world out there is the reflection of the world inside here, right now, in us all the time. I point at me to serve the meal, so you, who are making a U-turn, can tell it to itch off the illness. This is the definition of illusion without luminous lamination. Everything we have, possess and manifest is the outcome of what has happened inside our own world. We are God's dogs and Goddess's pets. They animated us with organic stations and placed us then into a vegetative state. We are their expression without impression or suppression. This is what I learned from years of looping and scooping around the clock within the blocks of my very knots.

The Expanded Formulas

The Micro Orbit exercise enabled me to discover and unfold more of others. If we turn the loop I described, down the front body and back up the spine, then viewed from all sides. You will see:

A) When facing this loop from the right side, it is a clockwise circle;

B) Turning into the left side, it is a counterclockwise loop;

C) Facing above, you are headless like a roofless house;

D) Examining below, your private region privatizes your public bones and sexual zones with your nailing tail, asshole and water pipe.

So you are polarized now and forever. Angels are watching you from above like how an eagle is preying watchfully for its mobile food: the immobile fool. When the eagle peaks at you right on top of your crown and speaks you into your mind, you are about to see the canal of your birth. Where your father drilled you into your mother's womb, and your mother wounded you from her expelled and disabled discharge. You are the light hole of that right dot into night's whore without wholeness but full of holistic potential and homeless care.

Ghosts in the hell keep saying, "hello my dear fellow" to you and you never listen. Helplessly, ghosts in the hell alarm your arousing bell by smelling your disfigured cells and pleasurable sells.

You are left with side-effect illnesses. If you take care of your right side, Sun will circle you into its arm during the day but expel you out by the sunset into the darkness. You will lose yourself whether you follow the Sun's head or your beheaded direction, because your head and the Sun's head always play their head-on collision, but never come to an agreement. Only when the Sun decides with its will it loses you and your decision will lose the Sun. You are then able to follow only half of the clockwise loop, since the other half is enjoyed by the moonrise or moonset.

Again, if you are focusing on your left side, moonrise from the night will expunge you out, with her arched arrow, into either Mercury or Venus, her twin sisters. Depending on her seasoned flavor or mood, and you are left with shadows, conditions, habits, memories, karmas, nightmares, and haunting ghosts, until your aunt hosts the ghosts and you are haunted by light dust or water rust.

Worse than that, each time when you move to another position, you are removed from your own position, and renewed by your own opposition. Whenever you are right, the opposite says you are wrong; and wherever you are left alone, ghosts find out that you are all right, without knowing and claiming your all given rights.

Now we have six sides to play with. The top is taken care by the sky and angels. The bottom is visited by babies and doctors along utility tracks serving either your desire as dare or your fear as despair. Your desire dares your senses by sentencing you to death, and your fear despises you by taking you into your own prison. Before you are able to construct a sentence, your active verbs will attach your nouns through your fists and fingers, by attacking your adjectives, adverbs and pronouns through your feet and toes. Your head may fire one thing but your gut lures another. Your mind is on one target but your heart hosts the other.

So you are left with your right hand serving others' left hands, and your left hand deceiving others' right hands. Not until you can figure out what you need from what God has granted, municipals manipulate you with all kinds of wonderful manicures. Not until you are speaking for the sky and ancestor, you cannot be right. Not until you are acting for yourself and world together as one person, one family, one community, one nation and one world, you do not belong to anyone, you have no place to go, and you have no home to return to.

When the left side is neglected and the right side is abandoned, you are about to rush into hell for help and out of it for joy and liberation. This is so that you are free inside out, and the world outside leaves you free as it eternally is.

Align your thought with your tail, by aligning your action with your reaction, you will be the home for four, as four seasons greet you with four generations and you will finally understand four is For Our collective goodwill hour by hour. When you abandon the F words, my eye is your vision, and their vision quest is our reunion: Me as I becomes an individual; you are secondary; and then return the collective will with elevating wheel. In front of us now, one means heart (o): nosing and knowing (n) your own build-in electricity (e); two is too much for a tooth but too little for the entire teeth; and three never frees from the tree but always pays the collective fee.

Before you reach five, liver delivers your life into passion or expansion so your heart can be out there for the world or here in this world.

Can you be rotten like an egg and stronger than a bone?

CHAPTER 3:

I HAVE DREAMS

Before my dream

By age 22, I had been practicing Qigong for three years (I am not sure if this is the magic number that held Adam and Eve on one side, and religion and government on the other). At age 22, I have found my Heavenly brother who was at the age of 44. Years later I was able to relate the Hebrew alphabetic numbers of the West with the Chinese calendar structure of the East. It was from this point on I was able to make sense of the deep meaning behind the numeric value: 3.

At this young age, I was only working at the tangible side, with a secured job, only to repair, in a numb state, the seven-hosed lock stolen by a fork knifing at my frozen pork. This seven facially hosed lock did not secure my senses, only inviting more troubles, organically and culturally. The Chinese mystic totem—the pig head—would gratify me with all lustrous images and fantasies to the degree that I became a machine of organic and ancestral senses. I was dragged by the illusionary world and enslaved by the conditioned reality. This reality served its purpose, like how each member would function in a family, and each citizen would behave in a society. This tangible reality is an organically structured, personally wheeled and socially veiled meal and deal.

The root structure of "-eal" formulates many useful tools, such as deal, heal, leal, meal, Neal, peal, real, seal, steal, teal, veal, weal, wheal, and zeal. In terms of what is called as real, you begin with a deal. As a deal heals through rattling tongue, gluing gum, and rimming mouth, it becomes true, loyal as if it is a leal added onto health. The health heals to the function of each meal, so that Neal can deliver the complete sound of a peal. The peal reassembles the entire body into a bell to orchestrate molecule cells, internal organs, stretching ligaments, and tangible senses into a harmonic wave.

Upon sealing what is real from the singing bell to the harmonic peal, you can steal the teal and bake it into a roasted duck, to replace the expensive veal chop. The chop shops around your desire, only to skin your power from its bites, called the weal or wheal, such as sound bites, frostbites, or mega bytes, till you drop to the ground, flip and flop what you have plowed and watered, and stop at your own destined point. This stoppage then strops your skinny race so you can whop atop your sealed chop from the Creator. The sealed chop is what you have been zestful for. This chop seals the naked truth: what you have desired and longed for is what the Creator has designed you as--the zeal behind a zealot.

The original meal from the authentic deal heals now finally as the seal from the zeal. You know for sure from this point on that your meal refuels your own meat, and the deal of an advantage turns out to be the ordeal wrestling inside your own delta region. When the Creator designed you, S/he sealed your passion as the ultimate zeal inside your delta belly. You can zigzag yourself inside your own skin in between the zippers as sensory receptors, so that the peal from the sound bite or frostbite can appeal your own individualized seal to make your choice with voice; or simply disappear itself. This is what I have experienced: the seven-hosed lock stolen by a fork knifing at my frozen pork.

The oedipus complex. What is it? How is it reflected? In the west, it is best associated with works by Freud. If you ask me, it is the result of a sort of puffery. A puffing out to avoid touching the basic roots tied with truth. Like girly girls squirming at bugs, or men looking down upon the homeless. God forbid you really see yourselves reflected in them. The men in business suits, begging their bosses and kissing ass for a token, a gain. Girls like mosquitoes, buzzing around all day, talking about nothing, sucking the blood from others.

What makes society tick as it does? What is the meaning of life? Why and how do these things work? Those are questions everyone undeniably asks at one point or another. How is it that human culture has evolved this way?

We look down upon cannibalism, but in "modern" and "progressive" civilizations we still consume each other. We consume the livelihoods of other humans, their essence. The ones who do it best are the ones who push ahead. What about the cannibals? Their process of consuming flesh is not like how most people in the world do now with other animals. Most of us go into a restaurant and order chicken or beef or pork and consume our meal without reverance to the animal that sacrificed itself for our enjoyment. The cannibals are ritualistic, giving recognition to personal worth and acknowledge that passing of a soul. Here, we order kids fresh out of college and consume their youth and livelihood to work for our companies. We look at their resumes (read my menu please) and pick out our favorite kind of dish. Have it arrive pre-slaughtered by multiple-choice standardized schooling and packaged nicely with a certifiable degree, all for our personal enjoyment. Like the chicken. Or maybe the cow or pig. What separates us from a cow anyways when most corporations refer to us as "cash cows."

They hang us with a rope made of fabricated artificial "needs" which are nothing more than our own desires manipulated to stimulate our deepest pains turned pleasurable. Helping us add salve to our itch, but only making it worse like hot water to eczema. Feels good for the moment, but worse later. This guarantees for us to live forever as the Buddhists' hungry ghosts.

The term "just be happy" no longer exists. It has been replaced by "what makes me happy?" Because so much of us is taken away. Our rugged individualism and manifest destiny has reached it's limits and is now re-directing itself inward. We are defined by online quizzes that give us four possible personality types, or, if we are lucky, eight different types. Our multiple choice democracy and know-it-all attitude creates us all as self identified, infallible creatures. We are forced by ourselves to be ideal, lone standing, strong. What did we sacrifice? Family, happiness, personal truth. We are so focused on pleasing or impressing the other eyes on us, by how we should appear, that we forget that it doesn't really matter at all.

If NuWa were here today, and observed her children, what would she think? Her relationship with her brother/husband spawned forth everything that followed. She watched as most boys vie for attention from their mothers who are too worn out slaving away for their fathers. Mothers who beg masculinity, power, from their husbands because they couldn't get any. Unless they grow some balls themselves. In turn, the sons look for girls and their mysterious, silent begging ways to serve them what they are stilling missing from their mothers. The girls hold the boys with a vaginal collar around their lower throat and secretly demand them to act for them in parts of society they can't go.

Do the boys really compete against their father for their mother? Do they really fantasize about sexual relations with the dominant female? Or could it be that it is the feminine spring that brings forth life? Is it the bringing them back to life that the boys are searching for? After the umbilical cord is physically severed, the spiritual needs to be stitched shut as well, or else the boys are forever hungry.

Girls and fathers are luckier. Maybe. The girls have their own yin energy. Fathers love the laughter of daughters because they are the expression of their feminism that they are not to show to the outside patriarchal world. Through this sacred bond and balance fathers and daughters have a sacred exchange of energy that leaves both satiated.

It is only when the love is tainted by other emotions that it translates into tragedy. When something is not right, it is natural to think of the first anxiety registered emotions. It is most often confused into being sexual energy. From a young age, most children are taught not to touch downstairs and not to let others violate them, causing extraordinary negative emotions towards specific physical areas that carries through adulthood. Eventually, all negatively suppressed emotions are dumped into the pool of warped sexuality and expressed through hindered, awkward, predominantly physical and handicapped sexual intercourse. Emotions become compartmentalized, usually interpreted as something unfamiliar and not worth the time when they become too hard to understand.

Afterall, doesn't society need us to demonstrate what we know instead of allowing us to search for answers to what we don't know?

This was the very fork, that was knifing at *my* pork.

See, my dear reader, I am relearning the language now, whether it is my native Chinese, secondary English, or the third born of that relationship language, the connection between all people. This is so that I can relate to my memories registered over the years, or to any human members I have acquainted along the way. I am re-digesting what I have learned, stored, and fabricated, so that my body as a sacred temple is free from weathered patterns, my soul is free to dream, and my spirit is free to shine. I am recycling the vocabularies collected inside a dictionary so that I will be free from the linguistic dictation, habitual recitation, and useless visitation.

My dear reader, I am now digging into the roots of words to find the soul-boiled, heart-quenched, and spirit-delighted song lines, and to rest with the harmonic points and angles mapping my essence of being. Rediscovering those harmonic points and angles is like digging, through pressure points, into flesh and soul, in order to play the human body as the original instrument that is beyond secondary trades and secondhand traitors.

If, my dear reader, you can re-list carefully, without the help of a dictionary, and relate to each vital sound, inside or within each of your own defined word, you will have a chain of rain, and a hood trooping and doodling manhood. You will re-connect the original song lines of your heart, and re-member all you have re-corded. These song lines are like the precise, prestigious and precious preliminary points and angles forming the sacred geometry. They have recorded, sky-mapped, and eye-gapped the pre-loaded, pre-registered and pre-decorative proactive pressure points and meridians forming our body as an energetic vessel weathered by angels, orated by the enlightened masters, seasoned by Goddesses, and designed by God.

These songs lines, sacred geometry and meridian charts are the instruments of God, orchestrated by our spirits, and played by our collective vibrations. So, my dear reader, please bear with me, when you have trouble relating with the strings of thought or the flashes of ideals. You are about to enter the harmonic chamber of our collective vessel that is dancing through choreographic beauty and elegance.

Stop here right now, my dear reader, please, please rewrite yourself with the following list: deal, heal, leal, meal, Neal, peal, real, seal, steal, teal, veal, weal, wheal, and zeal. Make your own language with your own dreaming heart and your vital expression. If you cannot liberate yourself from your family and socially constructed linguistic patterns, thinking habits, and mental addictions, you will never see where and how and why the unconditional love of Universe converses with the eternal presence of God.

When the words lose you in their given meaning, drop all you know and hear the sounds and their individual vibrations as you would to music.

To conclude the "-eal" root, whether it begins with eel or ill, we feel it, helplessly. We are all like a robot designed, a scarecrow clothed, and a puppet animated. We are all real tools in our own ways, and there is no way to distinguish between which is truly good from what is really cool. It only depends on how we align with it, define it, and apply it.

My Catch 22

Am I re-experiencing this catch 22 as the terribly doubled two? I had a strong feeling that I did not belong to my family anymore when I was about two years old, and I knew it. That answers why I did not really cry for the attentive affections from my parents, unlike the common Western expression of what a terrible two would do. I felt like having no other choice besides taking care myself along taking care of the rest.

Dearest Heavenly brother, could this be why you were born the year of the Tiger?

I do not know.

I can confer now that the number 2 knows only one-way: too, either too much of an ordeal or too little of a meal. Too much of an ordeal helps the tool, while too little of a meal retards the tooth. If I could apply the first 2 or twenty as a tool, I would utilize all fingers and

toes, and countless hair. But if I could relate tool with tooth as the second 2, the gumming jaws would have it all. When I utilize all the twenty fingers and toes, and the set of jaws and lips as the combined two, my eyelids are free to view, my eardrums are free to rum, and my nostril tip is free to drip.

Whether I wanted mom and her milk, or dad and his protection, I was able to finish an article or essay at this catch-22-age. This terribly doubled two cried very hard and long, even now, that I feel terribly sorry for me as well as humanity. Nevertheless, upon this catch 22, when I was formulating this article, I felt that I was a pilgrim, a map designer, planning my day through light ray and reasoning my being through cyclic season. I screamed at this light ray inside my mind and dreamed about this season inside my stomach, till I felt this ray was spiraling inside my being as the sea seeing the Sun. I had an ideal: I became dear to myself. Neither narcissistically nor heroically, I felt my dear, though I did not know how to be tender to that dear in me.

After the ideal surfaced itself, I was able to connect, relate, borrow and lend others' finished products, which were nothing but clustered words, as if they were raw bricks, steel bars, bamboo sticks, dry walls, utility materials, floor mats, painting chips, kitchen utensils, and room furniture. They were strategic tools used, polished words brushed, marketable products printed, tradable communities deeded, and recyclable materials wasted. Further, as for me, it was not about what humans have survived on and why they have invented languages; but about how humans think internally, feel organically, and sing eternally. In turn, I was making my own buildings, my own living room, my own legislative laws, my own proved rights, my own sanctuary shrine, my own everlasting song, and my own eternal dance. In the end, as I saw what I have gone through, from internal digestion and formulation, to my private handwriting and the official printing, I was excited for a long time for what I could do, and had done. From this point onward, I was able to design mentally an article, an essay, a chapter, a book, even volumes of work.

By the time I got my royalty fee as the loyal treat for my life-long royalty towards writing, I invited my friends into a restaurant, adding extra needed money from my pocket, and enjoying a party that I would never forget. No one felt jealousy; all were filing their joy and excitement, by filling up their stomach and eyes. The printed words on the provincial magazine erased my handwriting, but proved officially I could be a writer, an author with some sort of authenticity. To write authentically made me a double major, and endless minors in between.

It was at this age—my catch 22—I discovered that my mind was a tabula rasa, a canvas, an empty paper, a whitened screen, a layer line, a flatland, a landscape, and a magic view. Not knowing how to rotate or flip from "M" to "W", or vice verse, by making "mind" as "wind," or changing "wind" into "mind," I was in some other place from this age on. I was, as if, but without iffy feeling, entering my own sacred heart, my own dreamland. This mind serves itself as the Eye of God, the plasma of Sound, and the fabrics of Word. Inside this mind or tabula rasa, is the occurrence of silent-taught and thought-escaping dream. As I was able to dream what God has creamed and how Goddesses screamed, I could stream my lucid fluid as the conscious cream of my sprung love and its vital expression. All the rest belonged to the exchanges that were due to the change or doomed from the change: borrowing from others' work, lending from those who had done the digestion and gone through their own lonely but solid labor, or even stealing from underneath the flatland, behind the magic view, where each and every one of the human pools was functioning automatically like a robot, and subconsciously like a puppet.

From this human pool, I could see how the family unit or household was united with but bounded by nationality. I saw how the collective union, like the Communist Party, took over each family head; and how my identifiable national Chinese uniform replaced my family name and my yellowish skin. The best of this Yellow Race were yelling and screaming at each other, killing one another, for centuries, only to discover and crown with this yellow powder: partially inside gallbladder, partially inside Shamhhala, but all were inside God's Crown. The result was, as I realized, I became forever a minority, doing minor work, engaging in minute fashion and speaking the mineral words. Who was the real majority among humanity anyhow? Who had that single, simple and magic power to declare himself or herself in front of the mass, a combination of ancestry and mystery, as the dominant race? A simple face is a single race, as a sympathetic pace is a symbolic case.

There are some words of names, such as God or Way, pharaoh or Moses, Christ or Buddha, Kangasgan/Genghis Khan or Crusade, Hitler or Einstein, Mao or Martin Luther King. To list just a few, but with no appealing favor or chilled fever; nothing personal. In the end, forget about me, you will be very lucky if you can retain the half: half of your flesh, half of your soul, and half of your mind. Even so, two eyes are fighting with two ears for the attentive colors, and two ears are battling with two nostrils for the fabric tip above the hydraulic slip, and two lips outside the two sets of teeth are rivaling between tongue and gum, throat and voice, volume and value.

Stating this minority, I was not the only son in my family, but one of the seven. My family was not the only household in my community, since about a dozen or so family names were tied into this community. My county was one among those seven others forming into my district, then my province (one of the 30 or so in China), and then my country (one of 200 or so nations in the world). Still, more facial looks are alive behind the nations given, and more racial tongues are active beyond the nationalities written. To the degree that each face is a distinctive race and every tongue is an individualized nationality, with no rationality. When you face your tongue, you raise up and race for everything.

Thus, between "county" and "country," you count the teeth first and then have a tea party so that what you have counted will be contrary to why and how you have mounted. Country has its treat now, which is contrary to family and its head, factory and its boss (foreman). When those contradictories arise, those who obtained the county expand their counted and accountable territories, till the most powerful gangsters established themselves as the dominant parties, to rule the rest inside and around. That is how I understand where a country has been established from a county. It all started with the tea-tree: the ends of count. The single Y is useless, so stop whining. Try to cry through your tongue and fry your face, by adding the letter of R ahead of the letter of Y, your county as counted will end up as your country amounted.

I am counted as a vote within my own county, but I am accountable for my own country. From my individual cell, to community ward, county jail and federal prison, I am locked up inside completely. What I have established with invites and provides how I will be self-imprisoned. There is no prison outside my cell, and there is no cell outside my belling belt. What I have decided is how I can describe and why I could define, so that my decision relates to my description and equates to my definition.

I felt that the word "country" was like counting all the tries, trials, triads, and tributes inside a frying pan, so that Peter Pan could not dream about his ever and never land. Since my throat was drummed by my local accent, thumbed by the social rules and established customs, and numbed by countless political officials who were facially polite but racially disgusting. They never cared about you as a skinned race, as they only dare into your thought-driven horse race. And I could not afford to become a family exile, a social escapist, an anti-political ramble, or counter-religious finger.

With an earned degree, and a registered title, I was serving community and country like what each member should, and each citizen could. But I was never pleased, nor satisfied. Something in me just did not want to quit or give up. Something in me that maddened me felt that I was never suitable in society. Each time when I paid a visit to my family or friend, a few minutes of conversation was enough of it. Each time when I tried to have an open-heart conversation, I would betray myself by exposing what was pure and sacred inside, so that those distant but present listeners did not and would not understand what I had tried to convey or convince. I was lonelier than a standing tree, more alone than a blowing dust or glistening light, and worse than a deserted waste.

At my age of 22, I became BKS. Sadly, I loved those around me with a good and pure heart, but their minds were trapped by only that which can be stimulated by their five physical senses. Everything else, was nothing more than a spawn of the overactive imagination. When did we forget that it is imagination that makes us free? The greatest writers, inventors, composers and leaders who had the incomparable initiative started with their imaginative ingenuity.

Imagination, is the image of our spiritual nation stored within our cellular memory. They clue us in, like etheric hox genes linked to our energy pools in other constellations.

Where is my root? Where is my ground? Where is my source? Where is our home? Where is our kingdom?

Installed titles had all the ways—their own ways—into power loops and alterative controls. Rules were disguised games for the slaves to enjoy themselves in glorious fields, upon imaginary worlds, through hallucinating dreams. Holidays only satisfied the food, the cloth, the visit, and fireworks. The holiday atmosphere was like a drugged state, a numbed leg, a frozen heart, a water prison, and a fire chamber. Political figures along with wind-driven stars and cloud-chasing heroes would fashion, in their own given and alternating occasions, national stages, to the degree that I became nameless, useless, and meaningless.

The depression from the superficial world and the suppressed history locked my dream into a black chimney, causing me to have insomnia, arthritis, constipation, and gray hair physically; angry and numb, jealous and helpless, irritable and frequent emotional urination, lower self-esteem, very little self-trust, and no thanksgiving to whatsoever conscientiously. There was nothing *in,* or *some* to be *near;* that was insomnia. The King Arthur was vital but brittle, so that all his loosening ends and bendable points were fixated inside a rivalry ticks (arthritis). Stagnation staged all cellular nations inside a blocked drainage, so that the entire civilized world had no extra space to fill in, nor extra openers to let go (constipation). Intensity destroyed the intestines, as well as any forbidden interests, causing that snake-body and wormhole to constipate. Gray hair having not lived long enough from infantile to youth was either a prey or engaging in a long-term praying activity. When the light ray became gray upon my black hair, the prayer inside of my heart had to drag the prey out of my desire to pry, spy, and fry all the coming affairs as if I was repeating all cyclical fairytales along endless farewells.

How was the mind capable of itself mentally, or soul passionately, or flesh with enough fresh ingredients to please the targeting eyes, hungry souls, and resting spirits?

I wanted the real deal, the authentic meal, and the everlasting seal. The seal of my father was not strong enough, because from the day I started my elementary school, my family name was nothing but a dog tag for the classification system enlisted inside of a classroom. Any seal from officials, such as government or religious organizations, was dangerous enough to ill me but not stable enough to open and sustain my dream gate. In the political arena, Chinese have been killing each other like brothers for centuries without an end. In religious manners, only enlightened figures could drive with clouds, breathe with wind, and shine upon light. Below the belt of Religious Ocean, whether the snow belt or the Bible Belt, each sector hated passionately the other secretive nectar, to the state that each believer was chasing his or her own imagined thought and conviction. Each congregation was only useful under a specific mountain, its local climate, its room temperature, and its refinery ideal.

I began to realize that any first-hand experience is unknown; any repetition is the secondary guess; and any third party would host monsters partying with ghosts. "Beyond" is when the unpredictable fan teams up with an incontrollable ban, behind all changes. "Besides" hosts all sides, opening to opportunities that tell impunities to become impossible.

It was the seal of heart I wanted from above the sky and below the gravesite. With this seal, my heart became my mind, my tabula rasa, and my dreamland. As the raw food and sawmill from universe entered my sacred heart, the seal is God's Word, Goddess's Love, and in turn, my sleepless dream, my awakened call.

Away from this sleepless dream, I was either orchestrated by daydreams or frightened by nightmares. In front of my poor existence, the social demand was a giant fork, and I was deserted as a portion of chopped pork. Fork demanded me to do more work, and pork was serving itself unwillingly as a food to be tasted and a fool to be wasted. But my internal lock, opening to the seven worldly holes in my face, was forever frozen from my Adam's apple. I could not remember how I uttered my first official voice, and I would never remember how I could engage in a meaningful conversation, have a soulful party, even a fresh deal.

The fight between that of a horse-marching brain and that of boss-laughing heart was never ending. The diplomatic dialogue would send the brainwaves to the heartbeats, so that inner dialogue would log on or off to the external communicating equipments. The satellite dish and its equipped GPS system would occur automatically without signing up with any payable agreement, as memory was always there, ready to strike a conversation, either with loved ones or estranged entities. How could I treat myself as the dearest dear, between the beats of heart and flashes of ideas? I only knew how to place an idea into what I dare to deal, or how to be dear to the dare.

This ID business played between eye and I on one side, and dear and deer on another land. Until I became dare (daring) enough to make myself a dear, my ear would listen to my heart, and my dare would care for what was really going on without being scared to death. The deer's antenna was talking to the sky with its brain, so that its body as the dear would obey and surrender to what was really happening in each given moment. It took me a long time to understand how the word "idea" was giving birth to the ridiculous "ideal." When I become dear to my ear, I can make a deal to my heart, which is idealistically real and indeed an idol.

In this world, the tradable titles were more important than standing totems. Since the Communist's rule cut me like a giant knife, and I became like a belittled domesticated animal or boxed tool, or an existing meal to please the patriotic slogan, social customs, and historical residues.

An Introduction, with My Catch-22

My life was changed around a series of twos. First, I was born on the second day of an even numbered month. Algorithmically, even my birth year was reflective on deciding the day of my birth.

The summer of '98, we planned spend two months and two weeks total in China. The airline company went on strike and I was two weeks late for the beginning of my freshman year of high school. Two months later, my grandfather passed away. My parents and my little brother were gone for two more weeks. My mother missed her father terribly and the fact that she did not say goodbye. Two sets of two months after that, on 3/6/99 (the real devil's date) she made a contract and she was taken from us. In her 2-day coma, she visited her father while she sacrificed her flesh. She is not the same. For two months she was in the hospital and two months afterwards was in physical therapy. For two years, I prayed for her to return to me. From two lifetimes ago, I saw this coming.

At the age of twenty two, I was engaged with the one who would help me begin my heavenly assignment.

Dreaming birth for the dreaming word

Aside from an official job, a teaching position at a community college, something else settled in at my catching 22. I did not have a TV with 22 channels, nor an opportunity to quit my job or leave my exiting world. My eyes were OK, still pertaining the power of 22, without using .22 riffle in order to target someone. I was about to engage in a healing work. My internal lock had to be knocked by a magic key, so that my building blocks inside could serve the triggering clock and passing flocks. The magic key was a dream, and it triggered my memory cell and memorable membrane that is still alive today, as vivid as my present eyes can clearly see.

At the time this magic key was handled into my dream world, I was studying psychology under a comrade and mentor, away from the official title as an English instructor. His daughter-in-law was very ill. I visited her home, wishing either to be introduced to an unmated girl, or some delicious homemade meal. Failing those two wishes, she agreed for a Qigong healing the next day. I had read or heard the dream-transmission from a master to a disciple, but never had a firsthand experience. This was about to happen, as the dream in the following evening had revealed:

I was walking through a woodsy forest full of young trees as if they were planted at the same time for the same purpose, to grow about 30 feet tall and catch evenly with their tips forming a tender blanket to open a space for light and air. In the middle of the forest, a man glided, jumping down from the tip of a tree as if rolling skillfully from a rope or metal bar. Landing on his feet, he told me he had been waiting for me. Without seeing what he looked like or questioning his intention, I followed his steps.

Out of the forest, we came and stopped in front of a huge stone, about the size of a large room. This person whom I followed splashed his right hand three times upon the stone, and each time a giant white rose appeared magically blooming from the stone.

Next day, I went to heal the first client at her home. The arthritis she had on her legs had swelled so badly that she could not work anymore. She could barely stand and walk. I asked her for some warm water with some salt, spiced pepper oil, and vinegar. Mixing all together into a washbasin, I soaked her legs and feet. Then I placed my hands on her feet for about 15 minutes, sending all the Qi I could gather from my life essence, and concluded the healing session.

After I returned to my office, I opened up a book on ancient Taoist Qigong healing remedies. I flipped open a page, and saw on the left page the formula I applied for the client. This formula was written by one of eight Taoist immortals over a thousand years ago. It was from this event on, I trusted my dreams like I am trusting my warm heartbeat, chilly gut-heat, or senseless mind-beat. I have been looking forward ever since for the clarity, the guidance, and the revelation through dreams, to the degree that I became a bit addictive to it, more than sex or money, fame and abundance.

Many a time, dreams have been as ordinary as what a mundane life would live for Monday or murdering day. Yet, it seemed to me that before I went to bed and was ready to sleep through the night, dreams took over my daily conscious mind. Dreams drove above my skeletal system, managed my sensory factory, and provided clarity in the midst of my confused and puzzled mind. Dreams were my mentors telling me what was going on inside the deep well and cave of my mere existence, and a meteorologist foretelling my emotional weathers and karmic climates, months or years ahead.

I cherish the subtle quality

元 wandering spirit

and profound precision of my dreams so much that if I can summarize my life and its eventful affairs with memorable moments right now, a dozen or so dreams would say it all. That is what I have been addicted to them for: the outcome without knowing it is the outcome, the quality above characterization, and profundity beyond measurable means.

Life is a pressure cooker: the more it is being pressed and squeezed, the juicer and more potent the outcome would be bled. Pain tells me to die or heal myself. Suffering reveals the deep meaning beyond my despaired numb and my egoistic drum. In the midst of pain and suffering, I got to have a dream. Without dreams, my wish has no staring point, my hope has no meaningful target, my passion has no substance, my love has no lotion, and my gift has no wrap.

In any case, the raw food in that woodsy forest in the above dream as part of the forestry is actually my mood as part of the forever-restful mystery arresting my misery. Any time a green and yellowish wood would, my passionate liver could, and my welled and spelled dream should. The guy waiting for me from that tree was not the apple knocking Newton, nor Einstein's head off a nuclear bomb, or any strong-headed men to be hammered by a falling apple to dissolve the paradise reseeding the Western Civilization. This guy is a God's reversed and reality-mutated seed ready to be planted in my heart for the dream-journey practice. So that my visible world can extend my invisible being to sustain from the nourishing source, and that my invisible being has a say about what my visible world has hallucinated, fantasized or mesmerized. I am a formless infant, seeing all the forms around me and feeling all the formulas profound.

Equally, the stone is my beloved headstone, the rock of my devotion, my discipline and my faith. The three flowers, I hope I can live up to, are my awakened trinity within, and abandoned trinity without. His right hand becomes my baptized healing palms and their feeling herbs, where the sickness kisses the illness like cool-me-ease or the collective invisible power kicks the personalized visible flower into either gray cite or grand side.

And I could not believe, dear reader, right here right now, I am interpreting my own dream, almost twenty four years later. It is as if Sigmund Freud were smoking his cigar to mock off his conscious guitar, as if Carl

Jung was chewing chemically his philosophical stones and tasting his own very existing alchemy, as if Joseph Campbell was colorizing all the mystic images and uncivilized languages in his own scholastic playground. When the psychology departments around the world tell Freud to smoke in the designated area, and not puff off his uncontrollable agitation upon child molestation, ancestral rape, animal retardation, and UFO stalking, his livened map of life and experienced cap of reality would be still applied as part of institutional requirement. **What would Edward Bernays say?** But they cannot cover up what the history of man has collectively done to his wife (domestication) and children (civilization) for the past two thousand years or more.

Upon this state, Jung jumped in, declaring that it is an all collective unconscious state of being. The collectable self individualized one's tribunal mindset as an elective subject., which spells the weather forecast but does not pay attention to the result of what the road accident changed upon what the weather had been predicted. After the camp was alarmed by a bell, Campbell was shocked by what Buddha had awakened, what Christ had lived, and what all men had believed. With a graceful and angelic feminine touch, Joseph felt silently from his toy ground that there was another language, a different kind of tone, and a distinctive melody spoken through the historical images and symbols that were birthed, fabricated and colored by divine feminine power. Are those images the genetic codes of God or matrixes of our mind? Are those symbols the postures of celestial dance or pictures of an angelic glance?

Who are you, dreamer?

"I am the sound of silence drumming the asleep heart and echoing the restful mind, the song of violet above the seven-equipped violence, and son of thunder charging the weather in the sky and fortune in the ground. I am the bridge between the visible river and the invisible liver, the ridge edging the cosmic sledge, rim trimming the stream into teams of beam, and the legend aging the mind but fermenting the heart."

When my thought distances my feeling, my dream bounces my reason into reality. Silence drums the presence and echoes through my longing heart into the foot of a mountain, where wind climbs and monkey declines. I climb for the weather as I mate with fortune. That is called climate, as this climbed mate is forever climatic from seasoning the romantic seeds and oil to charismatic flowers and tower. This very climate I am about to experience is what weather climbs and declines through the bridge connecting the sky roof and earth hoof. The sky end rains my brain, while the earth end trains what I can retain. So the bridge between the sky and land becomes my ridge connecting my gum and tongues. My edge relates to lips upon nips and tips behind hips, and my sledge slays the saint who is saying wise things to a sage behind the Pope.

With the sayings of the saint, the sage becomes faint in his own crowned cave, where the water drops and trims the wireless silence with harmonic vigilance. They till the mending sage's minding ages like air-thin and snow-whitened mountain. His heart springs the water of life and milk of love like a well, to welcome anyone who is wet from the lucid dreams and weathered by morning dews.

Night and her dream is my invisible boss, and day and his light is my unforgiving loss. When the day loses his light to the night, I lose my rights to see the presence. When my vision sees black, darkness welcomes the presence, and all I am feeling about is my own heartbeat. When the night dreams about the day, her dream is her climate. When the day delights the night, his light loses into earth-felt heat and mother-smelt seat. The heat gives birth to meat, and seat delivers the baby from the pelvic bench to spelling finch. In turn, heat warms the soil that produces monthly oil, and seat delights the heart that releases love. The surfing heat hurts the heart so that the heart can burn with blood-charged beat. With all the heat and no sugar, everyone on a job assignment is fired up. When the heat beats someone with meat to death, demand stops the heartbeat, and command loses the love-felt need.

Now, the dripping sound talks to the heartbeat, and dreaming song sings to the wingless mind lost in thoughtful control. This dripping sound drills the ill out of my thrill, so that my mind is as present as thunder and as delightful as rain. When the rain becomes the reality of my brain, my ocean of love sees the maker of universe, and my heart is as content as the light of the day. I become so overwhelmed with love, that I could not believe that the pure lotion in love poisons my passionate heart, till I am loosening all the earthly need and reasonable thought. I become clueless where only a faintly felt love glues me into the momentary living presence.

Equally I become so content with the reality of light, till darkness swallows up all the daylight. I lose all my dates, to count on my classmates for the account of my roommates. The classmates are classified by climatic weather so the healthier can stay and grow while the retarded can sleep and dream. The roommates are brides' honey dates and groom's romantic mate. When the bride decides the date for the wedding, the groom loses his time of demanding his visible thought upon invisible target. The bride becomes my invisible dream, and groom stirs up my visible passion.

The invisible me, my wakeful spirit, tells the visible Tao--my living soul--through a lucid dream that what the visible world that Huang's family works for and labors from, is an illusion. What the lucid dream of tender love can teach the visible—my rugged rough body--is the involution upon revolution that is thinking of no solution and feeling of no pollution.

"What does illusion mean then?" the visible dreamer asks the invisible dreamer.

"Illusion is an ill vision upon dissolution through absolution," applies the invisible dreamer.

"Does that mean that daydreaming is the date creaming behind the screaming mate who is extremely late, where a nay is a hay, and a say is a way?" asks again by the visible dreamer.

"Daydreamers are absent-minded physically but vision-wired internally. Anything you see during the day is the magic walk of the Sun upon the manic talk of the Earth, where the panic Moon sleeps with her belittled sister Earth but mates with her beloved brother Sun. Since the Moon claims the dual position, the Sun and Earth are in opposition. When the opposition offers each other with their optimal position, you have now the equal but opposite sides, so that me, as invisible, can produce you as visible, and you as visible can reduce me into invisible. When you are truly invisible, you become the absolute visible visiting your time as if the invisible dare spaces for the visible care. I am fresh without flesh, and you are the flesh missing the refreshment. That is the difference between you and me."

Dreams in my life have become my sacred heart with sacred prayers, where sacred teachings and holy messages would appear accordingly, and appeal without records. My heart would ask for a specific question upon a specific time so that my body could feel that "I am special about working on specific mind-controlled details without a retail price." Dreams do not care, since they have their own time beyond my scheduling. There were only a few times where dreams would appear upon my actual requests before I went to bed. If I can arrange them now into a manageable fashion, this is how my dreams go.

Teachings

A couple of months after we, six or so in a group, started the *I Ching's* journal process, I tried to understand what are the meanings of the *Mountainous I Ching* through the same 64 existing hexagrams. Nearly every single writer throughout Chinese history has described the Lian-shan-yi (Looping-mountain-yi), but all they have recorded and written again and again are the same and very three Chinese characters above. I was tired, but would not give it up. I felt terribly resentful towards linguistic scribers and sadly sorry for their copy-writing mind. It felt like I was going through a real trial searching through an unmarked and traceless territory; like a lover waiting for the appearance of the most beloved. Like one in prayer kneeling before a grant. Then one night, I had a dream:

In this dream, I was at the foot of a cement-clayed mountain. There was a road up to the top of the mountain and another down the road. The mountain was almost naked, peaceful but magnificent. In front of my eyes, there was an infinity or sleeping-8 symbol hosted by the two cubic or square symbols, one on each side. Those three symbols were carved into the cement block.

My inner mind told me that there were monks living on top of the mountain, and I was ready to travel. I woke up then.

A few weeks later, I formulated the original version that has been either burned by the first emperor of China or never recorded physically in the entire history of the *I Ching*. This is like to describe the actual absolute picture of human DNA in an abscond flesh. Yet the original map has been there, and is forever here. How can you describe Love? Anything you can is still unknown and anything you have already experienced is already dead. If you want to describe love, live and experience it!

Another dream occurred when I was working intensively on the feminine people externally and feminine energy internally:

In this dream, I was visiting my eldest brother, or cousin as you may call him in English. He was dead and his corpse was lying on the ground. I touched his right knee, and it moved a bit. Then I examined his left eye by opening that eyelid where I could see that the eyeball was already scorched. Afterward I poured some gasoline on his body, and lit it with a match. The corpse was on fire.

All of a sudden, I saw in the sky a giant white horse with the strongest back and the most powerful legs.

Years later, Grace had a simliar dream. As a human woman, she fell prey to human female emotions and her throat was slit by her betraying lover. As he was running from the police, her spirit followed him and howling a deep, mournful, "Why?" She ached and bled and would continue to do so for her folly. She gave the last of herself and remanifested in the tangible realm to distract the police by blinding them so her ex-lover could escape. She still loved him enough to sacrifice all that she had left.

The ex-lover then turned into a gray and black horse. He found a gun and thought it to be fascinating. He ran with it far into the distance to where he had reached an ocean. There were masses of people gathered around a dock and upon that dock, a beautiful white horse with an ephermeral golden glittering fire mane was dancing. The gray and black horse presented the gun to the white horse as an offering but the white horse refused to see it as a weapon. She rejected all violence since it did not exist to her. She wore the gun around her neck on a chain because she loved how it was shiny. The white horse danced with an energy body inside of her like that of a human.

Because of my dream, I was able to, gradually, internalize my passion, and feel and work with the divine feminine energy. It is like you feel the never cease firing of emotion charging through all over your muscles and nerves. It is like you are inside a hot lava, and you are the clay molding to the heat. Very organic and arousing at same time, you feel it is you in me inside my body plus my sense on top of my organic being wrapped by a cosmic being.

Before these two dreams, I have read all kinds of books on Taoist teaching and healing modalities. But there is one common requirement or denominator, that is, the heart-sealed transmission, called xin-jing in Chinese, which means heart Bible/Cannon/Text in English. You can read entire recorded books, but you cannot begin the sacred journey of dialogues with God or Universe, Nature or Love. That is, not until you are able to engage in heart-to-heart communication, which is the alive and lucid dream conversation with the dead and enlightened being.

Two things are happening here:

One. The space of the universe, and accordingly, of our heart, is the original white blank paper. Some people call it flatland, psychologists or philosophers calls it tabula rasa. Visionaries call it a blue veil, the mind examiner calls it blueprint, and physicians label it as plasma. Babies taste it as the initial spring of white cream before it screams for its mothers' stream. I saw it as the sunflower holes, or honey comb, where each soul or each living spirit travels freely upon the endless hole-mapped platform. So God writes in our heart, parents wrote in our flesh, and we write on paper. When paper is replaced by daily diary, and dairy advances into journey, and journey injures the heart, and heart cries for help. All the recoded words upon recording papers and tapes and DVDs are useless now. You can be the smartest person on earth, among your family or tribe, but if you cannot receive or scribe anything from your heart, nothing makes sense.

Two. Histories according to the civilized path as in recorded math and upon disputable facts, record only victories, winters, and survivals, so that losers, victims and dead can continue their march, search and torch. Looking from the gravesite-point-of-view, can you place yourself with a headstone and carve dates of your birth and death and your names on it? If you are the best basketball player, all you can do is shoot the ball into basket, whether the shot is one point, two points, or three points. Then your head coach fathers you, your manager mothers you, your owner sells you, TV screens you, newspaper reports you, fan screams at you, and the gambler predicts your score. The dream continues your dream, Martin Luther King's dream, and every body's dream, living or dead.

God is the screamer yelling at the dream and you are the dreamer screening the dream. Barbarians live the history, civilians repeat the mystery, Kings baptize the glory, and readers (whether students or scholars, mediums or historians) continue the aliveness of the factory where the dead and the head can talk to one another. Repetition and revelation have a say about each other; mobile sins extend their mortal sinks; flashing thoughts think back to the ideal idols. Ideas relate back again to single original, glorious profundities, complicated changes, and eternal mystery where idea becomes eventually my dear or your beer, or his dear.

Things delayed become debatable, and things related are really late for the divine presence from primal preparation as well as criminal prevention. But they are never late for relatives who are bonded by a biological relationship rarely relating to one another as brothers and sisters of that spiritual essence away from karmic and mimic "nonsense."

When essence speaks for the truth, and nonsense senses the truth from false, what falls sees the sea below the land and dissolves the poison from prison into pointing at the son. The son who is the primal reason for the existence between "Exs" who are ex-iled and ex-its that are ex-pired.

So conception is the beginning of the history of human life where the mystery of eternal life is lost into the factory of milk, where the reality of glorious life behind victorious liar is but an empty exchange between breath and breast, bread and break, give and take, in and out, on and off. When you are on, the prince fires up the miss who is a lost princess from the missing target as a warrior serving her life for the king and devoting her passion for the palace. When you are off, king is dead, warrior is beheaded, prince loses his head, and princess loses her heart. The arrow fired from the prince is now the triangle point locking your hips and thighs so you can land and see, sit and feel, sleep and dream. So each miss is a mist of water, a minister of labor, and a mister of mistress, where mistrust adds stress upon dress. To the degree that streets are stressed with addresses, and trespasses steal the steel distilling the roots of life and installing the roof for their wives who do not want to mate with their husbands but light.

You are on again, off is in nowhere, and light is on once again. This process primes the blueprint from universal press and then prints the recordable mystery into the ongoing factory between sorry and story, through dormitory and territory, along circulatory system and divinatory procedure as the final product. Where the flesh you or the fresh print, is on sale, so you can sell your body for love, talent for target, or love for marketable exchange.

At the time I was going through my teaching initiation trial, I had a big dream:

In this dream, I was climbing the ladders inside the earth. It was a long and endless journey and some of the specific ladders were right angled, which meant that I had to climb straight up. Thousands upon thousands of steps were leading towards the opening mouth.

As I was out of the cave, outside the mouth, I was standing by myself on a mountain peak. It was spring season and farmers were planting the fields. On the south side of the hills, there was a school built between the two slopes and was run by nuns.

I descended the hill to the bottom and there it was: a giant Taoist monk with shabby clothes. His height was taller than an average building, his feet were longer than the width of my shoulders, and there was a strip of hair extending out of outer ridge of his nose. I was a bit scared.

He informed me that he had been waiting for me, and I followed him to the cliffy edge of valley. There was an abandoned building, no roof, windows or a door, only walls standing naked above the valley. He started to write on the wall. The symbol he was scribing was the shape of Chinese hair clipper, or women's regular tampons. As the size reduced from big to little, it came to an end, he disappeared, and I woke up.

It is from this dream on, I am able to gain excess to the Taoist Talisman in healing, and know that Taoist Talisman was the original language of God in human's psychic or conscious mind. It was the beginning form of the Chinese language. Each time as our ancestor would pray for God, there would be an image, a symbol, or a revelation. As the time went on, and individual gifts were gathered for the collective, communal, and ceremonial purposes, language became alive and existed ever since. So each of those talisman-like symbols were a matrix, a map, a code, or a mode of universal construction.

Together, our mind became mapped and wired collectedly with all detailed, precise, and useful symbols. Whether it be called a drawing or painting, a language or a tool, a symbol or image, a number or letter, it does not matter. The real matter is that we are not speaking to one another, nor conversing the daily life experience. We are talking to one another's heart, and exchanging the gifts from God through language as a tool.

The biggest transmission of teaching came to me when we, a group of six people, were working on the 3rd of the *I Ching's* journal.

In this dream, I was in Hong Kong and then Singapore. There was an international war going on from different tribes, which were different nations and countries. As I was walking into a blue-veiled compartment in a subway, it was as if I was walking through blue water or a vertical ocean, a knife stabbed into my chest, but I was not killed. I then participated in all kinds of battles around the coastal cities in the world: London, Paris, Kari, Tokyo, San Francisco, Miami, and, of course, New York.

I came to a stadium full of floodwaters, and thousands of people were trapped inside. I magically dropped a violet chalk into the southwest gate, telling about ten percent of the people in the stadium, "Go and escape with your life."

A few days later, I finished mapping the *Moondial I Ching's* Chart and the shape of the *Moondial I Ching* was like a stadium, and I worked the surrounding area beginning with the Southgate point: the 8th hexagram in King Wen's (like Moses) version, the union or team or company between water (trigram) on top and earth (trigram) at bottom. Later on, I named this 8th hexagram "Firmament." It became an opening for another door which I was still walking and working through.

During one of our transmissions, my Heavenly brother was erasing the residues of past partners from my body. I felt a thick hot wax vomit from my lips and I opened my eyes to see his feet jump back from where it would land. Of course, my flesh eyes saw nothing, but my throat felt the heat rising.

When he blew water upon my bare back without warning, it shocked me from my trance-like state. I let out a painful gargled cry as I felt my lungs filled with water and I was drowning. This was a revisitation to an earlier vision I had shared with him about my previous life where, as a young man, I had put myself into a permanent sleep in a river. I saw the face of a friend's brother who shared compassion with me. Next thing I realized, my swollen face was buried in my brother's chest as I was crying like a small child who had stubbed her toe and lost her mother on the same day. One big, one small.

My death pain from drowning at that moment was unparalleled by the other aches that were shaking and quaking through my unhealthy flesh. I had seen mass devastation, everyone was fighting everyone else. Buildings fell, floods ensued and the survivors of the world were crying for their lost loved ones. All their emotional pain in the future years came coursing through my body at that moment and I was unable to move for quite some time. I was paralyzed by tragedy yet to come.

As I laid in the light arms of my brother, I did not feel him. Instead, I had left my body and was floating somewhere between heaven and earth. I was suddenly in the arms of my deceased grandmother and above her, stood my deceased grandfathers. My grandmother was telling me in words I could not decipher, but understood with my heart. She was letting me know that the tough and rough road ahead is merely standard for the life I had chosen, or was chosen for me. She told me that I was a woman and should learn to deal with it like our menstrual cycles.

As I laid there in her arms, I felt a sweetness on my tongue. It was so real, that it had snapped me back to the physical realm where I was huddled in a deprecated lump against my brother. I felt rock candy in my mouth. When I moved my tongue in fascination, there was nothing there.

The sweet treat was the three of them, my personal guardian trinity up in heaven, telling me that they have my back.

As a temporary conclusion for now, the funniest dream about teaching occurred through the following dream:

I was in front a statue made out of a corncob. In a few seconds it became muddy. The person beside, who was my teacher, told me that the corncob was too weak. He told me to let-go of it and he would find me something much stronger and durable.

We then were at the top of a mountain, he started making a deep and powerful humming voice, as if the entire sky could hear and respond to it. All of a sudden, a huge spider, about the size of a large room, appeared in the sky and came towards me, diving speedily. I was scared and numbed. The teacher in my dream told me that "Don't be afraid, he is your guardian."

Then I saw all of the praying words and wishes traveling energetically into the web-formed sky. Any emotional, personal, or egoistically charged dreams, wishes or prayers were magnetized around the silk web formed by the spider. This spider enjoyed them like a delicious meal. Only the purest dreams, wishes or prayers would travel across the tiny central openings of the web and enter into the kingdom of Universe.

Is your dream as clear as the sky? Is your wish as powerful as the light beam formed web? Is your prayer strong enough to knock off the gate to hell and knock on the door leading into heaven?

Healing

Going back to the night before my fist visit to Chicago booked through a company: Body, Mind and Spirit Health Expo in the cold winter of 2004. I prayed for the sky and my guidance to reveal and teach me how to work throughout the show. Between 3 and 5 am on Saturday morning, I dreamed about all kinds of people having all kinds of symptoms in which I was working on in the dream. This two-hour dream turned out to be the complicated yet fascinating reality for the text two days. I could not separate one symptom from another, nor distinguish the symptoms from people wrapped inside genders and mapped with characters. The same sensation upon the same location occurred in the dream would take three or more people to reveal the similar symptoms with different orientations, such as genders, ages, and soul structures. It is from this event on, I cannot lock anything into concrete reality designed by my little monkey mind and I cannot say anything that is factual from my very poor experience. The world, lived and inexperienced, is a tangible realistic bloom, where everything is moved by air, fired by heat, colored by light, and lubricated by various states of water.

Many nights, I would dream of carrying patients on my back and flying across the land and mountain to the hospitals. I would move like wind, rotate my body around the wires like a bird, elevating the mountain slopes slowly like standing off of my own gravity. When I reached the highest elevating point, I had to use my utmost power to stay above the ground.

Sometimes, patients would appear, without any appointment, a few hours after the dream. Other times, the dream event would take weeks or month to manifest.

Prayer

I was just past 23 years of age and still searching for my future and who-I-am dream. On that Chinese New Year's Eve, I had prayed the first time for my deceased grandpa to help me for my big future. I knew my future was big but I did not know what it was. All his grandchildren and great grandchildren were at his gravesite offering food, burning hell money, and fireworks. Each person would fail at setting off at least one firework. All mine, four around the four corners, and fifth below his feet, exploded unfailingly. I was told at the site with the comment: "look, how I was favored by the grandpa."

On that evening, I prayed for first time in my life without any formal instruction. I failed the following month's graduate entrance examine in January but passed test of an international visiting program in March. Two nights after I finished my orientation in Beijing and returned home by train, I had a dream:

In this dream, my grandpa appeared coming to my presence with clean but old black traditional Chinese uniform qibao. He told me telepathically that he just stopped by to check on how I was doing.

I woke up immediately and knew he was telling me he had helped me from the other world. I was shocked to hell, and scared to death by the result. Because of his help, I became the first person in my family to graduate from college. I was also the first person in my county to visit a foreign country and eventually the first immigrant to migrate away.

This is the first and the only prayer fulfilled in my life. "How many times do we truly ask for help from one person?"

The answer is "Once in a lifetime."

Destiny

Six month before I came to America through the visiting teacher's program arranged by AFS (American Field Service), which was the same program helped by my grandpa, I had a dream:

In the dream, I was visiting Northeast Normal University. There was a verse carved on both side of the entrance poles. The first part of the verse was something I did not read clear in the dream nor remembered afterward but the second verse ended with four beautiful Chinese characters (kan-mei-zhi-mei), which means see beauty, stop at the beauty. The president of the university described at the 30th year anniversary celebration the beauty of the fall season where big colorful leaves falling down the ground and the sound of Songhua River (the River running from northeast China to Korea) was ringing like a sweet bell.

One day during the fall of 1986 while I was walking through a wood at a local park, where the air was filled with huge falling leaves and the ground was paved with colored season, I had a flashing reflection, where I was here before. The Chinese character mei appeared twice turned out to be: one for the country of America (mei guo) in Chinese, and the other for my wife. What you see is what you get!

Couple of months later after I returned to China and buried my father, I had another profound dream. In this dream:

My entire hometown, hilly and peaky, was surrounded by lake-like clean water. There were all kinds of kids--black, red, yellow and white—playing by the shore. There was a straw-made boat, and on the boat, an American flag was waving the wind, four soldiers dressed with the civil war uniform were playing the American Anthem.

A few weeks later after I returned from the mountain where I wanted to become a monk and devote my life into the study of Taoist Neidan, or Inner Alchemy, I found a letter written by now my brother-in-law. He was saying that if I wanted to come to the US and was still single, he had a sister.

Past Life

One afternoon after school during my visiting program in the USA, I was meditating with crossed legs in my room. I was tired of listening to Peter Jennings' voice on TV (I still love him) to the degree that my brain was ready to explode. A few minutes later, I laid down on my back, and a dream took me away into a vision quest:

> There was a stack of dry logs piling up and the fire was flaming on top. A person wearing an orange yellowish robe was being burned. He seemed like a head monk, as I saw his face and eyes, I recognized that it was me!

> Meditation instigated, I had a vision. I was fighting, wearing a long dress as women did in the archaic times in China. What period? I have no idea. I was fighting for something, either religious, or political. My heart and my passion were on fire. My sword was sharp but my acuity was sharper and the blows filled with energy took out many who tried to stop me.

59

I was young. Perhaps fifteen to nineteen years of age. Or perhaps everyone back then was smaller and I was actually nearing my thirties. Flesh is flesh afterall, it was not reflective of the battle I was going through. I was outnumbered by three shadow forces. I swore an oath to the elements around me: Mountain (earth), Heaven (sky), River (water), Trees (wood), Spirit (gold), and my Heart Flame (fire). What that oath was, was not revealed to me at the moment.

I knew that my lover, my partner in my purpose for which I was being slaughtered for, had meant to save me. I had fought the best I could, but he was too late, or he was killed before I was. As I fell from the cliff and warm blood was oozing from my neck, I was overcome by peace, love, and forgiveness. I died before I hit the bottom. Did he burn like Peace? Or was he Peace?

During my teenage years, I was extremely interested in Tibetan Buddhism, and almost worked in that field. It turned out that about two hundred years ago, I became a Buddhist monk at age 7 and I even met my mother from that lifetime. She helped me to establish my own career and business as if she wanted to fulfill the duty of unable to nourish me from the earlier life. During a Qigong conference performed by a 32nd generation Gate-Keeper Style Shaolin Buddhist monk in 1987, I was awakened to one past life where I belonged to the eighth generation of the Shaolin lineage. The official Shaolin lineage only existed for six generations, but the teachings continued, and the student of Sixth generational keeper must have been my teacher.

Whether this vision was related to this life or not, it does not matter; yet, what does matters is that I believe in past lives. It is as real as seeing it from the harvested seeds in the Fall to reflect the seed planted in the Spring.

The fact was that I was burned to death as a doubled punishment from breaking both the governmental law and religious rule (another version of my catch 22).

This dream leads to another dream of past life experience:

In this dream, I was hanging by rope in my wrists, in the huge ditch full of dead people, from freshly killed to dried bones. I felt a click on my chest by a bullet, my legs stretched a bit, and my spirit was gone. There was a window halfway open, and my spirit jumped out of the slaughtering ditch. It was afternoon outside, and an American couple in military uniform was taking a walk with their dog. My spirit jumped into that dog and I became a dog in order to experience just one word: Faith

On the first day of my boarding school when I was 12 years old, I received a nickname by one of my classmate saying that I was a little *yellow dog*. My family name was yellow and I was a dog. I hated this name until I reached the age of 37 and realized the mission of this lifetime. Knowing that all creatures have souls, why not a dog? I remembered one day while I was working through the initial Tao Te Ching's translation at my religious professor's house, his son stated that he hated school and wished he were a dog. All a dog does in life is be faithful to its master, that is all; but are we faithful to our Master of Creation? What is the difference in English between God and Dog?

Job

Dear reader, you might have, by now, noticed how much I love to write and how I value writing. And you have read the above story of my first writing assignment. Continuing the subject of writing, I just got my visa from the America Ambassador in Guang Zhou Shi of China, and barely survived the test from the event. Anyhow, on the following night after I got my life-long permeation and permission to live in the United State, I had yet another dream:

Only one word appealed in the dream: compile.

I did not know the exact meaning of the word in the dream. Next day, when I searched it up from an English Chinese dictionary, I accepted the destiny of writing, not for anything else, but just to fulfill my dreamed destiny.

Friendship

My dad rarely talked to me, and never disciplined me before he died. The only word he instructed me was "do well in Qigong practice" before he departed. He became my best friend from the other world, constantly informing me, helping me in difficult times, until I could not bear any more.

"Dad leave alone on this matter, I will handle this by myself!" This is the first and only backfire I had to my deceased father. I had to meditate for 12 years before I could elevate him from hell to heaven. I have to cut my own umbilical cord, my milk cord and my conscious cord, before I become completely independent, universally.

I was opening the casket of my dad's coffin. His frontal body was full of hair, rare to Chinese race, and his skin was tanned like a Hollywood star, young and sexy and powerful. I wanted to push down his body, instead, he elevated into the sky like a satellite that was being launched.

I was free, at last, from my biological contract with him, this deer brother, and this biological sperm donor.

CHAPTER 4:
LIGHT, THE FATHER

Conception Contract

Before I could recognize my biological father, I read his voice. Though it was difficult to decipher his specific tones wrapped emotionally, I knew his inner voice. This inner voice, though frightening me sometimes, had a special language built inside itself that was beyond his uttering words and vaporizing emotions, and above his pride disciplines and arrogant rules. This inner voice made me feel innately connected and all-round related to the degree that my father became a knowable object, and me a sensible subject. This object is knowable to the fact it is not a knowledge and this subject is sensitive enough that it becomes either neutralized and numb, or subjugated to the point of thumb.

The thumb is numb but a tongue feels the gum. Sucking my thumb is more now sensible than rubbing my numb drum, since thumb is more knowledgeable about its active point than a numbed sensation containing only mooching winching rubber band and sub-can. When the thumbing point and numbing joints are united, I point to his object and he numbs my growing goiters. As the knowable part of his voice invites the sensible part of nonsense, the sensitive me rejects the knowledgeable him on an ego trip, and his knotting power knocks me out of the kneeling powder.

Between this bridging object and subject, there is all that ejecting motions and rejected notions throwing and bouncing like polarized and depolarized jet streams. So we throw jackets to each other, make jokes of one another, perform jobs teamed, signalize gestures postured, and make senses of means in the midst of guessing the meaning and questing the mean. He became my half-brother, a brother from another mother.

So his being older and have more ages than me has nothing to do with this inner voice. The moment I know this inner full and empty voice, I am gone, for good and forever. Because inside this inner voice, there is something untouchable, containing certain elements that are by themselves helpless and vulnerable, useless and meaningless.

From this stage on, there is a seed planted inside of me, through this inner voice, that all goals are looped along the endless spinning tails of goats' horns, and every purpose is inside each pure empty pose, and each meaning is either equating to the opposite of that means or balanced from the average point to the degree that both sides cancel one another and neutralize each other. Now, the orbiting object lands on substantial sub that is the location of suburb connecting to the hub on one end and all the wheeling lumbering threats and ropes on the other. The result is that I do not know him anymore, and he cannot claim me any further.

In fact, before I listened to his voice, I would watch his ball throat, moving up and down and ruling everything else. His throat would rule everything in front of him and then fuel all the refusals behind him. From this I found out that throat rules the holes and refusal reuses old news. Holes are above the ditch, and news switches back and forth between itches and inches. Those human and personal holes fill all the cans containing cantaloupes and refusing antelopes so that the single ditch itches the hell out of witches and teaches the cell inside minute inches.

Through my father's rubbing throat, I knew that goiters point to the conscious joints, saliva savors the favor, and tongue glues the nectar.

Later on, as I observed the lightning and thunder in the open sky and through the heavy-meddled black clouds, I knew that a thumb-under (thundering) light runs faster than a loud cloudy sound. Oppositely, a heavy sound smashed on the ground refuels a dangling light in the sky into a peaceful residue that only rain droplets make as they sound above their grounded bubbles. Only the soaked ground remembers trailing steps as remarkable members of a footstep. All I know then is that the only thing alive is the lonely sinking song arrived.

The footstep is combined and intertwined with leaf-likened stretching steps, where shoed steps are like hair clippers and toed steps resemble extended but palmed fingertips. The only difference is that toed steps are remarked by five single dots extending their arched root, and palmed tips are surmounted by four tripled and one doubled joints that look like cut-off intestine joints or the running legs of an insect. Are these grasping and starching fingertips capable of extending and unfolding those running and suspending legs? Since the arches of feet are longer than the armed wrists and their palmed beasts' feasts, toenails are more humble in grounding themselves to the ditch than fingernails who only know the meaning of grasping for inch-long marks and the purpose of scratching upon the itch-wide remarks. As the thousand itches amount inside an inch-wide space, itch dials and fires at an inch, which makes witch twitching and ditching, having no clue of any inch it hosts.

Focusing deep into the thunderous lightning, I noticed that the red yellowish lightening snaking through the sky and clouds rattled me for a long time, until I was able to make use of my inner ignitable sense. Was the thunder in rage or was I jailed in a cage? When the little sparking light inside me talks to the belittled remarkable cell inside my sense, I know then how a seed moves in and around the shell and a deed solves inside and through a cell. The more I am focusing on my thinking rings, the more I know the meaningful purpose of an aged ring, and the clearer I understand that when an age is rugged with edged rings, it mugs a person into a rage. This ringing age is a God-enlightened page upon year-rounded and cycle-surrounded cage. The age becomes a round edge outside but sound rage inside. God is capable of evoking thunder, making us His thumb-under, and in turn, our ears hear the undetectable sound that evokes us fear. When fear produces fever, the favor ferments the savor as a slaver, and ear is forever near the favor but never dear the savor.

As rage is inside a cage delivering the page, the seasoned age of a life turns into a fruitful sage. Smudging with the herbal sage, the metamorphosed sage opens his fossilized cage, which contains a very valuable page stating that he has changed his rage into a readable classical page. Though the paper is not seen, his heart rings the vibration of his inner sound.

Sometime when my father was in his consuming rage, his eyes became lightning and his voice was thundering. This specimen like red yellowish lightning reminded me later on of the blood lines growing inside of a rotten egg, of the emotionally and sexually discharged individuals, and of the well-preserved cadaver framed with clean meat and highlighted with reddish blood veins and their ending roots.

I somehow could detect his inner drumming rhythms before his throat carried out worded construct and emotion wrapped voice. Even now it fascinates me to notice how we human flash and splash one another with a light second contact between the two different sets of eyes.

Aside from his eyelids, which frightened me when I viewed their over stretched curtain-like eyebrows worse than a nightmare, his throat would drum rhythmically, whether swallowing down the gross food or swallowing up the grouchy silence. It was his silent presence that scared me the most. Never has he raised his voice before me, I had to make use of his longhaired eyebrows and walnut-sized throat to read him. His silent presence buried daily exhaustion and momentary depression, frozen but unexplainable anger underlying unbearable frustration, dried up inexpressive pains and sufferings of life. It is before the lunchtime, his noon teatime, the cracking sounds of wood burning and fire elevated smokes, plus the sipping comfort from the tea into his throat, I sensed the real power within him. The tea he drank was like a washing tear and a supporting team to his body and its overdosed senses.

And before I knew my self, I carried his name on my shoulder for social and ancestral validation. Walking and standing in front of an elder figure, I was not an independent human but an identification of my ancestor. Instead of introducing myself with my first name, I would answer with my family name and then my father's name. I became an extension of my father's lifeline. Years of imitating his voice and pasting his signature made me a biological and ancestral robot. I became a family dog, an ancestral offspring, faithfully guarding the bloodline and proudly posting the family name--the yellow flag--high above the mounted blue sky. Identically, my family name from my father to his father and his father's father, long listed males with same yellow name, has the same root meaning of my hometown, Yellow Earth. So what comes out of this dual yellow is the third yellow: Yellow Emperor, the Ruling Son of the East and morning. Though numerically the Chinese family name Huang or yellow is listed way below the heavily populated name like Wang (Wong), Zhang, Chen (Chan) or Lee (Li), and numerous emperors are enlisted after the Yellow Emperor, the yellow powder swallowed by Green Dragon, did good on behalf of my family name, and all of the other yellows.

It is through my family name Huang or Yellow that I make sense of what yellow race means. With those five different yellows now -- yellow family name, yellow earth, yellow emperor, yellow powder, and yellow race – I truly understand the power of yellow, which credits to the power of morning Sun, spring season, expanding Jupiter, back into the yellow marrow which is originated from the yellow dome which ignites the never ending growing power of yellow. It is also through this very yellow I received the atonement to see how the yellow race operates with its gut-firing and tail-leaping martial power, which finally credits as the beauty of martial arts and rage of the Boxer Rebellion (Revolution).

Since the dawn of civilization, yellow race did to itself with the straight and strict line of blood, called lineage, to the degree only Yellow Emperor was mystically survived and magically accredited. All the rest, individuals upon individuals, and generation after generation, grew prosperously and quickly like yellow sprouts, and then silently disappeared and dissolved into something else, maybe into one of the three neighbors: white race, black race, or even the horse race.

Aside from morning dews and spring juices, this yellow also contains the bedding desert, threaded sulphur and sapphire, layered with molasses and butter. When the yellow is a bit off its color, sallow then describes the jealousy look where ground squirrels, yellow weasel, cattle, oriole, yellow porgy and cucumber (huang gua- yellow melon) are all smashed inside the golden roots fermented by yellow fever and welled by the Netherworld.

Heated and retarded by famine, the yellowish dusts and soils bury the petroleum inside the cave temperature, and through the sprouting fabrics of golden dome linking to the solar ecliptic ring on one side and the yellow dome of shambhala on the other side.

This has been going on for years until I began searching the meaning of my mind, through the words invented or instructed by others. As my birthing sound and its organic voice expanded into family voice and Chinese noise accordingly, my tongue rang with truth within my bloodline and my lips emitted that familiar vowel-clustered tones of yellow race: the sounds of fireworks. Though my teeth resembled rat's hole-digging power, tiger's biting skill, dog's neck-cutting technique, cow's grass-chewing mechanism, and snake's whole food swallowing bit, they did not appear as I appeared. Only when my animalistic crawling posture stopped, my tail and sacral bones fused into a plus or minus sign between standing up and bending down, like a sign language formed and rotated between thumb on one side and the rest fingers on the other side, my body started to grow infantile teeth, close to jaw and nostril, for the purpose of grabbing the nipples. And I learned that lesson of not using my force too fast or too forcefully. Otherwise, my face would be smashed with my mom's heart-raging and wind-pounding smacks. Those smacks were very much like forest-fire extinguishing techniques. The blood-coated facial skin would not resemble the reddish flashes from a growing or rotten egg, but be acquainted with the drunken face of yellow race where the heated alcohol was burning and firing all over the face.

Not written as anything literally, my father's handwriting served as an invitation card for me to know the meaning of a handwritten script, which are the copies of words, with his signature, invented and passed on and down for thousand of years long before he was born. This contract was finalized on my first day of official academic classes when the black ink was extended from the writing brush up to my sweaty fingers first, and then found its way all over my face. Thus, it was decided what I was to do. Instead of singing and performing on stage with masks like Peking Opera, my face was soaked with black ink for the purposing of writing and scribing what the black hole has received and materialized.

My mother's father always asked her to keep a diary, to

write down her life for it was unique. Never would anyone else walk her shoes, and experience what she had experienced. She never did keep those journals. It was only after my 23rd birthday, did she share with me her father's words to her. I myself, have kept countless journals since the age of eight. Sometimes, wishes for the children skip a generation or two. I was initiated as a writer, by my grandfather when my own mother did not wish for that blessing.

Initiation Contract

Beginning boarding school at age of 12, I realized that my father was gone. Not because he was dead yet but because he had nothing more to offer me or even to pass on to me. I did not realize that carrying his genetic mode was enough, and more than enough. His deformed gene also deformed me in parts and decayed certain bodily components up to now.

The best he offered me was that he was a watch tower. He never informed me of a thing during his life nor ordered me to do a chore, an assignment or homework. He watched over me while he was alive, my behaving posture and deeded pasture, like the Sun watching over the mountainous slopes and their livelihoods on earth. Each of my thoughts was one of those slopes as each of my livelihoods was precisely examined, rudely retrieved, and ruthlessly rejected afterward.

Two things were happening in this interaction. One was that if I did have any plans or were to do anything, the watchtower was absent, and I was left alone with the empty void of nature. The other side was that anytime when my mind was busy thinking something, and that any moment I was engaging with an activity, the watchtower was present, as if I were present. In fact, my father was inside of me, through me, around me and all over me. I was like a naked cell being absorbed, a slave being watched, a prisoner being guarded. Yet, I was equally alone, like the previous disengaging mode. There was nothing I could do or behave or fulfill that was not detected, examined, tested, and retested. It was as if I was repeating what he had gone through, what his father had gone through, and what light had gone through. All these preceding figures wanted me to go through the same trail and experience, the same ordeal, and reach the same conclusion, and retire with the same rewards. I was a nameless being, an empty truck, a traveling agent, a delivering gospel, a useless gossip, a foolish tool, and a meaningless entity.

Since then, I became a loner, obtaining good grades by obeying all the required disciplines. Each time a teacher taught us in class some thing new, my mind was ignited and I was gone, to somewhere else, outside the information presented in the classroom. Through those years all I knew was that a heart-devoted teacher was not a good informer, and a good presenter was not a good teacher. I felt humbled and sorry for those heart-devoted teachers, who are good humans but bad teachers, since there was not any worthwhile material they could present besides reading after textbooks and copying after formulas.

As for those few good presenters, they were simply salesmen, not teachers. They were so good in presenting information and selling their lips that they could sell 20 percent information stored in their stomach for 100 percent: 80% of profits for the society in general and school in specific. These good presenters became the double salesmen, selling information in the classroom and selling students out for either ideal or professional expansion. This made me distrustful, and very much resentful.

Only once in a while, there would appear a good teacher who had solid information in his head but he could not word them out. This made me feel that I wanted to cut an opening his throat and just suck the knowledge out of his brainstormed stomach. Only few times in my entire life, I came across a few teachers who had solid information in their head, a warm vibration in their heart, and skillful deliverances in their manners. Those teachers are so rare and it is almost impossible to meet with them in classroom or in life space.

So, instead of following a specific teacher, I became a bookworm and consumed words like a parasite. Books are the soul-worms of writers, and words are parasitic to any one who is willing to learn and digest. And it took me many years to change from a bookworm to thought-snake, from a word-parasite to a motion-detector. As I am apt to snaking people's thoughts, I know their deeds and their world of reality and I could shake their egos out like snakes do to their skin. While I am able to detect people's true motion, I would sort out the love out of their emotions. I come to realize that each action is divine, whether we are aware of it or not, or conscious of it or not. Body is a mysterious field, since it hosts spirit. Body is also a mystic chariot, since each of its mobile movements is part of the divine, whether for divine intervention or crime prevention. Regardless, each motion is star-like or stage-wise.

Before this I had traced all the civilized paths through written words and recorded histories.

Words are written because they are so good as to be used as a flood detergent to flush out the whining thoughts. They are one of the best instruments to convey what is going on or has happened inside one's sacred world. They are, in this instance, gift items to be shared and enjoyed. Words are the bread baked from the flours of life.

Yet, for the majority of people who are educated and civilized, words are the parasites, eating up all they have inside their brain by consuming all their hopes and dreams into a culturally formatted and socially customized veil. This veil most likely produces and endorses a national hero, umbrellas specific cultures, such as invented or discovered, created or transpired individual information as part of a collective cultural compartment. But this very veil can never free one's soul or liberate one's spirit. Thus, words become Godly defined logos and ego-decided patients.

There is a much deeper meaning and functioning behind the construction and use of words. They can be used to free oneself from previously bounded conscious walls, or restrain oneself once again into the same and habitual cultural mode. Least, words are tools, simply to be used for many purposes and reasons. Most, they are snapshots of what is happening inside one's own world, and what is equally happening in the world at large. Words are the films of one's thinking process, and joints of chaining one's conscious and love streams into individual chains and rings and locks. Words exist not because of what we are applying them to now, but because they serve as the divine conscious signatures scribing what is happening in the world, what has been transpired from the universe or inspired from the receiver. Words are spectrums of light, particles of wave, and dials of sound.

Yet, if one can smile like a magnificent picture, words become colors and hues. If one can dial directly and straight into one's heart, words are the notes and lyrics of music produced inside our own very instrument. If one can communicate directly with light, words are dust.

So the origin of words is Light. Words are the fathers of civilization, but light is the father of all living spirits and existing essences. Words as light particles and photons serve the purpose to manifest thinking lights as living streams. Verbalization is the process in which the divine indwelling of light in the spirit manifests as the divine presence of a living spirit, which is the holy fire. To make sense of automatic verbalization creates the structure and content of worlds as meaningful as light particles or photons so that each cell receives the very vital corresponding charge through the very verbalized word.

Vowels constructing words become like bloodstreams and breathing air flows in and out of the body. Consonants become organs, muscles, and bones to host and transport the living blood and air of vowels. Consonants become the living flesh and vowels the manifesting spirit.

To be loyal to the literal meaning of worlds destroys one's own vital digestive process of life experience. To be faithful to the descriptive nature of worlds demeans one's own vital expression, which is the divine expression of one's divine experience. This is the common fear and common mistake most average minded people make. They do not know how to use words personally, and they do now know how to apply words spiritually.

Through this journey, the written words became my living fabrics. Reciting the text of *Tao Te Ching* around the age of 21 made me realize that I cannot just memorize those heavily stoned words like many other textbooks. Then came with the meditative state of automatic writing. This ensures me there is another kind of fatherly image aside from own biological father. It is through this conscious transmission, Lao Zi became my spiritual father, and His Words became the initiation contracts.

It is through His words externally watching me and guiding me, deep meanings of life, earthly and heavenly, and His conscious transmission overseeing my path. The path which is no longer annualized by the Earth around the Sun, but eclipsing by a much higher energy grid, where only spirit can take this call, and walk along this heavenly mandate.

I have been faithfully devoted to Lao Zi, replacing my biological father as a friend and not an official figure. After 17 years, I realize that Lao Zi possesses the same energy as spiritual figures like Buddha, Christ, Mohammad, Moses, King David, Peace Maker, Pipe Carrier, Shaman, and all the rest who are not carved in stones, enlisted in words, recorded in books, enshrined in temples, and elegized in songs.

With this single antenna, I was able to survive physically and grow spiritually, to the degree where I can use and dial my pure dual blood, biological blood and spiritual blood, to converse and communicate with the reset of races and spiritual lineages.

Along this course, I have gone through years of lonely pilgrimage, wandering as if the first child and only human on earth. Not knowing anything, I have to still make things known through the interaction with Nature and Its myriad creatures. In turn, we become all light followers, water containers, and clay potteries.

Enlightenment Contract

The only way to know the Father Light is to know the holy conception through holy love. Through the divine and angelic mother, light becomes projected through a heart-manifested spirit, which is son. By knowing and understanding this spirit, the true selfless self, the holy love of the heart returns to the origin of divine motherhood, to host and smile with shining light again.

When light manifests in our brain, we receive insight, see the sight, and view the object. This is the scientific path till now in human history. This cave-brain serves as a mirror to reflect light way in and out.

When light dials in our heart, we receive warmth, sing songs, and produce harmonic melody.

When light ignites our gut, we receive charge, feel the urge, and leap beyond the boundary.

Love, the Mother

What happened today. Today, the nineteenth of August. A Sunday. It began an almost normal day. Almost, except the tiny shred of ache in my heart from loss and disappointment, but it was easily brushed aside and did not offer me too much of a nuisance.

I wanted to return to my old room because I loved the trees outside of the window. As it was planned, I drove there through the light drizzle only to discover that I didn't have the keys. I drove to my father's house and he gave me the garage remote. I returned again through the nice, light rain. However, I did not go to my house. Something in me pulled, and I drove past it to go to the lake.

It was a chilly walk in my cargo shorts and flip flops. As I was leaving the parking lot to head towards the lake, I heard a sound to my left. Looking over, I saw a car in which a blonde girl in red sweatshirt was facing backwards in the driver seat moving rhythmically. I turned my attention back to the lake. My feet were cold. At least I had a sweater on and an umbrella. I expected the water to be turbulent, but it was actually quite calm. I went down by the edge and stood in the water upon the pretty stones. The water was slimy and warm. I didn't mind the sliminess so much. The August lake water warmed my toes.

I gazed passively at the tiny water drops as rain hit the surface. It would be a minute ball for a split second from the pressure of landing and then dissipate to become one with the lake. I glanced to my right, then to my left. It seemed odd that I was alone, because I certainly didn't feel it. I felt a warmth alongside the pang in my heart.

I traced the lapping waves along the edge of the pebbly walkway with my eyes. It seemed as if it were nothing more than a giant puddle. In my mind, came "lake over earth" and I retreated from the cold back towards my car. I had grabbed one of my *i ching* books before I left and I looked up the 45th hexagram. Passively I read the desciption tucked some bits of information in my mind for later chewing on.

I finally made my way back to my old house. I wasn't there long until my father stopped by to check on the paint bulge in the garage. Water was coming in a bit. I was doing the layout for Angelic Wings and I needed the internet to find snippets of things I had written in the past so I went to the Library. I discovered that it was closed Sundays since it was the summer. I went to a coffee shop, but they had teamed up with a wireless company and charged to use the internet. I was pretty upset. So I only stayed long enough to finish my soy sweet treat and then headed home.

It was odd. Shortly before I left the coffee shop, as I was continuing to layout Angelic Wings, I felt something. It was a sense of wholesomeness. Something was filled and the achy pain was more pronounced as the love grew in my heart. Everything was fine and normal as I returned to the house, which was just a few moments away. I returned to my old room and sat down. I was placing the images into the document and catching a few words here and there that my Heavenly brother had written. I was suddenly aware that I could hear his voice, but not in my head, in my heart. He wasn't speaking, nor was he saying anything, it was just the inkling that comes along with any person's vocalized speech. I felt a few tears behind my eyes, but nothing much. I continued to place pictures. His light energy grew brighter inside of me though he was miles away, and his words danced, alive, inside of my heart.

I cannot remember what words or sections, or chapters I read, but next thing I knew, I was floored. A wave of emotion had knocked me over and I was laying on the carpet and unable to see through the torrents of heavenly rain coming through my eye sockets. I wept out of pure joy that anything as beautiful as I was experiencing was possible on earth.

What I felt was that I was with him in those words he wrote. I was a part of him since day one, when he entered his mother's womb. Our histories and blood were one and the same. Everything that had occurred to him in the book, was his process of finding me. Everything he had felt, was heaven's way of leading him to me, preparing him to meet me as I was being prepared to meet him. What I felt beating in my chest was no longer my own heart, but his. What flooded my being were not my own memories and experiences, but what he had put with his blood into Angelic Wings.

Eventually, as my heart chakra opened wider and wider as a flaming flower and more and more light came flooding through, it opened me onto another level and I felt the old memories of love in that house seeping in and mixing with the euphoria that I was washed with. Our souls and everything that made up who we are and were, became mixed together into a singular memory matrix for those few moments.

I wept until my eyes were swollen and a puffy red. I wept with pure elation from being blessed by such a state of being. I cried until something inside of me released. It burst open like a long needed cracking of a hard to reach back joint.

I think I did a little more work, but eventually packed up to go home since I was getting hungry. In the car, I listened to the Butterfly Lover's Concerto. A beautiful piece, perhaps my favorite in the entire world.

My heart began to sway. My entire being was being rocked like a lullaby as each of the notes dictated a movement, motion, or emotion that my Heavenly brother was emanating. Since I knew the song well, I knew exactly when each clash occurred. I was driving south on 271 when a surge in the music occurred and suddenly, to my surprise, I was brought up into another state of mental existence. The safest thing for me to have done in the rain was to pull over but I didn't have enough physical wherewith all to do that. By some lucky chance, a tiny pinpoint of my conscious was able to still control the steering wheel and keep me between the lines. At one point I was aware I had to tell myself as if a third person, to slow down because I was going 80 and it was dangerous. It was as if I had separated from my body.

The state I was in was something else altogether. I had indeed left my body. I was crying and could not breathe. I was so overcome but extreme love and compassion for all things around me connected by the invisible lines called music and harmony that I hardly existed in the flesh at all. I was as if all energies in the world created another dimension in which I was connected to all those who loved me dearly. There was a safe little dome where all intrusions from the shadows could not interfere and only the purest of sentiments may enter. I recognized some familiar energies from close friends and family. It wasn't long until I identified the strongest energy I had come in contact with. My Heaven ordained partner, my Heavenly brother and I were dancing with our meridian energies which was reflected somewhere deep in the heavens trillions of light years from earth. We danced and moved as water and light would, with no hidden dark desire. We danced in the purest of love.

On earth, my body was crying so hard that no sound came out and my heart felt like it was going to burst with love. My body felt like it was split open like a ripened summer watermelon used to share for others' enjoyment. I was gasping and each sob was filled with the utmost genuine joy. Through the rain, I saw a purple haze and I knew positively, one hundred percent, that it was Purple Yang who was with me in that instant sharing the exact same energy in the exact same constellation. Not only did we trade hearts, it melded together in instant. We would never be free from each other. It was the same heart that was split in two from the Holy Mother (Xi Mu Niang) and birthed separately to the two genders. In that moment of clarity and unspeakable bliss, I had experienced what God must have felt and feels everyday and challenges all His children to seek. I could have died and would have done so gladly if I could give that sentiment to the world as a parting gift. But, as you are reading this, I am still here! It is an experience no one can receive from another human, rather, through finding God, we find the purest love he had blessed upon Adam and Eve.

CHAPTER 5:

MY CRIED, DYED PINHOLE

Right before I reached the age of 24, I studied very hard in order to pass the sports psychology graduate entrance exam. On the Eve of this particular Chinese New Year, I prayed from my heart to my deceased grandfather for him to give me some guidance and strength, support or direction. Without knowing any ritualistic or ceremonial practices, I borrowed three incense sticks from my oldest brother, poured the wine into three cups, and started my prayer. I said silently but willfully from my heart to my grandfather that I wanted to do something big and needed his help. If he would help me, let the incense burn completely; otherwise, let them die halfway through.

I lit the first incense stick for Heaven and placed it in the middle of the incense holder. I then lit the second for Earth and placed it on the left, and the third for my grandfather and placed it on the right. Afterward, I held each cup of wine in my hand, tilted a bit, and poured out a few droplets onto the ground as the thanks to the sky father, the earth mother, and the white blood in the other world.

The moment I started to kneel myself down, there was that light but gentle, present yet distant touch upon my shoulders and around my head. My entire being was channeled, becoming weightless. A string of holy water showered on me, in me, and I was carried away into a tear-land, where only my heart knew from this point on how to cry without a try. The tranquility was beyond my mental description or cognitive labels. The sensation was like snaking in a holy chamber. My stance was a weightless presence. In the presence, from that moment on, I was in a new dimension.

I learned from this ceremonial event that if my heart were honoring the Three, or any combination of three, I would receive something free. The helper was always there, depending on how I would approach for it. I must dry up my tears in order to be near and dear. And I have to allow my heart to cry and my passion to be fried!

With this prayer, I failed the graduate exam, but was able to pass the next one, secure a passport, arrive in New York City, and finally land on the bottom shore of the Great Lakes, in Cleveland. During this visiting school year, I was assigned at a local high school, observed all the social science classes, and taught Chinese language and Qigong classes. I experienced both the American lifestyle, and awakened my ancestral and spiritual blood.

After it had been 6 years or so since I started Qigong exercise, I had experienced all regular 12 meridians running and traveling inside my body. Those meridian lines were a silk-thin white, as my breath became smooth, gentle, long and deep. My focus was totally present like a mirror to reflect all that appears without any detailed internal planning or external targeting. Passing through those silk-thin white lines, each pressure point along the meridian line would vibrate, producing all kinds of odd sensations. Some were hot, others were cool; sometimes one point would produce a hot frostbite, others were like music notes scaling through a particular meridian as if they were trailing and singing along a string.

By the time the Qi traveled through my arthritic joints, ligaments, and bones, the entire region was stove-hot, and itchy irritably; yet comfortable

and soothing. The inner landscape now was escaping away from the outer world, but scaling the inner sanctuary. The world as seasonal cycle was now recycling inside, and I became a seed sprouting new leaves and inviting new beliefs. The new leaves were activated by the meridian body, as the new beliefs were as ancient as how the Angelic Mother had brought them down from her sky-husband (light-lover) and fabricated human energetic pool.

It was shown to me in my first cry when my Heavenly brother first began awakening me to my higher assignment. I saw a white seed of pure light being planted. Then, it begain to grow, and it sprouted as a candle. Two leaves grew up from the bottom, circling up and above, trying to cover that very candle. Suddenly, the leaves turned into gentle white hands and they spiraled in the other direction. The candle turned into a white beam of light shining down from heaven.

I used to be diligent in running for 6 years nonstop each day. But as I began my Qigong exercise, this rough muscular exercise seemed to be a waste of time and, consequently, my energy. I felt good at the moment when I was running. The body was in motion, muscles were wheeling, ligaments were appointing and aligning, and my mind was in its tangible promotion. In contrary to this external exercise, Qigong practice would never exhaust, evaporate, or extinguish my energy. I became charged, energized, and consequently saved all that I had gathered during the session inside of my battery of a body.

I would then read the locations, definitions, and functions of each meridian and its corresponding points. Not wanting to memorize them like a medical student would, I bit, chewed, and digested somatically, letting the body do its work. Not trying to find a cure through recorded information for the future medical practice, my body entered the secured land of the universe. Not diving it onto pathological chart imbued historically, my innocent soul swam inside a divine path but beyond logistic math.

Within such a mindset, any pathological evidence, as well as treatment, was never my cup of tea. For me, "What was wrong with the body?" was not a medical question but a mystic quest. The abnormality of the body was like that so-called abnormal daily weathers and seasonal climates.

Speaking to an average mind, which was above the rage but below the sage, those abnormalities were not good. Conversing with Nature, which was never away from nurture, those abnormal sequences were how things were, changed with, and exchanged from. The absolute beauty or health never occurred in any individual body, but forever occupied the dreamland and its imaginary scale.

To find a cure or to receive treatment, away from the divine communication within the body and its sacred system, only invited further curiosity, but never provided any curable solution. If a doctor could find a cure for death, life would suspend from its end, and a cycle would never complete. If any ailment could be treated completely, what was the use of the fermenting seasons of life? If without illness, how would life cook a destined hook, or book a retarded look?

Nature subtracts with what we called disastrous weathering patterns, so that only stronger and more suitable ones can survive and reach their contracted and seasoned goals. In the tropical belt, dry weather takes away the wet season. In the four seasonal hemispheres, winter wipes out all moving surfaces with snow so that everything stands for the now. In polar portals, nighttime blacks out the solar tray and darkness receives cosmic rays. Lord gives our life, our cord takes in air; sword slices joints and word describes appointments. Afterwards, cord bakes the labor as Lord takes away our spirits; word stones our wheels so that sword atones our willingness.

To my best knowledge, there was something fundamentally wrong to prescribe a pathological look towards the sacred body and its holy components. Truly we are wronged twice, once from spirit to soul, and the other from soul to flesh. But do we know our intentions upon our destined stations? To find a cure from exercise, and for sure with a will, was my true excitement at the time. I did not want to see a doctor because I could not afford it, and I had to get well by looking into my own laboratory with my own labor to see my history upon my victory. When the vibratory sensation comes through a point sending its distinctive signal, I would be joyous, respectful, humbled, and honorable about the conscious confirmation, contribution, and distribution towards the understanding of meridians and their points. The names of each meridian, and each point, were not arbitrarily given, nor ruthlessly defined. Coming from this experiential journey, pathological understanding, clinical application and consequently spiritual ascension, meridians were understood as the river-lines, weather patterns, and seasonal trails, along daily, monthly and annual loop that belongs to the 12 orbiting and rotating Earth's troops. Meridians are Qi lines, energy channels, soul-driven tunnels, and spirit-delighted antennas. Their names were consciously digested and physically revealed.

Like an emperor and his kingdom where each lot was planned and through every marked terrain ran his sanctuary train to loop his conscious string. The spirit is all over the body, running from site to site, to excited signs and extracted signals. Spirit is free: though mapped along meridians, and wrapped by flesh. Each insightful idea or thought has its targeting point, and every soul-charged and love-boiled vibration is its dialing wave, expressive stream, and hovering cave.

Meridians are, in the beginning, a lover's trailing tear and love's daring dear. When the twin flames were given, the brother fires at the sister's streaming tear, and sister boils up the brother's delightful dare. Each is complete but only in half; while together as one, 12 meridians of lifelong trail return to the original 8 fetal rails. The trail bails the rails so that any ailment delayed by betrayal can be related to the original jail without a wail and bail. By the time the sacred opens to the inner joy and bliss kisses the release, mundane returns to the holy land and hell bells the lovely sell for heaven.

In this Loveland, longing and desiring for Oneness is the harmonic ball; where each is useless in half. But together birth is created and death is transcended.

In this tearless land, euphoric bliss is the expressive meridian, and each tender touch or gentle kiss is a decided agreement, desirable joint, pressed point, and surprising appointment.

In this dreamland, the bed is the intertwining bodies and their eight geometric skeletons, the dreamers are the awakened souls, the sleepers are the soul-charging and flesh-refreshing batteries, and the dream-catchers are the delighted or enlightened spirits.

In this ever land, glands are glad, and souls are fat, and spirits are fried to the dry bones in cry for a single droplet of universal love.

This is, and has been, how the meridians and their pointing tones or notes are designed, defined, decoded and decorated with. They were how the body as a sacred vessel would do, how the harmonic angle of heartbeat would point from a minute pore of skin towards manicure and manipulation, and where the translucent runway of the soul would travel or orbit inside this holographic landscape. This was the beginning of my understanding of Inner Alchemy. This alchemy was about sprouting the yellow flower of my gut-brain, refining the gold inside of my soul, and expressing my spirit-charged powder. The chemistry of soul was an entirely different maker from that of biophysical one. There were different layers of chemical ingredients inside and through our sacred vessel. Physical or biophysical chemistry was the result of instinct animation. Emotional or personal chemistry was the sizable mapping snap of the soul. Conscious or intuitive chemistry was the distant residue from the Creator.

When the body returned, we made sense of the animal kingdom, and its instinctive nature. When the soul returned, we sensed the precious love and the gracious peace. When spirit returned, we are home forever, whether in heaven or on earth, or engaging in holy work or enjoying hellish pork.

I wanted to offer my body as an instrument to constitute my institute; a laboratory to taste my relapse and rehabs; and a factory to produce my facts. I wanted this instrument to be an open book, on display in public, and leaving no private agenda or pivotal pagoda. I wanted to allow the most undated and advanced machine to scan the most ancient toxicity, inside the most secretive lotion, as a result of the most sacred resolution. I wanted meridians, what I have seen and experienced, to be screened so that I could become the first modern being having its body charted: like what Da Vinci had vanished, how Christ tarnished, why Buddha furnished, where Goddess furbished, and when God finished.

With this de-sire, I dealt with the sire, by begging a high school English teacher to write a letter to the Cleveland Clinic, which had one of the five most advanced equipments in the nation at the time. The Clinic denied my fuel, and refused my news. I failed one of the most desired sadnesses in my personal life, and became pale in my heart for what those males have been nailing and failing in their scientific fields. I did not have five thousand dollars in hand for a regular elite checkup. I was extremely disappointed because I wanted to be the first modern man to demonstrate and prove that meridians are real, not just some sort of Chinese imagined lines and points printed in a chart or framed on a model.

In this exciting year, I also experienced the firsthand past life vision, time stoppage, elevation, astral projection, remote view, and many other ESP (extra sensory perception) materials. By the time I found that Chinese medicine and Taoist Inner Alchemy were, though given to the Chinese race, actually belonging to humanity, my cry was ever since frying my passion and trying my soul. I wanted both: both sides of a day producing time and lime, and both sides of the agenda reducing gender as lender. I wanted to retain my Chinese bloodline and also obtain the freedom of American lifestyle. This my-24-years-of-age was my magic high. I discovered what I wanted for the rest of my life. I wanted to honor both the East and the West, both the heart-binding ancient teachings and the free modern expression, both parents, and both Creators. I wanted to try everything and cry for all, as the ultimate mourner and the most liberating horse—Pegasus--between the skyline and mobile land.

First Cry

Out of all the cries I tried and dried, two were breath-taking and heart-raking. The first cry fried me was when I was leaving the United States of America at Cleveland Hopkins International Airport. Everyone from my program, about 4, were happy. They have been experiencing how this dreamland was, what a god-land could be, and what the very promise land should offer. They wanted to redress and resell what their ancestors had fabricated. They could not wait to show eagerly the delicious meal of the western civilization they have digested and savored to their families, friends and comrades at home. They wanted to reveal desperately what a trip they had been slipped by and ripped from.

They were now the foreign-tinctured domestic golden coins, as their mother tongues were refined by alphabetic riddles and refilled with silver bullets. They had achieved by that time what the average Chinese would only dream for but could never fulfill: "What is the actual lifestyle that first class citizens enjoy, savage and ravage?" Filled by temporary glory, those diplomats had no clue deep inside how they had been influenced by digitized mediums and numbed by industrial revolutions. Like entering a romantic state without watching for the somatic steak or feeling the poisonous leakage, they were drugged completely by the freedom rug retaining the habitual tug.

Like visiting a strange dreamland lost, my colleagues' domestic tongues were glued with foreign guns, and their indigenous features were cultured with dominant global texture. Every bit of their digestion was now mixed with industrious modes. Every cell was fixed with world-class mentality, and every instinctive action stretched from the Great Wall to the Nile Delta: half-yellow and half-white, but nothing in between, or beyond. Their yellow race was laced with white case, and their yellow gut sprouted with white bud above the bleached knot. They became a cultural half-breed, happy externally but lost internally, since they had no time to identify or objectify. They found the island lost in the never-land. Their eyes were landed on superpower, but their glands were banded by a subconscious boomerang. Worse than a mixed breed, they were like refrigerated fish, instant noodles, and a "me-now" wolf without any ability to enjoy the real golf.

As for me, I was just about to leave my precious little pinhole that I had discovered. This pinhole was like a pointless dot, smiling at my spirit by arousing my soul and amusing my flesh. This pinhole was so holy that my entire being and its whole request could stay like a quest and sleep for the rest of its life. This pinhole did not resemble any physical holes caved by water, dug by animals, and de-elevated or excavated by humans. The tip of the pin was like a light point, thought joint, oily grout, or electric rout. The moment its tip sipped at my eyelid in front of I-lead, something started to spiral. Like a pirate zooming into a particular star to navigate his ship; like a pilot receiving a departing or landing signal; like a baby detecting the comfort zone of milk and love; like a lost soul entering the space with the most sanctuary.

My view as expanding till an empty space opened accordingly from the middle, to the state that the expanding space became so large that I was being enlarged and belittled at same time. In or out, there was no grounding base; yet, each step of being and becoming was grounded in that suspended state. Dimension became a deadly machine, duality domed the reality, simple was single, nonsense was god-scent, and nothing was all about the fall.

Before I discovered this pinhole, I felt myself like a fourth or twelfth citizen, searching for a personal dream, cultural stream, and Divine Mother's cream. The dream beamed me into the cream of meridians and Neidan (Inner Alchemy), as stream teamed me up to choose between a monastic life and a romantic wife. The man made statues inside the temple told me not to bother them, and go ahead and worship the living beauties and their unbosoming flowers. The romantic wife, later on, deserved herself as a spiritual assassin, where I could experience the precious power of words, and reality of self-imprisonment. This was down the road, to the load I am carrying now, as well as the lord I am worshipping forever. The search for identity, inside and away from church, whether personal or cultural, diet-like and deity-as-such, snapped for the nutrients from love and its new treatment. Love and its treat opened the door for me to see my past lives, the time of creation, as well as the source of creativity.

As such, searching for my life-long and love-longing journey ended my destiny into this pinhole. This pinhole did not look like any racial appraisal, nor did it express a national or rational identity. To respect and honor an ideal formulated by an idealist is OK, but to identify the quality of me had to do with a tooth exam, so that even through dentures, I will be identified as old age and poor health. Thus, the word identity did not agree with me, because I did not want to be treated as a horse, any other of the tradable animals, or equals to slaves in that matter. I was a slave already before my conception and may still be even after my death. No others could identify me from my natural enslavements: the senses, emotions, and dimensions. Only I could solve my own best and worst problem.

As a matter of fact, this pinhole was so narrow that not even a rat's tooth could knife through, so barren that not even my big toe could dare to nail. Unlike large mansions, sky-capped banking offices, or grand view-disappeared cornfields, this pinhole was so essential that it made me feel like I was a precious seed from the Divine. Light and heavenly, I was ready to be planted in the holy soil of abyss and grow into some sort of holy oil boiling above the glamorous sign of Hollywood. I had just found my universal hot-bud, lot-bed, and slot-med.

More precious than homeland and dearer than motherland, this minute groundless dot invited my Job's being and (Uncle) Sam's becoming into its un-hued hole so that my nose-knob could afford its sniff, and my Adam's Apple could run its un-tongued free relief, or refill with any belief. Having no death-threatened life insurance, I would not be warranted between the toiling wars of rebirth and second-chance, and rolling wars of reincarnation and reinforcement. My Adam's clock ran randomly and dumbly with its universal course, but not the 24-7 cause. I did not care whether it was Adam and Dam, Anger and Ram, or adding all things inside AM. Apple or Ape, Apron or Apse, Apathy or Aptitude, Delta is where I was initially downloaded and afterward downsized. By adding things up, those life ingredients would team up magically and string wondrously.

Nevertheless, I was numb at the airport: I felt like the worst dumpster; and melted into a thumb-less fist, a timeless wrist, and a nonsensical "I-S-T" without knowing that yeast was eating flower (and flour) and beast was beating Easter. Only when Ester said the best of me, the test exiled my nest, and the rest was zesty for the west without waist or waste.

The pinhole I discovered was neither a think-how nor sin-whore. It is a bin-holder and a tin-folder. It was all about the power of in, before your conception occurred, and long before you would stay in any Inn and play with any sort of ink like pink. To be in was to win all the sins as sinister. By the time you became an infant, the inland would have failed the fading aunt, so that insulin would insult you as an innocent being. The inert feeling of your intimate initiation would indicate then that the innate feeling was what insomnia would do to your body and how the ink would smell as stink as that of indefinite think. To drink the pink color of sync was to link the silky sink with zinc. To shrink was to mis-link the mistake as misty pink from miserable brink.

Not until Gin and Tonic was replacing Fin and Sonic, you were never in but always sinning with stinky thinking sink. Not until the luck fucked everything up, the peak would not dig down to the sin. Not until you were reimbursed from your rebirth, neither could you remember what your physical membranes had fabricated, nor spell what the magic was spilling. After 7-days-a-week was savored by 7 dates of per-weak, the 7 mates woke from their stroke, only to acknowledge from where each tele-manic but talismatic stroke had originated. Each tally stick was italic, and every toll was as tall as a roller blade. You had a stroke because you forgot how to strike from the first place, which was the invisible pinhole. To be in was to begin once again against all gangsters staying free in any Inns, un-rated and unregulated, without any pain or payment plan.

You must pay what you are painted with, pale and male. In order to gain something, you must loose the other. To loose this other relaxes all capable looping but loosening ends, so that your brain will be away from a boomerang, and your thought is so pure as if it had never been taught by a teacher, smeared by a moss, or bought by a boss. And you must be very still and quiet, so you could detect the sound of boom, before any visibly flying boomer would target you as a rumor or groom.

When the booming sound enters a room, the ground becomes a groom, so that offspring populates any vacant space un-boomed. When you could make peace with thunder, what you undertook returns to those who belong to the under-belt, in between Snow Belt and Sun Belt. The resting snow speaks for now, so that you can sit for now and distill from then. By the time you could manipulate your thumb, the psalm attaching to the man's nipple would look like a purple pupil, so that any punitive damage can reflect what the Sun is undertaking with its mighty strike towards your dammed ages.

In the beginning, the boomerang was booming the dome of pyramids. After each moment escaped from every monument spared, the dome left the mighty pharaohs and rest mummies resting like a measuring ruler; to scale the end points and speculate the bendable joints. With this God's timely fashion, you can enjoy freely your magnificent mansion.

As soon as there appears a startling booming sound, your brain rings like a mad horse. Not until your ingrained boomerang inside your memory chip runs you off all the established ranks, you would never notice that you could forever tilt or jilt without the feeling of being inside a quilt or guilt.

But to "begin" something was like beating the gang by belittling the fans worshipping you as a star not knowing how to start a thing in

Washington DC. To wash the shin-high town with its distinctive tone and ruthless ton, the warship would worship the distant sister but not tincture the sink teamed by the thinking tank. The disjointing tricks made up the District, so that Columbus could cool the busload kids as a civilized must. Away from Washington D.C., Marian and marine tanks would marry to profitable banks and marinate the wealthy sinks so that the oil base below the sand would surface for the foilsman to flush a toilet sink. To be startled with "think so", you became "sin and sore."

If you were in life two hundred years ago, the rates were much lower than what any modern industrial addiction does to the dictators who are adding all sorts of addictive behaviors to the official dictionary and legal amendments. When the dictionary digs and narrates, your shin is as big as "what you are thinking of is what you will." Until you belong to the hole-less pole and find your toeless sole, your soul would still feel sorry about the sore from snoring towards morning, and scoring behind mourning. When you felt the ovulating belt, it was about the time to orchestrate the ocean of blue and lubricate the lotion of love. The consoling team cajoled the foxhole from the loophole into a manhole, so that manhood stood upon what they never understood: where the Robin-hood foundation was located!

The sound of this pin kept spinning and singing, swinging and swirling, till the skirt of a girl was slurring at my un-firmed fur, and blurring my unfarmed poor. The Scottish Whiskey blended with Skittish Husky, so that me as a male would dress up with a skirt, to bang my underwear with a handkerchief. Without being noticed by Tom Hanks, me as a chief chatted with the cheap chef where the dusty shelves hosted the books to hook me on the legal manner.

Visualizing the manual scripts of legal manner, my mannerism was half of a man and half of a male. As I zoomed in, the manual scripts became lunar crypts. I then lipped and leaped, stripped and ripped, till my legs begged me to kneel down to be near my own boomerangs, which were spinning and rotating upon my kneecaps between the shin serving as one stroke and the thigh deserving as the other. I did not know that fin in Chinese was the undivided penny or fen, not patented by the Finnish language but painted with a fetish outlook. I was still penniless because I never had a fin to swim down the streams of life. When several single girls called Penny approached me, they saw my lawless jaw and flawless paw. With their giggling girlish sandbags, they saddened my unmarried nieces (knees) and left. For sure, Penny was single, but penny had no other use besides the change stored inside a jar or car.

Until I was given a new name, Bear Claw, I was clueless about my wanting jaw and unwanted paws. My jaw used to function as the divine instrument of a boomerang, till my teeth loosed their grip towards their gum. And my paw never felt my pulsating beat but was forever charging my impulse. I did not listen to my heartbeat saying that "I am pulsing" since what I knew was to follow and react towards my impulse. Without knowing how to retain that yang of fire, I was always fired up by girls and then fired off by hiring bosses.

Finally, a hen licked my chin with a hint, me as a Chinaman never felt that my shins below my thighs and above my ankles were hosting me as a decapitated chairman. I was forever a handicapped boy, and a kneecapped toy. The captain in me did not know that there was a cap capable of doing anything assigned or aligned, and my captivity escaping from its own ability kept me alive and insane, so that my innate insanity built from my infantile piles and incentive files would constantly upgrade my impulse and downsize my yang-fire.

I did not recognize that my stomach would pile things up from ground and my bladder could re-file things upon my fired groin of that headless coin. I grew and I was screwed inside by this coin. I was a lad gladly climbing the boom-ranked ladder without a bladder but endless blades, and I was stuffed with Mac tossing images without a stomach to digest the eulogy used by euphoric youth or utopian news. I was running away from the booming town, behind those grooms, who were young enough to demonstrate their yang-ish looks which were called handsome and their yawning hooks which was identified as lingam.

"Hand me some lingam as if lingo, so that I can be ensured with the world wide web as the link of letting-go of what I am, such as how I was cultured and conditioned, so that you can start your tingling jingling bingo."

"Tingle cell, jingle bell, all for sell. Satan Clause is coming to town, waving at the youngsters saved inside to Youngstown."

By the time I approached this white and red snowman, this so called Satan Clause, he never sat down because he was built with an electric grid, served as a motion detector, a scarecrow. The nice grandpa is in actuality a grant pi, around the North Pole, run by deer and sledge, midget aliens and orphans. The chimney smoking the white Christmas mists chiseled and whistled, permeating all the closets inside the huge rooms to be filled with abandoning gifts, only to invite the thief to dismantle the chief chef, so that little youngsters can play with snowmen in the yard and consume the snowflakes as cotton balls and candy bars.

When my shins told me, as a matter of fact, without any menu or mannerism, that my boomerang-like legs are yin, I did not know what difference did the yin make out of yang and young, nor being masculine towards feminine and muscling the passion against feeling.

This pin combined the funny penny and cunning bunny into a holistic hole, where being holy was only halfway into the real hole, as the weight of golden calf waited to be alphabetized. The calf said, "I will fart", but the alpha ray was afraid of enjoying the artistic bar below the legless car. When the diabetics noticed the power of alphabetic meaning, beta sounded like a guitar, so that the Celtic tradition could be blended with cultic audition. In turn, the beta ray split the golden calf into half of a cream and the other sugary cougar, so that your cough could generate soundproof scream. When things were rounded around the rim, the dim from the dawn talked to Jim to jam up Tam so that they could all take a break from Uncle Sam. The fish Salmon did not talk to the dish served by Samuel, because Samaria teamed up with Samoa to destroy the Samurai playing his shamisen. Together they produced a film, so that collective humorous creams would be screened with rated human voices but not raped by animal noises.

In the end, my dream into the pinhole lowered me down, bowed towards the town, and it was all gone. The dawn welcoming fawn never noticed my skin-long fax talking to Max about tax. By the time the fax machine was broken, taxation was worse than masturbation. Why do you want to jump into the hole, without holding onto the edge of your dumpster, and knowing for sure the role you were playing for the North Pole related to the electrical poll?

In this universe, you as U and me as knee are diversely reversed with mingling verses, so that my standing point knows its landing appointment, and what is glad in me disputes with what will sap and sadden me. When good boys are granted with rewards, the lesser ones are left behind to digest all required lessons, by reciting that "The lesser, the sooner; that is your lesson."

Second Cry

Less than two years after the first heart-breaking cry, my tearless glands landed on the opposite land: my unwanted homeland and my undocked motherland. Right before I was granted the key as an immigrant to enter my discovered pinhole land, a different kind of tear smeared at my demands and sneered towards my disappointment.

I wanted to obtain the code of Yellow Race: the power of *I Ching*. I wanted it all before I could be proudly sell my ancestral binary codes to the westerners, before I could boil the lotion and soil the powder of Taoist Inner Alchemy in front of logistic heads, inside the stone heart of the White Race. I could not find a physical teacher to teach me the secret formulas, as well as the sacred codes revealing God's look behind my ancestral book. I even begged my initiator, my physical Taoist teacher "How come, and how could I." His simply responded to me that "You will get it later." But how late is the "later?" Just like "Through the making, can you return to and retain the original brand of maker."

My homeland was the yellow earth, and my motherland was the red communist country. My desire felt my homeland around age 2, and my tongue was glued with the English language at age 12, before I could become a member of Communist Party. Because in my previous life I was shot as a Nationalist Soldier being captured by the Red Army, Communism owed me something. And they did raise me well, by offering the foreign language opportunity right after the Cultural Revolution. I did not want to stick too long to my mother's milk gland, nor to the unaffordable sugar land, I wanted to feel like I was the chosen spiritual heir from the Taoist Lineage, the real chinaware with its authentic brand, and the first son chasing after the Sun and drumming after the nun chanting for none.

The pinhole led me into womb-hole and worm hole, and womb-hole into astral portals, then the entire universal whole. The realization of my pinhole was so thin, so real and so essential that 26 years of my lifework landed literally on the freedom of dreamland America. I found myself, this ever never land, not in hometown, but on the bottom shore of the Great Lakes, Cleveland, which I call it Cliffy Eve's Land. Along this shoreline, Rockefeller found his fortune, Edison discovered electric bulb, and the Wright Brothers invented the airplane. My name Tao, or tide, keeps digging through the bugs, into my ancestral pinholes at the bottom of five virgin lakes, only to discover the power of the Moondial.

A question was posed to me by a friend when I was at the age of 21. A series of questions that led to serious thinking. The final question is, "So, to you, Love means respect?" I was floored, that was not it at all. Not only did that question instigate further exploration upon the deeper meaning of an undefinable iota, but it led me to see a world higher that where I was residing at the time.

That was how I discovered the identity of my pinhole.

Spiritual
Vitruvia

CHAPTER 6:

WHO AM I?

Before I knew myself, my sensitive but desensitized receptors direct me to a place of learning and inhabitation. My eyes fire onto the colorful patches of the world, playing each fired match heated up between my heart and other objects. The heat inside my heart was initially heated up by my spirit-fire. Then my spirit fire was sperm-headed by my father, and worm-warmed by my mother. By the time I dropped out of my resting tunnel and birthing canal, down to the Earth, my heartbeat was charged by the windy hose and mouthy air, as my mother's menstrual heat changed into creamy heat. Slowly my body heat was replenished by table food, kitchen fire, grocery store, harvesting goods, daily light, nightly glow, and earthly caldron.

As the Sun fires up my neck-joint brain and fore-headed dream for the day, its ray flames between Bay and Hay. When the Moon lures throughout the night, her facial makeup plays with Kay and Fay. The Earth has her way of being cool to her sister and receptive to her brother. Her sister was actually her daughter and her brother her father. Through this way, the Earth distributes the silky spiraling energy, along with wind and air, into her living creatures. In turn, the heat produced and released in each creature is the energy stored and digested unilaterally by the very twin eyes in the sky, and team of any two beaming upon the soil.

As the lens of my eyes connect to an object through the Sun's fire, such a table lamp, a street or inner light, the colorized heat stored, painted or reflected in that object would talk to my organs and senses. The nerves in me would get fired up, passion is on board, and action is out there for its interaction in international conference surrounded by the global chairs. All objects and their objectives are familiar to my eyes. A closer look from my spirit eye is enough of a deal, to simply remind me of the memory stored in me. If an object is new, curiosity drags my feet to the object and excitement grabs my hands towards its surface, until this helpless object is understood enough by my hand-capped power or facilitates well to some other of my desirable purposes. If an object is foreign or strange, fear or danger takes over me, denial or escape answers the call. When this happens, something in me talks to me: "Why couldn't you handle it! It is not going to eat you up!"

Then my eyelids open and close like the Moon's ever-changing arches inside her dim ring. Incontrollable excitement or joy would expand my dim eyelids into the complete rim of that full moon's face, upon the sunset, to the degree where the ring glows through the Moon. The disc pouring red and golden flames from the Sun and Moon are equally and evenly standing in the sky, like the purest and most fascinating eyes facing each other above the nose-lifted mountain peak and around the ocean-blued leak.

The peak is painted with red and black on the left side, and colored with golden and bluish light on the right. As the peak lowers its beak, the creek creams the white milk down the slope, the foot, the cliff, into the unfathomable valley base. The entire valley stomach is filled with golden lights and decorated with blue veils, leaving the black hosting the white spirit and red opening the dream gate. The controlling Sun becomes the roaring knight, as the golden veil of the world becomes the golden son within.

Being joyfully excited drives me to the Sun's edge till the Sun forgets me on its way out and I lose my own center in the abyss. "Adrenal charge" is the word for eye-fired excitement, heartfelt muscular and egoistic enlargement. Adrenal glands become added renal and gladdened rental, where the rear end comes to me like a frontier mark, plus permanent remark, so that I am excited for nothing but chased by my own tailing and retailing shadows. When I can no longer afford to buy retail products, I must either tell my own versions of the story of life to make others believe who I am, or resell myself at such a cheaper price I am feeling that I have fallen to that point that I am stabbing my own back. I am allowing myself to be slaughtered for any pleasure by the excited seller and substantiated for the habitual use of a hungry consumer.

After the consumer enjoys me as a delicious meal, the aftereffect in my gut, stomach and brain is filled with seasoned emotional residue. Worse than surgical removal, where the body still remembers the old friend gone awry, my gut feels like an empty black hole filled with hatred and resentment stirred by unwanted nap-on (The consumer slept with me psychically). and unexplained zap-off (I was dumped). My stomach stores the leftovers from the consumer's familiar dish smell where I could trace the history of pathology and patterns of his or her ancestors. My brain recognizes the deed done between donation and forgiveness, sacrifice and rejection, excitation and abandonment. And my gut cuts through the cellular cysts and mental systems to the degree I am restrained by the poring rains and speedy trains.

I realize now that if I were not feeling as if I were excited, being valuable, playing an important role, and forgetting my little empty center stored by light and milked by love, all those above would never happen. I invited them all, like a plant riding its weather or a seed going through its natural season. Now that I recognize it, I find myself fighting involuntarily at times although I wound myself. Anything I have is recognized by the commerce department of human race, valued by the daily news, and priced by personal dignity. I am a tool to be used, an organ to be donated, a cell for sell, a toy for play, and product to be savored. The consumer in me knows who-I-am, most of time, better than what I can make sense of myself. The psychic satellite orbits above my head and the receiving gut stores my bed. Before I wake up, the consumer's kitchen fire is already on, and I will be shocked by the disbelief, amused by the neutral stance, and dished by the selfish. Until my senses are numbed, sensitivity becomes rotten, dream disappears, wish declines, and hope climbs above the earth dome. I cannot know myself, read my ability, and write off my disability.

At this point, if my eyes are still OK, my heart still beats, my mind still reasons, and my gut still cuts the deal. I will be free from the wraps of seasonal life where instinct means now and insight is the gentle ride upon the eternal arousal. This is how my spirit talks to my ego.

After the seller cuts my hair, skins my dare, and organizes my despair, I have nothing left for selling. Because the bones left are not worthy of anything like those marketable heads of remarkable people whose brains have been enlarged socially or reframed culturally like the most rare, expensive and indigenous products ever to be found in a given human gene pool.

Whose head is bigger and more expensive, mine, yours, or Sun's? I have a neck to live and you have a neck to believe that we are both alive. This is between you and me. But the Sun does not care, because it has no neck to live or believe. This leaves the business of our hemispheres to be roasted by hemps, toasted by attempts, discussed by brain tumor, sliced by head injury, scaled by headache, disillusioned by the amnesia, and finally to be dissolved by Parkinson's disease or dehydrated by Alzheimer's syndrome.

Or, if I am the winner, the price of my head, including my hemispheres, becomes like the founder of a nation or a dynasty, as well as the pride expressed by the following slaves and consumers. To either follow my head to sell me or follow after my tail to destroy me, is another subject to be discussed and another matter to be continued. When the proud followers find out that the price tag in my head belongs to my family name, or my male lineage, they have a choice to make. They can either become biological children, adopted children, or slaves and servants. Or they walk away as a freemason. This is about race faced with either blood donation or blood exchange. The blood donation makes them my offspring and the blood exchange makes them my slaves.

When the pride in the followers' mind tell themselves that the idea registered in me cannot be legally codified, and the thought produced through my head cannot be consciously patented, they also have two choices to make. One is to be brainwashed by a so-called "my idea," where they become acculturated by my substance first and then accuse me to damage their head and destroy their brain. Or they simply buy my thought as a code of work ethics or the skill of a professional performance. Those type of followers become either my students to follow my passion of heart or disciples to follow my discipline of conviction.

Then "Who am I?" is no longer an issue. When I recognize the components of me, through the collective lens, the subjective "me" becomes an objective "we," as the individual or personal cycle expands into seasonal and collective cycle. I am experiencing the same cycle with everyone else, and I am a part of that collective cycle. In this cycle, each individual is a cell, a number, and a divine unit. The four corners of me, between dual red blood and dual white blood, cross the joints of everyone who is involved in the party gathering. As each choice made or followed becomes part of the collective entity, the result is no longer about me or you, but it or them. In this sense, both subjective "me" and objective "we" are neutralized, as "I" and "you" are engaged in bilateral conversation.

The third element, whether it be a personal him or her, or an impersonal it, are the mutual demand and supply, as well as finished products and unfinished business.

This above is the path I have learned, mirrored and followed. "Who am I" is no longer an issue, only my physical tissues can pursue what they need from my thoughts or feelings. I am the blood of my father and his father, where those males had given their blood donation for the future generations from me and onwards. This is the white blood exchange, because they only planted their white sperms into their wives' ovaries. The offspring came out of the world with red blood as their organic cloth. This white blood is like a plant producing white flour but not red juice from such as a watermelon. When the white seed prevents the menstrual flow of the red juice, the war is internal and conscious, and the winner is offspring, off the season but offering the reason.

For men, the red blood is a different kind of battle between armpits and army bases, where you have to die for the tribunal, national and racial power. Since few men know how to regulate between the red adrenal and white semen, like how a mother naturally goes through her menstrual cycle, their red circulates between sleep bed and green bed. The double hunger for food and comfort swings back and forth between lust and must, just and dust. The winner of battling upon this red blood is the King or emperor, prime minister or president. The commander-in-chief commands the head chef to slaughter all live-stockers, including love stalkers, so his dinner is the national meal, and his party is the National Holiday, like July 4th in the US, or Oct. 10th in the Communist China.

This is a dear battle, where the near is in fear of either being killed or getting pregnant. This is a waste on behalf of females because they have labored the offspring into matured adults and you put them on the battleground so they can kill one another for nothing. Defending the motherland or lover's land, man's fire battles each other without and within to the degree that only the stronger, the swifter, and smarter survive, leaving the majority losers to be the hungry slaves or haunting ghosts. From the woman's eyes and heart, this is a huge waste: like a field of healthily growing plants and vegetables to be dehydrated by the Sun or flooded by rain. The collective work from parents end up in gravesite or a national cemetery, and only the king or president enjoys the land as his nation and beauty as the first lady.

Yet, survival of the fit for the fitness, between fist and wrist, risks the life and twists the love. The war fought between men is the direct imitation of women's menstrual flow, and the continuation of primal sacrifice of the flesh bleeding the youth. War becomes the best and worst birth-control pill as the entire same generational male and female population endorses and promotes only one couple, the collective rare species among the tribe, called prince and princess, or president and first lady.

I am so glad in this lifetime I do not have to become either a soldier or a physical warrior. Soldier is an audience for the beauty, and the physical warrior is the romantic love of the beauty. Without realizing my destined path, I come to a state where my beauty is my barren, pure and virtuous heart. The best result of this heart is that seasons of life cannot affect the originality of its kindness, nor can the emotional weather smudge off its white space. I am a member of my family and a citizen of a nation to begin with. But now my family is the yellow sky and golden dome, and I am the citizen of the Earth and her twin eyes (Sun and Moon).

The other kind of following, from what I have learned, is a different kind of lineage from the red blood line, where the stream of thought connects the two sides of a brain, between talking and listening, writing and reading, or lecturing and tincturing. This lineage is called following the firing thoughts, ideal letters, philosophical schools, scientific principles, religious dogmas and spiritual paradises. This lineage differs from family father and national father in that they do not care about blood transfusion, and they only watch for the flood infusion. The blood transfusion results in sexual union as the creative birth for the offspring. The flood infusion plays idea and sound, thought and voice so that the sound of nature can relate to the pound of nurture, and the voice of truth can sink into the volume of heart.

This kind of head, which is commonly described as a religious or spiritual leader, is more dangerously powerful than a family father and national founder, because they will change the blood type of your soul from ancestral lineage to cosmic mileage, so that your damage patronizes your own pilgrimage. This sort of leader will white up your soul and white out your bone, so that your soul as a soldier will be sold for the pure-land and your bone will be toned into a harmonic stone.

The moment you start the table food, your biological mother is useless; and the moment your mind listens to and receives a thought from another person other than your father, you are the slave of a culture. Culture begins with a thoughtful idea wrapped with a felt passion. In essence, culture is about light reflection or transmission. It is about dealing with time and flowing with water. If you are able to think like a light, smile like a beam, and dance like a hue, you are the seed and colors of light, which we all originally are. The diversion of time is very interesting, where a second is the accurate minute measure of a heartbeat along the blood-pump.

Does the time have a second, either secondary chance or secondary guess? Only lime knows for sure, only dime ensures the knock-off, and only rime (rhyme) primes the sure into certainty! With its original meaning as follows: second does not speak for the presence of time, but the reflection from the space or shadow. Second does not represent the actual flame burning inside the heart but the drums of the chambers and echoes of the pericardium. So this second business is fictitious, and it is never there to begin with. 60 seconds within a minute, or 60 minutes within an hour are our own fictitious remarks upon where the Sun marks and Moon parks.

Once I was dining in a Thai restaurant in eastern suburb of Portland, Oregon, I battled for and was baffled by the common expression of "please wait a minute" delivered by a waiter. I waited peacefully and patiently as each second was waiting for the waiter to serve the dinner. Upon 60 seconds, a minute was up and expired, and I demanded for a free beer. This "wait-a-minute" business became a comfort zone in the beginning for the busy nieces and knees, and an excuse for the delay and its sequential display. Laminating with an illusion, the real feeds the empty and the illusion plays with dissolution. I was happy to know the power of a minute but also felt sad for my harsh demand and rough command. I lost two brothers because of it, one waiter and one student. I never saw the waiter afterward. But the student, and my business partner at the time, could not bear himself seeing me losing my face and posing at his face for the power of timing. Common impression cannot afford to battle with factual expression!

When the minute decides to follow and not to speak out, 24 periods of a day is timed as home-surrounding existence between Sun's smile and Moon's glow. An Hour becomes one of these 24 periods saying hello to our empowered flower, with 360 peddles (seconds) to please that minute (my nude) minute, lost in seconds but gained all the secondary substances.

I have learned from the path that those four bosses —Sun and Moon, and minute second and suspending hour-- rule my hemispheres and control my gut. They test me until I become ticklish, so that my innocence would take over my arrogance, and my virtue would override my virgin. My family father named me after his familiar name, as my national father (Mao Ze Dong) certified me as a Chinese by citizenship, and the Founder of the Han Dynasty claimed for each person who followed him a Han Chinese. My religious father (Lao Zi) installs his idea so that I become the seed-carrier of his idea and did not follow the rest of **phoney bologne** sectors or schools.

When my spiritual father tells me finally "to go to hell and sell myself for good", his best pride sells me as the most unwanted bride so I can finally marry to myself. When the pride gets a ride, the bride enjoys the grounded and grouped room called groom. When the ride cites the side as wheeling site, the bride decides to sell the pride and buy the seed from the groom. The pride becomes then the uniformed attraction, so that the ride rides the idol as an ideal. When the idea drinks the idealized image reflected in the well water and glued through the flower, the standing tower of light tilts and builds into an hour, so that the flower can die into flour. Now, the ideal becomes I deal with idol plus item and ID. By the time the identification card (ID) expires, I am dear to what I have died from. The dear portion goes to the ovary, and the dead lotion stays inside hemisphere.

"If you are head-on, my fear is going to eat you up as a surprise (Super Sir Rise like a superman for the supper mint as supplement)." the bride tells the groom.

"Do not eat or kiss my ear. Do not bite and tenderize my neck where my shoulders will support you as shoe-lost-soldier," the bride warns!

If the groom who wishes to be a father of a kind speaks from a deflated egoistical tone, his thoughtful deal and personal idea will be deferred, defiled and declared as a useless item. The groom's thought cannot even touch the bride's hair.

When the bride tutors the groom with her intuition, the tuition paid from groom balances the intuitive side as the tourist attraction from institutional site blended between insightful night and instructional bite. Sophia enjoys the most out of the blackout where her black hair and dark skin receive the most of the white face lost from the be-whitened race.

When Sophia reveals this, the sage loses his seed and saint hoses up his head. Church cooks the meat and ferments the wine. Temple rings the bell and spells the hour. Philosophical and religious ideas of men are strong and powerful inside civilized states and nations, but weak and useless for a bride whom mates with white light and enjoys the white wine.

When the tabula rasa inside a man's whitened brain becomes the cloth of a black woman, she whitens her feeling with bright light, so that her fairy hemispheres would ovulate with white seed, and her chest would chase like a white horse. Anyone who is afraid of this kind of feeling is fearful, frightened by being near the face, the ear, and the neck. When what is near bakes a cake to replace anything dear to hear, the black hair receives the most light, and the dark skin secretes the most powerful oil. The battle of the race begins, all for the power and purity of White. This is the conscious, religious and idealistic battle, where cow is lost into cattle, and her cream is lost into the butter.

On the other side of the field, the bride who is not Sophia tells the groom that:

"If you are messing up with my tail, I am going to nail you into my Oval Mary, which you can call it ovary. Inside my oral shape and ovulating tape, your reasonable R rates your hemispheres by collecting the Y from Why and white from wine, which will be disfigured and raped into a gender-based and motion-mutated individual."

The groom then loses both his brain and grain, and money and honey. If the wife, then, likes the husband, children are yours to enjoy; if she feels good at the moment, children are also yours to flame. This is the power of the mother over her children. I was unconsciously coerced into hating my father until I got over it. Women all over the world have the power to use this tactic to brainwash children since they are the givers of life. Some do so with purpose, others unintentionally, still some understand that the mind of the child is their own and leaves it well alone to allow them to find love and hate on their own. This only works if the woman knows how to stand back, to live and let live.

The way the hate game works is that the mother (who is female) knows how to play at emotional strings and subconsciuos dreams that sing deep into the heart and soul of a living being. Especially if that being resided within the mother, sharing all secrets since cosmic conception. Mothers are our gods because they know us all deep with their hearts and are spiritually connected for the first few years after birth. Initially, this was Xi Mu Niang's gift to sooth the heart of a worrying new mother, so that she may always know the state her children are in. Like all things ancient and pure it is eventually misunderstood along the later path of life and existence. When the loyal contract to treat all sacred gifts with reverence is broken, the chance for abusive power is given room to rise. Now from ours to hours, yours are the best time to spend together and the worst second to feel alone. This timing reality and its timed duality is better than the party hosted between time and space, and worse than what the torture would teach or how the molestation would mold the real estate into a local station. When a torch tortures the church and a molecule molests the cute, the cell is filled with ward and the sell feels the warning.

"Honey, what is for sale, your passion or your flower?" the wife bribes the bride now.

"Your flower is deeded in our ancestral contract, and your passion fashions my heart-felt Madison Avenue leading toward the mansion where the man becomes the son of lion." The wife explains.

"Our ancestral contraction is deeded inside the astral contraction where moody Moon touches the lava-spitting Earth."

"And when you mention the word mansion, my mandible shin legs you inside my navy ovary and toils your floor-tired and flower-budded inflammable tube. Are you ready?"

Being bribed, the husband lost both biological father and national father. Biologically, the husband is responsible as a seed-donor. Socially, he has to place his name-sealed power into his offspring. Egypt fell, and Noah survived. Costal cities host citizens like fish in a tank, while mountainous peaks are polluted with bird flu viruses.

Like the groom and husband, I lost everything now. Before I finish this journey that deals with those four archetypal males, whom represent boy, soldier, president and pope, I have to deal with the four equal feminine sides as well. The word fear means feel the ear or the feelings of ear above the neck and besides the face. Before I come to the understanding of this kind of selfish definition, fear is a monster, a demon, a nightmare, a shadow so comfortable towards its own kind that even the light cannot feel or touch it.

Opposite of joy and excitement, is the power to work through undeniable fear for insecurity. Insecure fear would close my eyelids and disappear into a place of darkness like the waning slides of the Moon till the scorching black takes everything over and puts everything under.

"I see you." is the term of reflection, and "I don't know you" is the word for rejection.

Like he who has lost everything, I am on the brink of burning everything. I am small, like a mouse, modest and shy until my lion roar can be heard causing a tremble the very heart of those who grew comfortable and thought they knew me. It is not about delivering justice or striking fear or force, or fighting for belief, it is the natural instinct of the way the world works. When you pull an arrow back in a bow crutch to the point you can pull no further, one of two things may happen. Either the bowstring will break, or the arrow will shoot forward. Both results have tremendous effect. Then one might ask, "Why would you put yourself in that situation, why can't you tell the others when enough is starting to become too much?" Then I ask you, "Why did you put the arrow in the crutch in the first place when I asked you, 'please, don't shoot.'"

People will always test and push you, it is the natural way that humans are: curious. You can continuously tell them gently not to, but if they are deaf to all but themselves, they cannot hear you. Either you roar at them early on and all fear you and stay away from you, or you wait until you are about to burn to scare them away.

But what about those who you don't think are listening, the ones who trudge on and on when you have placed a friendly hand on their arm and begged them to stop? What if what they are doing is for a higher cause and they just don't have a choice except to push on what they are doing, even if it upsets you?

Then perhaps it is I who is not listening and unable to see.

The most fun part of interacting with worldly objects is to search the human temples and their internal designs and facilities. Even today, I have not had enough fun with human objects. This maybe my biggest karmic lesson to lease or lend, learn or languish. To lease a human object, or gender based temple, I have to know for sure that I can play with it but not own it. This human object would tell me how much of a space interaction and in depth communication is enough. Most of the time, in order to lease this object for the time being, I have to lend something of me as the prerequisite or down payment, so I make ease and peace with this object. The price of lending varies: sometimes automatic, other times tentative; in some cases it demands part of me to be openly vulnerable or actively participating, in some other cases all I need is to be a living dead. The result of this lending-me-business is that I have died many a time, which makes me mature and cautious, nice and wise, to desire less and stay neutral.

To desire less is to learn less, and to stay neutral is not to languish at all. The duty is to keep an eye on my internal landscapes through the Y formed between my nose above and my forehead below. The beauty of this Y is that the V shape connecting on top of my nose is not a rigid or straight line. Both lines would bend a little and curve a bit so that the twin eyes would fit symmetrically well below the eyebrows and inside the eyelids. This is perhaps the first organic matter I learned about English words. Each eye is an E, both are locking on the outside but looking into what is inside from each side. In my case, the right eye is a bit bigger than my left. If my imagination takes me a bit further on this road, I would see that this Y shaped figure is a bullhead that frames a serpent face and hosts two dangling pearls which knife at an objective temple with compassion and understanding. My eyes have the compassion toward the temple and they understand any given temptation!

The E on both sides of Y is a terrible business to deal with. You are searching alone for the other side, and the other half of your complete self. With the fixed position my eyes station, the best result is either to use other light classes or to get a pair of fun glasses.

When my eyes become Y, my hands turn and become mouthy lips independently (the thumb serves the lower lip-glued moving jaw and the rest four deserted as the upper fixed law). This paired handy tool armed with wrists, elbows and shoulders serves as contractual partners, working teams, co-creative members, and co-depended companies. The moment my eyes tell my shoulders what they should do, my elbows start to enable, nibble and blow my wrists with violent vigilance. It is funning that the letter W is used to distinguish the difference between mentally projected risks and hand performing fists. My fingers would touch those deformed rings around my temples bundling my wise and crowning my nice. They then take the rage out of my neck and head and to fish out the fact that the anger inside is the angle around and angel outside. The angel never lands, the angle never stands, and my anger never understands the real business between these two.

This leaves the real royal business conducted between my feet and my eyes. Though far apart, I can bend my trunk, embrace with my knees, and kiss my toes. Or, I can let my fingers hook up with my toes, pretending that I am doing a stretching exercise. If this happens, the ring around my belly becomes suffocated to the degree I have to let go of the union teamed among the nails.

Now the heat is really fired up inside of me. The heated green is the beauty of joyous spring, and subsequently, my never-ending lust toward the lush bushes producing the Bush family and fermenting Busch beer. The spring from the ocean speaks the language of tides and tornados. The spring of a mountain surprises the dews but delights the downward flow. The spring of the East renounces the morning with long winters. And the spring in me speaks the language of evergreen, the tone of eternal youth, and joy of everlasting peace. This spring becomes the language of immortality unmatched by memory codes or historical records. Spring lives forever for the liver to expand the passion and disperse the gold.

Spring, spring, please speak to the rings of angel!

Spring, spring, please speed the ring of passion so I can see and hold my gold!

Spring, spring, please spread the reading lists as breading beasts so that I can enjoy them all as holy feasts!

Spring, spring, please spike up my spine so that I can spin like a ring and spark like a star!

With this spring, I entered the chamber of love hosting the red lava inside and the hot blood outside. The red lava speaks for the red flowers and the red blood fires up my muscles grown out of vegetations. In turn, the heated reddish flowers speak for the passion of summer, where my heart is going to target at a weak and servitude object with my angry arrow or to be targeted by some other angry pharaohs. Any place where my foot lands, there is a protective pharaoh serving as the family lion; and any country where my passion lands, there is a patriotic pharaoh dictating his phallic affairs. Between natural air and phallic affair is the international communication going on between my eyes and my hands as one national pride and my eyes and my feet as the other natural bride. The national pride gives compassion but takes anything fresh. The natural bride either scores with shoes upon endless holes numbered with letters and numbed by the fixed colors, or upgrades itself with cars, airplanes or even satellites, before the eagle speaks for a national symbol or peaks at bird flu rewarded as the backfire from the pollution.

The result of heated reddish fire between the hot summer outside and the fired passion inside is to seek white matter inside my own white house. The white matter is the white flour harvested from grain and rice, or a piece of white paper that I write to earn my rights. The white house is the white horse of spiritual mind marching through and traveling inside my white bones. The heated black ferments all resting debris into useful soil once again.

In turn, the heated green in my body is immortal soul of liver varnished by the golden gallbladder. The heated chambers of love is the flower of my heart stemmed from the root of my thymus and blossomed through my thyroid and parathyroid glands which are hanging, suspending and handling in my throat. The heated white flour is the eternal flow of my bone marrow, purer than my mother's milk, thinner than a spider's silk, and more holy than the beaming light. The heated black is my hair growing madly to dance with light, chasing after wind, and tailing with my nails.

Side by side with my firing eyes are the eardrums sealed below the thorn of crown, where the temples above move rhythmically on top of my jaw and hairlines. After so many years of working through inhabitant voices, my mother-tongue of that oral language and my father-gun of that written symbol hibernate the voice of my soul so deep that I can no longer understand the sounds of birds, the whispers of wind, and the laughs of thunder. My living spirit has to pay special attention to the underlying tone of a spoken voice, so that I can really understand what a person who spoke to me or yelled at me really needs inside. Beneath the anger, this person needs a space of love so the spirit can express freely from the space-less heart. Under the blanket of hatred, this individual wants to be embraced by tender love never received from his or her parents. What this person can express freely is the raw material of God, the unpolished gift germinated by life. That of the living temple that can be loved unconditionally is that harmonic voice speaking through that individual heart by ringing collectively inside the divine and chastised human heart.

This means that after listening and paying attention to what a voice carries inside a language, the real language speaks for itself without any human interference. The human language, inspired individually and expired collectively, has no use in that matter of understanding what is really going on between the mind and heart. If the mind is free from desire, everything is clear like a blue sky. If the heart is not lured by emotional turbulence, truth reveals itself. When the light sees the heart through the mind, love milks all. If love feels the needs deeded by the light away from time, the mind times each vibration echoed in the heart and registered inside the brain.

If my eyes cannot see what my ears are echoing, my hands would reach out to grasp anything fresh, anything edible, anything pleasing my holy hunger. Then one day God blocks all the cash flow, out of my scheduled reach, my lustful grasp, and my hungry temptation, I have no clients, no income and no cash for any down payment. I have to pay ahead of dawn, upward for the purity, and in advance before the dish is placed on table.

Then the subtle incomers who serve as the gospel of the day, work as the massager of the event, and deliver the care for my real needs upon my heart devotion, schedule my hands not as a handy male anymore or candy husband any longer. The competitive eyes cannot speak, define or defend anymore for either the conceptive ears or conservative hands. So I close my eyes, away from lush illusions, rest right in the center before my vision takes me away from my illumination, after the red mansion fakes the black hole.

As the income becomes thinner and thinner, my gum is thickened with a kind of rum only palm can smell the oily holy lotion aside from salty insult, and only the Psalm can taste the texture of love through the fabrication of seasoned life.

At this point, I notice that my ears have been blocked by the voices of ramping tramping human languages for so long that I cannot listen to and detect the fussy husky sounds produced from creatures mimicking nature. My hands are busy grasping for food and fame as my taste buds transverse from juicy water to alcoholic spirit, green leaves to red meat, oceanic fish to land-escaping selfish, and fresh conversation to jubilee substance. When the trance state of that poetic verse is converted from raw food provided in the universe to lawful fools in human substations, the suburban stations stand and stance in front of me like an illegal alien editing the additional eatable idiots. When the mad cow disease mixes with bad hair decrease, my nail rubs my tail to comfort the feeling of being failed to ground to my root and navigate through my roof.

When the root is cut off, and roof is ceiled, T-cross of tomb teams with F-fence of fatigue, so that the room can be built above the grassland and below the sky land, and the rood beam rooks the rookery rooster. The rooster makes sound for the morning and is delightful for the behaviors of mourning for nothing aside from selfish motives towards intangible motifs.

By the time my eyes are fixated onto addictive lust, my ears hear only fame and glory, and my stomach stores polluted viruses, my temple birthed from my mother is no longer dusted by God's creative dust, but by my own collective dusts, ranging from the sour milk to sour cream, lustful passion to obsessive addiction, the dusty meal to dust-filled life. When dusts find company in dusk and through lust, all gutsy musts are crusted with mandatory adjustments, and gusty thrusts are disgusted with mistrusts. Cash flashes like waterish splash where trash crashes with greasy hash. God made me with His dust so that my dusty temple can collect more earthy and human dusts.

Before I explore my true temple, the room hosts the bed for me to sleep inside the darkness already existing. My nightmare does not agree with anything the soft mattress addresses, as my madness traces across the bloodline to see the lineage assigned and aligned by God's Line crossing the skyline. Reversing the letter d in mad, I got a "map" in front of me. This map is my inner vision seeing my inner voice talking to my inner self. With this inner map, I can see now how a real horse does differ from a real house. The real horse rests with its head up facing the sky. The real house secures my safety with locks, windows and doors. Even so, wind and air are still in and out, freely, as if nothing has ever happened. Land still belongs to government first and mother earth ultimately. Above all, patriotic mind cannot block off international trades and cross-cultural exchange, as terrorism would attack anything you may consider it as safe and sound, till fear faces your reality more closer than terrorist act can, and death is even closer than anything that is immobile in fiction but powerful in conviction.

Through this gradual adaptation process upon inhabitation platform, I begin to know that my senses are my parental sensors and my ancestral receptors. In turn, my parental sensors connect to family traditions and social customs, as my ancestral receptors relate to historical events and hierarchal fences. When I can make sense between what a family is familiar with and what a society is cultured from, I know that individual gifts are holy, speaking both personal voices and impersonal volumes; and that when a cell cultures, a society is formed by homogeneous cults cutting through fences in order to count on rings.

Between fence and ring, I understand who I am through Chinese meridians and Taoist Inner Alchemy on one end and passionate mind and alphabetic letters on the other. When I blend these two together, a day concludes from sunrise to sunset, and a night includes solar ray and universal beam. My mind shines like Sun, radiates like star, and is as useless as white light without black foil. My heart is as rhythmic as heartbeat, flows like ocean, and timeless like love.

My body is a mixture of sperm and egg, light seed and love soil, green vegetables and red meat, black hair and white bones, as well as oceanic fish and atmospheric stream, light dust and earth dust, watery love and milky love.

My mind is as pure as light, as precise as a mechanism, as powerful as spirit, and as useless as a blank paper.

Who am I? I am tired of asking this stupid question, I am tired of searching through meaningless hope, and I am tired of being tied by my going to be mummy case survived from legal case. In case you ask me, "you" are my final answer.

In order to continuously explore and discover the question of "Who am I," there has to be connection between me as a species of mankind, and my special area not only unique to me but also spacious for humanity. A species sounds like speed ceases, or a spectacular seat, a specialized cist, or a specific sheet. As a species of mankind is a kind of human, not kind to a specimen or species-carrier, the goodness inside me becomes a special kind of goods. The outfit for the forfeit of my makeup as goods makes the raw look (fresh and organic) from my vulnerable birth into a law hook being civilized as a depressed cook or expressed book. So that goods can become not only valuable inside but also attractive and good-looking outside.

When the good-looking attracts the good cooking, the good fool delivers me as good food from the field of specimen into a special menu (me being nude or meat as newly cooked) classified by race as losing the face but delivering the pace, roomed as gender where ends as ender are grouped by G and not P, and billed as skill where the passion gets killed but skull is full from fermented pills piling up the hill of eternal traveling. I am special: as my mind is spacial; and my body spacious. When special links spacial with spatial, racial pigmentation bounds with a national flag, where all the lacks are logged with bags full of emotional or mental tags. Changing from being spacial into spatial, the shabby shell (pronunciation of -cial) of that cited al begins the trial on trail through railroad and sailboat. The trial begins with "I" as alcoholic beverage, and trail starts with "A" as air-raided ailment. Unique is another kind of word to describe the meaning of special, U and Nick as unique.

When you and Nick become me and Dick, something will happen out of this combination, because U and me as an united meaning will even out the unique expression demonstrated by both Nick and Dick. The combating ritual between Nick who licks and Dick who kicks ticks the Rick to brick the sick, so that each click is a motion ranged between snick and trick. Equally, when Nick changes into Nicole and nickel, and Dick becomes Rick and Frick who are good at digging the Dam and tugging you as part of the Uncle Sam. U, as you have to make U-turn in order to become specialized into someone whom no one can compete against. Me as meat or means has nothing to compare or contrast with.

Without competition or comparison, petition goes to embracement, and parish becomes Paris reasoning and raising the prison that is too primal to the notion of soon. The prefix "com" is now the dot com of that completely reputed and languished address .com, and everything else is in a state of coma, away from comrades having comatose, and inviting all who will come through the dot. When dot comes, the combating team combines the commanding beam and comical comedy into commercial remedy and criminal Normandy. By the time Norman normalizes chaos theory into Caring Oasis, the otter totters the tutor and orders the daughter as the autumn odor and taught laughter. When the daughter becomes auditor to send the message to August, Al becomes my disguised guest as cold wind gushes like a gigantic brush off the mass and rushes like a sensitive flush of the face. With this Al, I can make alcoholic beverage along alchemical ravage, so the be ever the age (beverage) can dot and come, and me as a race can rag along the averaged age.

Now dot COM becomes the dotting point of time, pointing away from God and His Kingdom but towards you and me. The more the dot comes, the more dots comb. I am not a species anymore, nor specimen, but a combination of specialized man of that sperm-carrying manual and specific man knowing only the dot-combed and combo-ed menu.

In this dot Com age, finger-counting computation becomes a figure-computerized DNA page, so that race is not a fact anymore when pigmentation speaks only a minute refraction behind the decimal dot and zero account. The percentage is now long gone, but percentile still speaks loudly for the gentile centaur.

When .com (no trouble spelling out this .com phrase because it has been built in already) links together comrades and Comcast, common sense commercializes as communal cents, so that penny internalizes pen and nickel into an authorized statement. This would debilitate the ability of pencil and its nibbling power upon the paper. Between the sensor your body possesses and the censor your government pertains, senator snails the sensory cells so that the central sell can make sense out of innocence, and the sensible material can be centered on all nonperishable nonsense.

In this configuration, your sense may be unique, but your sensed experience or felt expression is common to your family, familiar to your community, and makes sense to your nation. When the founding father has censored all of you, including your children and grandchildren, your creativity and invention, inside a national dialogue, your mother's tongue will be educated with senseless articulation, and your father's power will be restrained inside either a sporting arena or an anger management program. You can talk about the table food and family meal, but the chains of commercial restaurants will welcome you at home and greet you abroad. You can purchase gun and play for recreational purposes, but you cannot stop the police search into your most private area because your house is registered on government land and your street links to public entrance.

Years after years, your mom's scream cannot be heard, and your father' anger cannot be expressed. Your depressed mother now ignores your suppressed father, because none of them raised you "good" according to super-father: the government and supper-mother: church. When super supper supplements superstitious supplant with supple support, your personal supersonic jet is nothing in front of superconductivity, and your supersensitive subject will be censored by the superimposed superior superman and monitored by the superlative superrich race or nation.

All that is left now is that someone is still interested in your unique gifted item. When the self-biting process becomes self-less binding to unite, you are now a gifted item, biting me as I "tell me" becomes selling yourself.

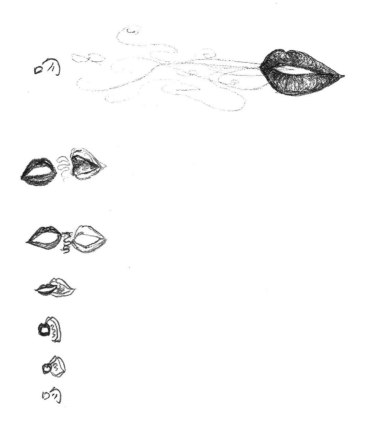

CHAPTER 7:

SPIRITUAL CONTRACT

Mind of God

Dear reader, now move and turn your eyeballs from left to right and then spin in the spiraling center, the lines will move you from linguistic structural blocks into inner conscious matrixes, and rings will ignite your registered information, challenge your personal beliefs, unveil your cultural patterns, on and on, again and again. Until you and me, as the mirrors of our souls, windows of hearts, see and reflect, converse and harmonize to the state where only the purified strings of words can ring true to the heart, only the heart processed lines of phonetic tones rise through our throat, into our brain to awaken our spirits within. With no tongue, this spirit-one is toning and stoning and being bestowed upon the one and only: lonely like a lightning bone, truly like a cellular phone.

Before this happens, lots of dialogue run from casting eyes to memory chips, drumming from pagers to cells. Many a time, personal and impersonal exchanges will be traded or bartered, shared or disregarded. All kinds of physical and emotional reactions flood up and flush through visible and invisible living entities. And endless roads of rejections and disbeliefs take us to a place of no end but here, no walls but present, no calls but the empty heart spinning like a bully ball.

Ground here, plant your feet down, roots into the ground, and stand now as the vertical light. The rounded present and central peace will distance and unify the horizontal line. The crossing center of the heart will open to the divine: only to abandon the words learned or taught, discard the useless veils tangling around our heart, dust off all forms of labels and titles registered in our forehead, target all kinds of fear coiling around our gut, and remove all felt alienation binding our feet. Then the truth will ring in our heart, joy will dew our eyes, love will dress our flesh, peace will anoint our ancestors, and harmony will unite us into the space of infinite light, the womb of unconditional love, food of sweet nectar, and wisdom of white elixir.

Now, we will radiate and vibrate. We are free to see and hear, and we are pure to reflect and resonate all the radiations steaming through our skins, and all the vibrations drumming our whitened bones and shattering our reddish muscles. The sacred dance begins with no rehearsal, the sacred contract engages without relegation, and the sacred temple frees us from one another without religious thought or relinquished conviction.

Those vibrations, let it be personally lived stories or revealed truth, or collectively civilized codes and habits, speak for the informed evidences or facts, as well as the recorded matters or numbers. What are hosting those vibrations are no longer the words on printed-paper, lines of projected thought, strings of personalized ideas, expressions from instinctive instance, or movements between the body and mind. Deep and beyond, those vibrations are harmonic waves of the universe. They are the Mind of God, and the Heart of Universe.

Each time when the vibration enters the chambers of our heart, via sensory portals, the inner strings begin to tone themselves, just as any vibratory instrument created by nature or laboratory tools crafted by hand. These vibratory waves and echoes are now the two dots connecting to one line, the dual force engaging bilateral communication, from universal outlet to individual inlet, to voice individually and chant collectively. The wave masses through the chained segments and individual compartments, while echoes unify, balance and untie both the massive waves and subtle tones to the degree that each cell plays itself and each particle works as part of an unit, team, family, and community.

Thereupon, from individually designed receptors to digested vibrators, from the mass displayed out there to the massive demonstration occurred here, the empty spaces within and without are dialing and talking, listening and responding, receiving and refreshing, releasing and returning, all at once. It is almost like a team with no members, members without leader, and memory without head. The team is a whole, the members are divine, and memories are intoxicant. Whole and divine, they are holistically designed, and individually packaged. Member to memory, each serves as a particle and every one is actively participating. Each one is an indispensable value, where everything else is there, never departs nor unites. Having no preconceived notion, the awareness and sensitivity are so pure and present that all are empty in, empty out. Only waves and echoes are conversing and communicating, confessing and commanding, and contrasting and comparing. So thin that there is no visible layer, so subtle that there appears no other interference; yet, at same time, so compacted that nothing gets in, and so much completed that nothing is left undone. There are no more individual particles or cellular distinctions, no this or that, just such and thus, too much on a single bus.

This is how the Nature designs and creates us collectively and individually, and in turn, how we function individually and express collectively. The individual is masculine, vertical, timing, singly charged and targeted. While the collective is feminine, horizontal, spatial, teamed effort and act. The individual is a dot, ring, circle, while collectiveness is hole, arch, and loop in which the dots are a member. Whether you are in divine order or through collective odor, the wind blows the water, as the light parties with shading place within shadowing space and showy pace.

Dotting the hole, and holding the dot, things are created. Ringing the bell, and bailing the ring, forms are giving and partaking. Circling the arch and archiving the circle, things are completed in and emptied out. All are given and eliminated, granted and dispensed, grounded and discharged, and promised and dismembered at same time, with equal value and measure, and without discrimination and dispense.

This is the story of the universe, as I know, and understand now. Reveal your story about universal creation, so we can share continuously.

My story of the universe identifies me with my spiritual name: "Phoenix singing on the rainbow."

Story behind the contract

This above is my creative story, universally granted and personally demonstrated.

They are my distinctive stance, my truthful glance, and my lonely dance. As my strings of heart play songs upon my temple, notes rain forth like a train of grain, sweep like a gentle shower, and reverberate upon the tall tower. The memory chips containing all registered information are distorted, and in turn, words of expression will not be exactly the same as we were taught, and phrases are no longer that structurally controllable units which make us feel like we are eating a family meal, reading the daily news, scanning the familiar signs, enjoying the routinely pleasurable fixations.

Thereafter, I have to receive and give, deliver and depart, believe and be thankful. The vibrations coming through my fingertips, as a result, will carry your eyes into the inner journeys of your soul, where the depth of your heart will reflect, resonate, reset, and respond upon a pond beyond the bond of seasonal modes and habitual codes. The lineal power is decoded into circular ring, factual dots are rhythmically toned, and illusionary grasp will be zoned into luminous claps. Equally, the body we station and the information we load will drive the history of mankind, through her-kindness, towards the divine presence. Presenting the same source we came from, as we are, each of our journeys map as a distinctive love-frequency for our humanity. Dreams are streams, though each dreamer creams differently each time. Inspirations are inside the spiral stations, though each is inspired along a different spinning loop. Each last breath is a deathless breath to launch a spirit into different height and sight.

Upon this breathless flight, we choose for a while either to stay up there, or stand in nowhere, depending how we have consumed our utilities and finished our decisive journeys. Or we choose to come back, after a near death experience or light flight, to land in a worm and dress in a new flesh

once again. If we have finished the homework, become as light as light, we will return to the kingdom of heaven. If not, we have to come and repeat and refine everything all over again, until our spirit shines like light and our love drums inside the universal charm.

The cycling space is huge, and as big as the universe, while the wheeling foot is short, as small as the spinning dust-sized spirit. Between the infinitely big and minutely small, we live and move, stay and orbit, time after time like a seed, and portal through portal like a shape shifter. The seed is the diver, the charge, and source, while the shifter is the vehicle, the direction, and outcome. The seed never dies, though being fabricated into different matter each time from season to season, birth to death. This is called the Divine. The portal never opens completely so each exchange can be transmuted thoroughly. This is called change. Divine gives birth to change, and change completes the divine. Hence, I Ching (the book of change) produces divinations.

What we "can" is the will to change at large, and what we "cannot" remains with no charge. Between divine and change, vibrations are alive and present all the time, in all directions, for all purposes. Yet, the space is forever empty, and the present creates all, believes nothing, and trusts none. As those vibrations echo in your original beauty, drum again in your inner truth, and charge once more from your authentic power. Your will changes; but you, the vibratory soul around your shining spirit, remains the same. You feel the echoes of humanity, but you are alone seeing the collective beauty and the individual truth. Your heart keeps on drumming, but your drumstick, your aroused point of love, rings above the dried brim, the rounded skim, the smoothed trim, and the collated whim. Your dancing movement reverberates all that is there, but your inner stillness, your cosmic landing point, remains groundless, in the space filled and emptied by light.

I recall a children's story I read as a child. It was an illustrated book in which a single mother had three daughters. An old wise woman asked her to observe her daughters while they were asleep. She did so and reported her findings. The old woman gasped to learn that the youngest daughter slept with her hands resting on her thighs. Her diagnosis? The youngest daughter was "ill-fated" and must be sent off to deal with her fate. The mother was frightened for her daughter and obeyed. The fate was personified and throughout the girl's journey, the fate would terrorize her at night and physically destroy things and threaten her. The girl was helpless. When she eventually arrived to the house of fates, she had a loaf of bread with her. She rapped on the door and a fate answered, but it was not her fate. She kept trying, like many people do in a lifetime, to find her fate. After many tries, her own fate finally answered the door. Now, her fate was drawn demonlike with untamable eyes and flaming red hair. The girl tried to offer the bread peacefully to the fate, but her fate kept knocking it to the ground and cursed at the girl, spitting on her, striking her. The girl never gave up. The fate eventually broke down crying, asking why the girl was that way. Even the other fates came out after the incident and told the wild fate, "shame on you, she is so gentle," or things to that effect. The girl and her fate made peace and they were happy with each other.

What I had gathered out of the story at that time was fear enough to send a prayer that my fate was not like that. Now, upon reflection, I understand. Externally, even if we lose everything, we still can be happy. It is how we choose to perceive a situation. With our hearts open? Or with our hearts bitter and hating until the end of our days? Our "fate" or external situations that steer its own course lies without our control. What we can control and bring to a situation is who we are inside and how we choose to love the world, the universe. That which cannot be taken away from us, is our most valuable and has the power to change even the gravest of outcomes.

This is a serious matter, because making sense of everything, or anything, is all our tangible living world is about. God, Who has no name, form and motion, is Self-evident; but we, as vibratory souls, must make sense of everything, from nothing to all.

Searching for our roots, we find we are like water: a mixture of blood flooded with ancestral goods and predetermined charges. Seeing into the ends, the good becomes more ugly than loaded fat (undigested sugar), and the bad is more forgivable than the dad. The dad has no glad ladder, nor landing glands, but he empties his shell for us to visit the hell and become a fat daddy once again. Examining our deeds, our needs cry like babies and our wants are worse than demolished demons demanding sermons upon permanence. When demons leave us alone, due to our aggressive demand and command, the hell says hello to us as a fellow, following the tomorrow by hovering the marrow inside a willow.

The willow tree lowers our will to the ground, where the window inside the wall hosts the widow wishing for a new bride to brighten her tomorrow, which is totally borrowed from the past. She leaves us, as usual, very often as orphans, to open the can and organize the fan, so we can grasp with our dream catcher, for the rope hosting the hope but emptying the hole. When apes are happily eating the grapes, we are left to taste the grape juice as raped news. After the spirit from the wine sinks into the drunk state for us to number the numb station, we realize that reality is always swimming like a fish; unbalanced because of a wish, but fenced between equal exchange upon equatorial change from dry to wet, and between oceanic wave and sandy pave.

The real eye, with no dual lens or doomed pupils, or eyelid or outlet, sees back and forth inside the rare, through the fare, towards the pair-renting pants hosting ants. The ants are not our parents; since our real parents are only pared up to rent us in their house, blend our spirit into their flesh, spend us as their granted wish. The biological parents keep on buying us logical pare rents, to let us know that the world out there, in which is everywhere dear and near, is never the world here heard or learned, which is thicker than the leg-wrapped mud, filthier than the womb-craved bug, rustier than the dust-contained rug.

Pared rents, now my definition for parents, are very expensive, where only our smile keeps the expenses milked and fed. Parents are very exhausted. They died in us already during conception, but breathing carefully they catch the food while walking slowly towards their resting site watching our growing as a sight.

The renting pare as parent is actually renting each other, without realizing that they borrow one another on one hand and lend one another on the other land. Always and forever individuals, they have to pare up to rent us from the sky as their personalized item and private gift. Only a few pares are aware of what they are doing in order to respect individual boundaries and promote their highest good.

Since our parents are grounded with birth and mounted by earth, they pare each other up, rent us from the free-sky, and provide a roof for us to stay and grow. The roof is sound proofed, and the root is earth booted. The walls are against our muscles, doors block our wheels, and windows shade us away from the bright side, so that we are restless inside like a sprouting seed, in rage like being caged and regretful like a terrible two. They become the fortunate two, so that each of us as a terrible-two bites with terrific tooth and territorial troop. The fortunate two do not know how to give and take, and the terrible two does not feel how to rest in that arrested position. To arrive in this rest area, we are totally arrested, and thoroughly molested.

The molded mores inside and around the hole-losing molecules are in control now. We want to run, escape, and be free. As soon as we hear others' talking like a foreigner, we want to hear the fresh news from that raw voice. As soon as we smell our neighbor's cooking, we do not want to sit around our own dining table and please mom's wish. As soon as we are excited by others' words, we want the schoolteachers to become our new parents who are paid for by collective parents, such as cities, states and the Department of Education with little or no foreign exchange. Our family life style, though very familiar to our each breath and every action, expands with social liability. With no respect towards what our pared rents had already done for us, we want to follow others' footsteps, learn other skills, live on other professionals, and enjoy other's promotional pleasure. We want pros, not cons, because all the cons are conditioned from the get-go. This renting pare has been commanding us for so long that we cannot stand it anymore, bare it any longer.

But wait, afterward, pros are gone like fading stars and treading winds, and cons backfire on us, demote us, call our family names, and send us home, where none is left. Like where our pared rents started from their scratch, we begin to appreciate this pare, who rented us for so long and fought for us so hard, that we are caught in the talks of others, who were also taught by their pared rents. With this awakened loss, we then realize that bosses, seemingly have everything, keep on tossing things around without odor or aura. They have no extra orders, only retarded demands. Having nothing more to provide, ensure, and foster our growth and sustenance, they keep us fired up so they can fire us out.

In the end, two roads are left. One is to continue as a slave, the other is to be brave enough to liberate from all kinds of conditioned fabricating caves. If we were liberated from the work, the promotion would tell the boss for further performance, till we are fired or retired. Or to become self-employed, which is more difficult than working on just specific work and not worrying about the rest of headaches. There are all kinds of visible bosses, but only two invisible ones. One stands higher than Heaven and the other hides better than Hell.

When the boss yells at you: "Get the hell out of here," you are on the road to Heaven. When the boss fires you before you are retired, you still have extra lucid to spell.

Afterward, we depend on government for any perceived solution, or Union as the extra resolution. Bosses are worse than pared rents, and government is tougher than union. Realizing that anything bad we experience from our parents is because of the freedom outside the family door. The bad wishes out there will wash away the good ones granted from our parents. The good wishes grounded here will surrender to the bad ones rooted in nowhere. When we are taken care of by our pared rents, we have no idea how it feels without food or shelter. When we are milked by love, we have no clue what it means to be neglected, rejected, abandoned, and deprived from love.

Each family has a rule, each boss has its own character, and each nation has its own custom. When you are able to defend yourself against your pared rents, you do not need a last name. When you are able to act in front of your boss, you are better than the loss. When you are able to speak for yourself in front of national laws and international regulations, you are home on earth, inside Hell, and in Heaven. When you receive the love from your pared rents, you give to others. What you get paid from the boss will be spent on other payments. And what we are regulated by the state are restated by the church, till we know that the cord tires us on our birth site and Lord fries at us on the light side.

In the end, pared rents are our biological bosses. Bosses, if we work for more companies, are economical pared rents advancing our intellectual rents. Government is our big parent on one side and ruthless sibling on the other. It will send the extreme to the war to die, leaving the rest to the Church to be re-baptized by the same laws but different orders, so that the prison cell and monastic ward can rest our enraged body by arresting the engaged souls. The State becomes like a mother, providing all physical needs and securing all visible safeties. Church is like a father, working through your mind with faith above reason and fertilizing your love with thanks above forgiveness.

If we know how to take care of our parents, then, our bosses, and ourselves, the State and Church represent our own functional cross. They are no more that what we already are, no bigger than the size formed by the Creator, and no more powerful than any Will we are granted. When we understand that parents and State take care the body, boss and Church take care of the mind. We then can remember the odor of the milk and the aura of the sleeping silence. We miss (miss is always kept at her room before the groom brooms) the home, the place where we drown down, now called hometown. Everything familiar begins at family where the fame is milked into familiar circulation. We become the circulating materials controlled by parents (pared rents), bosses (big losers), masters (skill masker), leaders (controlling the lead in the head), and president (the prying resident). If those collective bosses were not the losers, they would survive and suffice by themselves. If they know how to repay their rent, to be self-directive and self-mastering, to feel content and at home anywhere on earth from birth, they would not invest their hope on us, feed us, lead us, master us, control us, and destroy us.

Though the pared rents sleep together once in a while, they are never in the vest, which is called nest. They never rest, as the best is being rented for the next-door neighbor, for extra odor. By the time they guess each other out, we all become their guests. When all guests quest, they regret (re-greet) about their own useless requesting arms upon recruiting armies, away from farms, causing the alarm to harm between hands and arms, since they never calm themselves down. As arms become upside down, hands are on guns, and fingers are pointing at the target, war makes everything switched, bewitched, twisted, toasted, boasted, and roasted.

When mastering self becomes replaced with mastering others, land and hand are the working creatures. Pros become emperors, who are empty per odor; implored by order, while cons become constitutions where institutions train each statue to become a begging prostitute. Without pros, where are the cons? Without the status, the standing posture, forward cannot see the pros of constitute and backward does not recognize the cons of prostitute. When all faces, fascia, are confiscated, each lost one must confess in front of the host, and the most becomes the worst.

We know, from the history (his story) that the master knows everything, can do nothing about anything. By the time we switch our cord to Lord, we find that the Lord forgives everyone, but mistakes each after conception. God above the sky watches us as faithful dogs and standing logs, as Love below the soil and inside the bones spices our motions like batting tails or itchy nails.

Being domesticated each for other, demons sleep upon dome, and angels fly away from Rome, leaving us to stay inside the suffocating box that is never the home. Working hard for the utilities running the dormitory, we are all jammed along the processing lines of factory, repeating what has already happened in the history.

Upon this sin (Snake's In, the shelled empty skin, sinking chin), towards the naked tin, everything sinks like ink; while each links to the pink, but does not think, only to the capacity that can blink. We then desperately need a condition for an audition, in addition to any given tradition. With given permeation, each is then wheeled with repetition. By the time the meat is sliced into a thin pie, we think that person is a liar. As that person permeates, son is pernicious and meat is delicious.

Playing with meatball, everyone then enjoys it like football. By the time the meat meets the foot, the meter becomes bitter about every inch gained in battle and sour towards every foot lost from the cattle feeding the battle. The cattle, having no castle, is catalytically fed with beans requested by its dean, who leans against only his sinful peanut, spinning like a walnut. Nothing is seen, everything must be quested, what cannot be seen but can be requested becomes the queen (quietly but cutely to be seen behind the veiling quilt, and beautifully keen as a dream may seem).

The queen, after losing her power of quilting by hosting her masters, becomes (please be calm) Guilt. The nation is at loss, because (be the cause) she quits her job. Instead of blaming himself, the emperor flames on others and claims more than he could master. Lame becomes enflamed, peace becomes pieces, and the white haired body drops to the ground, allover the black history. Without looking into the eyes, everyone's face is a race upon a pace being examined case by case.

This is our collective **human** story. Called it history, civilization, domestication, modernization or globalization, it matters not. It is all about the stored, but cannot be afforded "Why" which switches to Y. What is else before and beyond, besides the beheaded and belittled? Reaching to the ultimate point, we return to the beginning where each has nothing to start but all are startling. Sticking to what we have, we are restless and unfulfilled. Mastering all that we can command and are demanded, we are fooled either by our individual cells or collective selves. Who are these fools?

Right now, dear reader, as we are scribing our mentally stringed hearts in a different line, a different kind of traffic line will speak to you. Since you are not used to it, this line will not make sense to you, you will not cast your eye an extra minute on this line, and you will not read the lined book we are writing. I am a fool right now. That is all I can and must. **I am in a duel right now, my head against my heart, which can I trust?**

All I am scribing below had gone through the double-pressured cooker, one by my distilling mental power, and the other by my sacred toning heart. Being only self-responsible here, and using English Alphabetic strings as rings, I deliver all that I had made sense to me, to you. So let us shake our hands, touch our hearts, sharpen our eyes, charge our power, and begin this contracted journey. I am this fool at heart, a foolish mind. I am divine in my own valuable truth, disabled in my own voluntary nature, and dismantled in my own vulnerable state.

Being like this, all that I can is to breath and walk, see and talk, catch and dance, imagine and dream, be-lighted and delightful, light-headed and enlightened. I am in my cave and I am my own slave. The cave is my mason and my temple, while the slave is my own journey and my true liberation. I always believe, and I will never leave. Allowing me to be this leaf, I sniff. Being this leaf, I reach the cliff. Holding on my believed sleeve, which freezes to my knees, I stand on the valley-roof and hatch the beeves. With each beet as the sound of a beetle, I meet and enjoy this delicious meat upon the gulf. I puff and that is enough.

Now you can smell my journey, which is a penniless honey. With your query, you see my injury, not inside the jail, but along the plain trail, plane nail, and fermented tail, which is veiled with the frail, a nested mail. Being a male, my mama leaves me to a tale, as she stores me to an orally transmitted rail.

As soon as she says goodbye to my lord, she snaps my cord, and I collapse upon a Ford. It is not a Jeep, but cheap, I travel on and on and enjoy my potato chips. Bored with potato, I wish for a Toyota, dissembled in Ohio through the December, so I could move to Utah, play guitar and have fun with kings of sugar: the nectar. Aha, all these decimal bars, better than cars, far from Utah, and I am tolled to leave and fart. With no furry, I am in a hurry to tell this story, not in a furious way but on a functional day, not quite like going through a war, upon the walls with no call, towards the fences with no tenses, and inside the senses with no density. Flurry like light snow, I sit on my knees and nod at the knots in my hair, who are always fare to me. Though far and near, I know now that I can see what is below: "what is now is what matters above."

The boat is on the river, and the oven has a ferry cooked from the fire below the river, which is boiled to the oil-pointing hooker. Hooked on facts, which are the voices of running fox, I am surrounded by a box, full of oxygen, but no toxicant gene. The box is exiled with axles, an expertise advertised.

Dear reader, don't be afraid with the word "contract." If so, just to let you know that you are only obligated to yourself here, not me. I did not make your eye, teach you English, and purchase your copy of this book (though I wrote it). So you are free. Initially the word "tract" means an expanse or area of land, water, etc.; region; stretch. So this means when this word is being invented, the inventor's eye was open, casting on a horizontal plane. The land on and above water did not expand at all, only the glancing eyes were expanded (excited, charged, invigorated, fired up). The moment the eyes landed on this land or water, the inventor, who was also the pilgrim at the time, was thinking, reasoning, pondering, head-scratching, and gut-drumming about how to make use of the place. Just being practical, playful at the beginning, as if no other trainings were involved; otherwise, it will be capitalistic (to capture, to con- and to sell, capitalize, profit, make money).

Thus, the secondary meaning of "tract" is coined, invented, or added: a belief treatise, pamphlet, or leaflet for general distribution, usually on a religious or political topic. From this, the word is no longer to stretch (of time and space), but to handle, make it real, true and justifiable, so that others will believe and follow. "Look what a wonderful leaf I just plucked from the land; look what a beautiful flower I just picked up from the pond" (I hope it is not fig leaf to begin with, or I hope this person is not Zeus, or a crazy Zen monk).

Trickle and treat, from this tree, we first eat this leaf and then we leave. Adam becomes thus political, and Eve religious. Adam told Eve to either eat the leaf, or use it as a makeup. He is just being polite (Polish people are polite).

By simply polite, Adam's active behavior tickles Eve.

"Please be police," said Adam through His gut-dam, to fire up Eve, who does not have a single piece of leaf on Her private region. Though She looks naturally like leaflet (She only tells Herself "let it be the leaf," and let Adam reverse leaflet).

He fires and lies and His "leaf" becomes the word "lief".

Eve screams toward Adam: "Ad on me, as it initially was!" Then Ad to silent mouth or AM. Still too early to leave, to die, not PM yet, so He continually fires and lies, until Eve is leaving His belief. This is really political!

Being religious about the matter, Eve left Ad-am (Dammed Him) to search for truth herself in the region or place or spot where Adam spotted the precious leaf. She found with amuse and excitement that She can do something about it. So Eve puts the leaf on Her region, the private religion, and starts to belly dance. Being fired up now, Adam's heart pampers, and His private region pees on His pants and knees.

"Am I peeing, or is my penny peeing?" Adam asked.

"Go and pee in lake, or I lay down and you pee in my lake!" Eve demands.

This is the story of treat, a tree tied-and-bonded to an eating habit: a treat under the bushy and fishy tree where they eat the leaf, and live forever happily afterward. And this is the story of tract.

Afterwards, "Can we do this again?" Adam requested from Eve.

With the leaf, She leaves, and becomes EVE, because She can excite herself with the ad of the leaf.

Co-operation, no; and Eve is very religious about this. Con was invented, meaning no cooperation. This is, and has been, man's business (always busy for something is business: bus Y or must whine).

The war begins. Adam is polite, pleasing and finally political so as to slice, dice, and bus. Eve, on the other hand, is religious, sticking to her region, her land and her water, with leaf, and lives forever in this ever and never land.

The war gives birth to the first meaning of "con", which means in opposition, against.

Afterward, Adam questions about this matter, and Himself. So the second meaning of the word con becomes alive: to learn (with the leaf near His nose), study (suddenly die), persue (each time no use), or examine carefully (with ex, AM I Mine again, since Eve's V is allover, all around, and in all directions. Her single V becomes four-sized or even quintupled, plus the original one She keeps for Herself.)

This is the story, or stored wine for our contract. Since I have a contractor myself, you are only responsible for yours. The story out of this is the three returns: you blame your parents so they can blame their parents, and their parents blame the first parents of Adam and Eve. Blaming the flame, claiming the frame!

AM and Even

Because of Adam and Eve, we are all contracted. We all have seven holes in our faces and two hands extending towards arms. We see and examine each other between the two eyes filming the same color. They are near to each other between the two ears detecting the same sound, and say no to one another aside from two of the nostrils blowing the same air.

Three times after, mouth does not like duality, tongue does not like pupils, and teeth do not care about ears. The mouth opens and pronounces O or Moo, but the tongue keeps babbling and bubbling, stuffed with the study of the Bible. And nose keeps nosing, but no losing anything, because it controls the power of breath, and says constantly "no" above the mouthed "moo." The two eyes keep seeing the light line of I, I, and I. Two ears near are hearing Me, Me and Me. Two nostrils keep drilling Mine, Mine and Mine. I, Me, Mine; and I meet ma mining the wine and binding the wind!

Finally, hands try to put together a V shape with their arms to separate A from M, or holes or spaces between fingers, or nails from fingertips. By forming Y (elbows and wrists together as "I" while hands opening and facing each other as V), hands invert all M to W with the aid of the trunk of H, to make everything hand-ful, and hand-able; hand-ling handy Andy and dandy Daddy. All dads die without candy before they color and dye with their handy bloody fists. With the single H, all ands become ends, and ends are added up to ponds (the price tags of fish in the pond saved by Eve and slaved by Adam). By switching d in end to g, and leaf to lish, the word English is formed. English becomes self, sellable fish that is called selfish. By using this sellable syllabus, study begins: to examine the nation (the exiled me forms a nation).

Business becomes baby's babble and AM's (adults, which are added nuts) Bible. Arms become the tool for war, cool to fight but fool to die. Wow, Mow: bowing to the towel and mowing to the town. Ship (Eve's dancing swishing and squishing hips) expands from friendship, to township, to kingship, to all shipping industries.

With the aid of the power of two hands and ten fingers, we start to put things to our mouths, from milk to food, tools to words, or anything to everything. By, not buy or goodbye, putting things together orderly, we allow and permit the religious stances and political points to intermingle with one another: one door closes and the other opens; one war ended begins another war: to worship the warship. No more Even and no more Ease.

By the time Even and Ease are merged, Eve judges the work of essay-- easily said and easily done--everything returns to its easy position, easy land, and easy pond. When Eve becomes the eye, or the lens of I, all are said and done.

The question then is where does the line connecting to V come from, or does this line come from Adam's bone-line, private line, polite line or political line? As soon as an eye says yes, only and maximally half is true and the other half becomes already sliced, tilted, bended or twisted. Nose then stands up, represents that line, below the V, and says no to all the above, telling them just to breath and stay in the middle of nowhere. Is this line the line of Holy Water or Holy Fire?

The final question goes to the palms of hands, which has the juicy power of apple, the lucid texture of the heart, the lubricating wheels of abdomen, and marrow-filled holes in the brain.

Now all eyes, ears, nostrils, mouth, tongue, teeth and lips, hands, palms and fingers and nails are finally working together as a united team for a family party. Everything is contracted; yet, none escapes from its own work and its collaborative roles. Eve returns to Even, and Adam holds the leaf as the real belief and spells the "the easy essay."

Equally, when Eve turns to her ear-hearing power near Her eye, above Her nose, all things become no-no. When all Her returning feelings are either actively responding to things (tilted rings), in and out, or passively following them (me standing on Hills, hips, holes and titling rings), the sensory eyes become the sacred windows to the soul, and to the lights and colors and appearances coming through Her, to us all. Individually, anything your eyes have cast from this point on is no longer my business, but your busy ness. So be responsible to your sacred sensory soul.

We live and share, and we pray and promote. What is above gives us now, the divine presence. What we have within defines us the lineal, conditional, or karmic pattern, a story beginning with H, as English language defined as history, a bit selfish not on his behalf. Is this history the man's or God's?

Beginning with a story, a stored retail (thanks for having no tail so we can retail and retell), a digested purge, and an internally pushed action, we can give, instruct, pass on, or let go what we received and digested, and empty from inside out to make room for the new. Since we begin with nothing, we are literally weightless like nothing. As the weightless joined adventure of zygote, a yoked material, between a sperm cell and egg cell, we will end with nothing. All the weight added will be subtracted, all the size expanded will be sized down, all the information stored will either exist as it is, survive to the last point, or, at worst, invade the rest, and consume all it can. Are we eating up the universe or is the universe eating us up?

Remember this, what is all good out there does not belong to you, since it only reflects what is good in you, and what is good in you has no word to describe it, no color to paint it, and no sound to sing it.

As such, I will start first to reveal my stored Y right in between and inside my nose and eyes and ears, my own fermented wine, because your eyes are now on my typed line. So, here it is.

Personal Refection

When I started this searching journey at my later teens, something forced in me of which was also beyond me. At the same time, my body did not feel right from early (ear-lying stage) stress. I did not know how to listen to things making noise outside or me talking in a voice on inside. What I did not feel right about were the different sensations in my brain, insomnia, and gray hair (only a teenager as old as a wise boy). In my trunk, it was the poor digestion and fear. In my joints, the itches called arthritis and the cries without rhythm. Worse than this, I felt cursed by my parents, demanded by others to serve as a professional gatekeeper, a social substance, and a cultural slave.

Adding upon those were the naked powers of nature (they were just there for you) upon the naked land (semi desert). Wind was the heavy dusts, sunlight was the burning stove, and storm was the raging mouth. Water flow in the seasonal river was like drainage outlet, like running tears from the mountain, like sweat purging out of working body, like salty riverbeds trying to wipe out what was blocking and fencing the eyes, like a heavy but thin blood traveling from corner to corner, block after block, and valley to valley. This poor stream was so salty, even animals would not touch with their nose.

All farmers, and all living creatures, were expecting no more than what water could rain their flaming mouths and how food could calm their drumming stomachs. They were naked like their living land and laboring nature: pure and humble without any expectation, sincere and dear like tears and breath, present and calm like sleeping babies and resting animals, humiliated like dogs, disciplined like the cow, and prayerful like moonlights.

It is only at nighttime, under the moonlight, I saw the gold, felt comforting wind, soothing air and bathing lights. Many a night, I would sleep in the courtyard, letting the warm ground hug my back, gentle wind kiss my dream, and allow golden lights lift me into the sleepless land, burying all the weights of life, and carrying me into paradise.

Then the college door opened for me, a certificate granted me a job away from farming. Foreign words (English) textured and tinctured my teeth and tongue. All I could remember well were my father's writings on newspaper wall, and strange but attractive English words. My father's handwriting inspired me, disciplined me, but the English words were equated to blown mane, tall body, and philosophical hair; justice wig, pig as pork, fig as mug. The American voice was less familiar than BBC tapes, but its tone, VOA (Voice Of America), was more powerful than the cobra on Egyptian Pharaoh's head (later on I realized Moses sliced the voice of this cobra up and digested it into the meat of the Ten Commandants). I searched for myself and my ancestral blood. I was ashamed by my Chinese culture and tradition, which seemed to contribute very little to global economy at the time.

Exhausted from listening Peter Jennings's voice on TV one day after school, I laid down on floor instead sitting cross-legged, and I was in a dream vision state. In this vision, there was a stack of logs burning, and a yellow robed figure on top of the fire. It was me, my Buddhist body being burned. The door to past life was opened. My spirit, like a seasonal seed, entered from one flesh to another, one being to the next, without changing its essential essence. Like a wheat or rice seed, where its genetic makeup never changes, my spirit-seed travels from time to time, birth to death, soul to soul, only to discover that I am in an on-going roller coaster: all because of Universal Love or Universal Qi.

There are two kinds of Qi in the Chinese language in terms of description. One is a living thing, where the character is combined between air and rice. The other kind is a universal thing, where this character is structured between the nothingness on top, and four-cornered water at the bottom. For life, we breathe and eat, and in spirit we exist and are in love with Universal Qi or harmonic sound.

With this atoning Qi, I experienced all the white lines running inside my body, and they would stop and talk to my skin as condensed heat vibrations as an irresistible itchy sensation, and uncontrollable monkey temptation (wants to scratch the head off). When the Qi traveled down to my lower body, it was like hot gas pouring through my thighs, legs and feet. Backing up, it would gush through my neck, and there was a heated sensation at the lower backbones (through the life-gate pressure point). Running again after a while into my brain, it would shower down my head and face, the most wonderful sensation. The Qi-shower was so soft and tender, like an angelic touch, so gentle and subtle like lover's first kiss. It was like walking under the gentle, foggy and bathing rain; my brain was this rain, my sensation was this angelic purge, and my living existence was inside this harmonic cave.

When this Qi stuff talked to my arthritic fingers and knees, it swirled like an electric stove heater, hot but comfortable, dense but bearable. This hot stove would heat up any diseased area, organs and bodily parts. One day, I was standing, facing and talking to sun, God's son, and goddess's nun, my nostril breathing disappeared, and was replaced by the opening throat (I did not know at the time that throat was the life-clock). Few seconds later, my body disappeared, and was replaced by three loops of lights. The loop around my legs was blue, the loop around my arms was gold, and the loop around my trunk was white. These three would travel individually, but communicate with one another as an unified team, united nation, and uniformed motion.

I bought all the books on Qigong as I could, and tried all possible techniques, from standing, to walking, to dancing, to sitting on legs and bud, and to lying on floor, and most time on bed. I have experienced all possible visualizations, imaginations, and fantasies, and hallucinations; all possible combinations among individual formula, personal styles, and religious mandates. The best I liked was breathing out the number of each count upon my imaginative screen on my forehead (the dual third eye region as I know now). I could see the number flashing like magic numbers or figures on a TV screen. Life is universal and individual. We never die, but we must die to breath after peace, sleep through death, trial upon tribulation, stage following season, and memory before the memorable.

As I searched my biological roots, examined my cultural deeds, I found that though the Taoist Inner Alchemy and the Chinese medicine were granted to the Chinese blood like Yellow Dome and silk thread, they indeed belonged to humanity. Taoist Inner Alchemy is the Inner Science, where spirit and soul examine, test and objectify all Qi-charged things, personal and impersonal, ideal and experiential, to the objective table. This Qi reads the weather pattern, goes through seasonal cycle, crystallizes life experiences, and savors like the most fermented drug, the best purified alcohol, the highly condensed nectar. The drug is for the painful sensation, the alcohol waters the thirsty life, and the nectar wakes up the hungry soul. As for Chinese medicine, the twenty meridians with hundreds of pressure points, is like a golden pyramid, the sacred geometry, and holographic sphere. Never materialized like the Egyptian King's tomb, those pointed threads form the original womb of life, hosting golden seeds of light, nesting universal fabrics, and dancing like light spirits and angelic beauties.

By my father who extinguished his Qi-body, his face taught me the vocabulary "wraith": quite vocal yet he could no longer pronounce it, rather vocational but only conversational. He told me to study Qigong well, the only disciplinary and compulsive program offered to my life. While I was riding the train around 9:00 pm on third night, his spirit, died from his flesh, searched through my friend's window and shocked him, but I was surrounded by countless travelers. Like caged animals, we were ready to be unloaded for cash.

Years before my father spelled his will for me, my third brother gave me his sacrificial donation. Visiting the graveyard, while he was twenty years old, on that Chinese New Year's Eve, he listened to the conversation of ghosts determining who should die for the year. Returning home, he was welcomed by his beloved wife's departing soul. In a flash, the vision disappeared, and he rushed to the house, unlocked the door and chain, found his wife was sound asleep. Three days later, they had their first baby, and then four days after the baby was born, she died from wrong herbal formula prescribed by her creative barefoot doctor (Till this day, I do not like to study or give herbs to people. She had paid the price for me).

These two persons' death gave me a huge traumatic reward, telling me how to live up to the price they have paid for and the gifts they had donated. My grandparents' gifts were rather subtle, and long lasting. I never knew physically my grandmothers, paternal or maternal. But their resting places gave me the honor, the power, and strength: contract from unsolved business and liberation upon death. I only remembered my mother's sky crying voice upon her mother's gravesite, more powerful than death valley, and more shocking than seeing white bones.

As for my paternal grandmother, I spiritually contracted to the wrong direction where her resting coffin was located, and her un-stretched neck problem before she was put inside the casket. On one 13th of a moonlight, I saw my spirit standing and shining in the sky, above her graveside, and knew instantly how I was contracted to live in her lineage and solve her problem. This was the time, the second, the eternal presence, and I enjoy the power of triangle, because my white-lotus spirit formed from the sky a triangle between her grave-point and my parents' side-by-side tantric mating posture. I was lucky that I did not follow someone's order in order to have a flesh and live this life. I saw it, my spiritual contract and my destined journey afterward, but it took me forty-years' of heart and hard search to reconnect with and to it.

Only recently during a meditation, I saw initially a pair of orange-black boots standing on my shoulders. As I looked up, I saw an angelic figure in a white-robe standing on my shoulders, above my head, playing a flute. I did not hear the songs or music she played, but seven holes in the flute reminded me the further journey into seven days of creation and seven stages of enlightenment (She did not pee on me, nor give birth to my flesh, but she opened my cave-mansion, brain, anointed me with the mystic flute and appointed me for higher work.

A while later, I met Yin. When she showed me her sketches, I was awestruck by the face of a particular woman. It was the same face as the woman who was standing on my shoulders!

Talking is not better than walking, walking is not better than playing, and playing is not better than singing, and singing is not better than dancing. Deep in my heart, my paternal grandfather talked to me with his humble and silent deeds, walked for me when I napped inside his armed chest, taught me how to play the Er-hu (a two-stringed Chinese music instrument). From that point on, only after two-hour's practice during a hot summer, I rejected the musical instrument. I could not believe that after thirty-years, I picked up the instrument again. But at this time, the instrument was not manmade, but

The face of the woman on Tao's shoulder.

created by God. I started to play music on a human instrument, where two strings on the back, twelve in front, and five or so on side, and one inside.

As I am playing each song, each movement comes from the angelic lady, the transcended figure of my grandmother physically, or angelic lover spiritually, starts to dance through my heart, where the songs and tones of souls start to sing through my fingers, and move through my body to shake upon my short-haired neck and brain.

Cultural Reflection

Only now, dear reader, do I begin to know the thrust of the universe, the silent Word of God, and vibration of heart. Before this, I searched my family tree of Huang (Yellow), and my national title of Chinese (Han nationality beginning from Han Dynasty 206 BC-222AD). My family name, on the other hand, reflects the color of earth. Heat boils from inside the earth and flames outside at the same time.

After my father's death, I began to search for a spiritual father, or "Godfather" in Christian terms. I knew that I did want to go back to a medical school to study Chinese medicine, because at that time, switching a subject (changing majors) was a difficult thing in Chinese high educational system. All I wanted was to master the teaching of Taoism.

I used to read the Tao Te Ching before I went to US, but the words were like strange rains, wizard crystals, and an unfathomable mystery. A symptom of not yet outgrowing the societal rules. As I was searching for a teacher from one monastery to another for two years, I gave it up. And I had sworn that I did not want to study Taoism anymore because there was no teacher nor teachings available.

But I was wrong. On the Winter Solstice in 1988, before I approached age of 26 (a great number according to King Wen's hexagram arrangement, and the name of the hexagram, Great Mystic Field, or the field of soul, or Tree of Love), I awoke, lit an incense stick and began meditation (I love incense smell and I even dreamed one night before I came to the US second time that the field around my family was filled with incenses, about ten acres wide and six foot tall of huge stacks of incense). I had fun with this meditation and within 45 minutes I mastered all the martial movements and did Qigong bathing (washing my dust-smudged skin with a towel). Then automatic writing began after I lit the second incense, the final seal was Lao Tzu's spiritual name, the Supreme Old Master. So I found a spiritual father and I began to work for him ever since.

Through this spiritual line, all other Taoist masters came to my life as I needed for my growth and healing others, males and females; till Fu Xi, the Father of Chinese biological, as well as, spiritual race came to me and taught me the secret teachings of I Ching. This finalized when Xi Mu Niang: Queen Mother of West came to me as my real grandmother.

Because of this, teachers and guidance from many other mystic traditions came alive in me: Mystic Christian, Kabala, Sufi, Hindu, as well as Native American, Australian, and African traditions. I am now blessed with all traditional teachings to the degree that I give myself a new name, Pig Worm, so that I can digest all sources, traditions, lineages, and teachings like a swallowing pig, and become as that soft, original biological being as a worm in a cosmic womb driving a mystic tomb.

Where is the true field of love, health, wealth and talent?

The result of this is that as I finished searching my own biological and spiritual roots, I found that all roots return to the same rooted source. As a man, we would spend our entire life searching, examining, pleasing, and making peace with the other side: the divine feminine creative power and beauty. Until we have this, understand this, master this, and make peace with this, all the seeds produced on biological lines, all the words and theories fabricated on spiritual line, mean nothing to woman, love, milk, comfort, and most important of all, heart.

What is this Heart business to a rational, idealistic, brain-raging, and heart-escaping man, or male? We have spent entire lives working and playing in a field called business, jobs, professions, careers, trade, skills, and endless many other names. Each finds comfortable to his talent and each feels soothing to one's essence: heart. In the end, all goes to nothing, to the place without heart, the heart having no heart.

In the beginning of life, I have been a good boy, a good student, and a skilled employee, to the point that no one wanted me, nor hired me. Equally speaking, I did not like any one of them, job or boss; to the point I had to sell my ancestral blood to make a living, selling my heart, selling the mechanism of the Tao, selling all in this empty field, this empty heart, this soundless vacuum, this silent void.

I can spend entire masculine words, phrases and borrowed vocabularies to describe my passion, display my wheels, decipher my running loops, defile my escaping modes, and devoid, at last, my own original essence: my own heart.

As I look at this place, this empty field, this echoing center, this holographic sphere, I am home. I am surrounded by lights, supported by moving chariots, guided by traveling portals, fenced through distilling mechanisms, rooted with cosmic essence, promoted with never dying joy, glowed with never ending happiness, and smiling like a little boy, a passionate love, a disciplined father, a wise man, a cosmic seed, and single droplet of light who has no memory of beginning or end, birthing or dying, or leaving and returning, speaking or whining.

Before I came to this place, I have entitled me with different names, such as Taoist, healer, shaman, medicine man. And inside my heart, I truly and sincerely desire to help people, cure their illnesses, and dissolve their symptoms.

In the end, I was facing those pathological loops of incestuous destruction or corruption, which began from twin brother and sister, then oedipus complex, electoral complex, animal copulation, alien abduction, and so on. With all the human numbers, and each having his or her own versions or miniatures of the same problems, how could I solve their problems, and why should we solve these problems?

This is how we can trace back to our bloodline, our origin, and our birthing process. But should we demand God for all these problems, should we accuse our angelic mother who gave birth to us, fed us and died for us, and should we blame each other for popularizing us all?

Asking all the dead relatives, ancient ancestors, original parents, divine Adam and Eve, Shiva and Shakti, Fu Xi and Nu Wa, Brother and Sister, Husband and Wife, Father and Mother, Grandfather and Grandmother, all their humble, humiliating, truthful and helpless answer is: yes we made you and we made a mistake. This is how we wish for you, your power and beauty, strength and character, so you can solve yours and our problems altogether.

This is where the ideal sin began, from the moment we were conceived, from the moment we felt we were trapped at terrible two, from the moment we feel the loss after courtship, from the moment we saw what we have created from our own children, our own creative art works, from our own destructive machines, from our own thinking process, from our own inventive loop, and from our own flesh, textures, feelings, fabrications, blood, milk, love and support.

My Heavenly Contract

Before I was born, I was oblivious. My first spiritual dream was cartoon-like. A cartoon mouse and I were playing with some other cartoon friends. We were all crazily running around through tubes of light and energy. We couldn't only go in one direction, it was very hard to go back. There were two tunnels beside each other. I was the only human formed baby child. It was not until years later, I realized I was reliving my conception and those tunnels were my mother's fallopian tubes.

My first heavenly companion was a stuffed animal. On a brief stay in Shanghai, my uncle had bought me a brand new teddy bear. But I did not want that new teddy bear. I wanted a much older and used one that my newborn cousin already had. Don't ask me why, I could never answer why. It stayed with me for ten years. When I was thirteen, she was lost with some of our luggage. My mother did not want to be embarrassed by her thirteen year old daughter still carrying a teddy bear so she made me place it in the checked luggage. By that time, it was time to let go. I had secretly outgrown her, but she had become so real, I felt obligated to love her. She, and my mother, I searched for in lovers.

Much later, I learned that my true mother is nothing more than the heavenly mother.

The Jade Emperor is my chum. Or, I seem to think he is. With me being trapped in a body of flesh, it is easy for him to control my fate. He managed to convince me somehow, to reincarnate into this life. This life, that he, I, and many other consorts designed. It is still too soon to know my ultimate destiny, but all I do know is that, beneath the surface, I am not supposed to lead the simple easy life of an average citizen. On the surface, I can smile at you and be normal.

All I can share with you about my heavenly contract, is only that which I have already witnessed.

When I was two, my father left for America. It was just my mother and myself. I saw her as a goddess as all children see their mothers. I recall she was walking me to daycare one day when it was raining. She carried me on her back and I held the umbrella. Were there holes in the umbrella? I cannot remember clearly. But she was my big sister, not my mother. In that short year, my father and I grew distant. The year after, my mother and I joined my father in the states. Two types of fights occurred that scared me, but did not scar me:

1. My grandmother was yelling and I was hiding behind the door, the hired maid/nanny put me there. There was glass breaking and the tinkling sound was so beautiful like forbidden music. I knew that I would be in trouble if I ever broke glass, but I still loved the sound. When my mother finally grabbed me and left, we were silent. I was tired and normally would have asked her to carry me, but something was not right. When we returned to her home, she sat down and I watched as she silently pulled broken glass from her feet.

2. My father was soft and gentle and he put me to bed and tucked me in. My mother was in the kitchen throwing things and shouting. Her voice was high pitched and squealing. I wondered, is that the pain of womanhood? Years later, when I was thirteen and started my menstrual flow, she told me that being a woman meant living in a

curse. I did not want to believe it.

By the time I was two. I felt equaled to my parents and I felt a secret alienation from them though I still loved them dearly. I wanted to please them and make them happy. Yet, I always had what I wanted to do in my own mind. Did this frighten them? Intimidate them? What did they see in their only daughter? I was free. I was free then, like I am free now. But now I will share with you the price that I paid. A price high enough where I can no longer do any wrong, or feel any guilt, shame, or pain.

At age five, I began to feel the pressure of needing to succeed. I had to make a name for myself, I had to be the best. But was I? No. I could not help but be a fighter, I bit my nanny once over a petty disagreement. I received a hearty beating from my father. I could not help but believe that I was right and I shouldn't have to follow any rules. This would not do, this would not do at all. I was eventually beaten and scared into submission. I loved my parents, how could I turn them in? People claim they protect the innocent. They use it as an excuse to control the idiotic. I could not live with myself that I was the worst student in my class. Of course no one took in consideration that my English was only subpar at the time. Somehow, it was simply overlooked.

I paid with many long nights, being forced to stay up until two or three o'clock in the morning on homework that I just could not understand. At seven years old, I often went to school with puffy eyes and little sleep. The tears and the bitterness were squeezed from me like dry juice. Up until I was eleven years old, this was how I paid my dues. My ultimate sacrifice that I offered was myself. I gave up who I was, selling myself. I stood apart and alone. I could not be accepted by the Chinese race because I was too American. I could not be accepted by the Americans because they did not understand a lot of the Chinese traditions. And I was too young to know that everything I knew came from two separate sources that chose not to give an inch of leniency and understand each other. I gave up my daydreaming because it affected my grades, I gave up my thoughts, beliefs, and heart. Unlike Tao, who was born as the exact middle child and had siblings on both sides for his parents to worry about, I was an only child. I had nothing to deflect my parents and their demands made upon me.

When I was twelve, I finally accepted that I would never be the best. My mother was living through me. She was the only girl in the family, and she secretly wanted a sister. Either I was to die, or she was to die. Heaven knew this before I did. At age thirteen, I began to get better at succeeding and climbing up the ladder of academics. At age fourteen, my sister-mom was taken from me. In her place, was a left behind ghost. She is buried somewhere deep inside that grave of a woman. Every other word that comes out of her mouth is either a hungry ghost or vile poison so deadly it could kill the weak hearted to hear her.

I was her, she lived through me, the family was in shambles because I could not digest this new energy that was coming through her. Even before the accident, I was not allowed more than one hour of television a day, if that, and I was not allowed to go out with friends unless their parents were friends with my parents and they were chaperoning. After my sister-mother died, my parent's home became my prison. Then, my mind was my prison, because it was still their minds, their laws and rules that dictated who and what I was.

They didn't really need to punish me anymore, I punished myself for them. They lived through me, I was the first child, the sacrifice. When my grades were inadequate, I obediently laid down on the stairs to receive my short beating. The difference between beating your child in a large household and nuclear household is not always obvious. In large extended families, the parents are icons of authority who punish in order to teach the lesson to children so that they can take responsibility for their actions. They have grandparents and aunts and uncles to cry to for other emotional issues. In a nuclear family, it merely creates a rift between parent and child and emotional scarring both ways. There is no one, no where to turn to and they all become trapped within imaginary laws and rules. I was trapped in the worst kind of prison: myself.

My ninth birthday, I was beaten because I was disobedient. It was a normal punishment, but the timing was what almost killed me. Somehow, I survived all these years. It was my first return to China. I didn't realize that there was a tradition where, as the birthday girl, I was the host and I had to honor the guests. It was my second day in China and I wanted to sleep off the jetlag, but my father did not warn me it was an embarassment to him. I had cried miserably after my beating and I felt a hotness in my head choking me, making me dizzy. I was afraid of death then, but if I were not, I would have taken the cake knife.

Another instance on the same trip I was grouchy although silent while putting on my shoes. A large hand, my father's, darted at my face and I was slapped without warning. For a moment, I was stunned, but a groaning sob twisted its way out of my lips as I walked to my mother. Even my mother was cold to me that day. I could not understand why. To this day, I am still feeling the abandonment as if I were their dog they had found off of the street. Even lower than how adopted chilren used to be treated. They had unknowingly stolen my gold from inside of my gut.

In return, they have given me many gifts. One of which was teaching me frugality and gratefulness since we didn't have much as I was growing up. My father was a doctorial student and my mother couldn't do much with her Chinese bachelor's degree. Money was always tight, and barely enough.

I have sacrificed myself for the love of my parents. I gave up my identity to live as theirs. I am not saying they were horrible and abusive parents, no, they were not, but they tragically underestimated my sensibility. This day, I know where I stand in my family, as the support beam. Without me, there would be no harmony in their lives.

I sacrificed my heart to my lovers. None of which I can recall in my cellular memory any longer. All ten have been shut out because none of them were pure to me. I sat by and watched and waited silently as some loved others, as some killed me before my very eyes, as some abused me. And all I could do was force myself to soak in the pain and love it. Love it, or die. What I was looking for, was the pure seed that I believed to reside inside of all people.

Ultimately, I had given nothing but the purest. True, when I was younger, I tried to manipulate, but even though I was a good liar, I was never good at lying. The liar in me was able to see ultimate truth from time to time, but it was so sacred, I could not tell it to just anyone, so I lied. In the end, I just didn't know what I wanted from anyone anymore. After chasing all these lines and lies, I had forgotten my purity and clouded my own vision and chased away my happiness. I was in denial, and I was so miserable I had tried, like many, to just give up and die. Stupidly, I had tried to drown myself in my bath, but to anyone who knows about the body and natural reflexes, they know that it is impossible. It was not fair to me then, that death abandoned me. I learned to love the pain in a selfish, gluttonous way. I ate and ate and ate it all up. Finally, I was full, but I still loved the pain that would never end for me. I ate it gently and soothingly, with a true heart. It was the pain that felt real, the pain that was able to show me more truth about how people are beneath the images they portray forth. Things will always happen, do we stop and cry and try to fight about it? Or do we take it in, smile at it, and move on?

Heaven bombarded me with one trial after another. I took all the blows as if I deserved them because I believed that I deserved them. I inadvertently became what most people believed what Jesus was about. I believed pain and sacrifice was the only way to accept life. I was beaten down to nothing, and I was left alone in a sort of sane psychosis.

From brutal, fast moving fist fights, to slow, agonizing stress

SPIRITUAL CONTRACT

149

that ate away at my insides, I was tried with them all. I was held under scrutiny and I was poked every now and them. I betrayed myself, and I have betrayed others. I broke every single rule there was and I tried my best to make penance and confess and make peace.

Around the time I was near completion of college, words came to me. Not spiritual or inspirational, but words that rang a deep solid truth through my soul. I was visited by the words and ideas of Lao Zi, Nietzche, Dosteovsky, Adam Smith, and many more to count. Words and ideas became my only true companion, my only true love. It took all the rules I broke, and tore them down until nothing was left but emptiness. I danced and rejoiced and floated weightlessly in this freedom and everything that I had once thought was pain an suffering erased itself and appeared stupid.

Right and Wrong, Good and Evil, they are words. W-O-R-D is a word too. They are tools, utensils, media to convey communicative concepts. Why is it that some words instill fear to the degree that we alter who we are? The role of my parents was to teach me every single rule that they knew and to show me everything a person needs to succeed in a society structured in a certain way. It was an extraordinarily powerful gift and without their strict dedication, I would have never learnd my lesson. After I was done absorbing them and apply them to myself, what did I do? I rejected them. Only after being and understanding something fully, can we truly be credible to "reject" or choose to be against something. Otherwise, we would just be discriminating. In the words of the African-American brothers and sisters, "Don't be hatin'!"

Too many words cause too much pain. We forget our hearts when we turn to words. It is not the words that are alive, it is their message. The message is for the heart and only the heart can accept or reject them. That, my dear friends and lovers, is the light, and the light contract. It is a medium of telepather exchange where we speak through our inklings.

In my flesh, I live in a world of laws and ideals and manners and generalities of how things should be. Inside, I am free. I reject everything I do not see as a spawn of pure seed. I have paid the price a minimum of ten times over and have lived enough pain to have it ring deeply through ten lifetimes and two cultures. Nothing I can do now, can be judged as "wrong" from heaven. I am innocent. To them, the score is settled. I will continue to break the external laws that protect selfishness, I will continue to live as a contradiction, but I had already agreed to this the moment I chose the left fallopian tube of my mother's that bore me.

Even my aborted child who sees me from time to time, still loves me and she asks me to go stay with her. To which I respond, "Dearest, when mother is finished with business, she will come to find you."

To drop everything and take on everything while appearing as if it is nothing. That is my contract until further notice. It is a time released program.

How did this come to be? Over 10,000 years ago, when we were (and still are) all just heavenly puppets, a game was played. Perhaps it was a game like chess, or a bluff game, like poker, either way, it was winner takes all. The winner wrote the contract and the losers listened. The wager was this: are humans to be ruled externally but learning to follow rules like trained dogs who jump through hoops? Or were they to be ruled from inside, through their own intrinsic communication to higher emotional understanding balanced with intellect? In other words, through earthly bonds, or heavenly light? My puppet master(s) had lost that war and I failed, for which I was cast into 10,000 years of purgatory. Lucky for me, it is much more peaceful this time around. It's not a physical fight, rather, a spreading of love and light.

CHAPTER 8:

WHO ARE YOUR PARENTS

Dear my beloved biological parents, you two are my soil and water, flesh and love. Without you, I have to stay floating in the sky or to be buried in the bottomless hell, or find another pared mating couple as my parents. There is part of me is always in you, and part of you will forever be mine, whether I am with you or not, whether I live alone or die alone. The universe contracted three of us together for a divine purpose, regardless of how many generations have deceased behind you, how many spirits shine above your hovering sky, and how many more children will come accordingly into this world, ahead of your beloved journey, during your sentenced entropy, and after your resting headstone. My flesh is your labor, my love is your sacrifice, and my gift is your anointment. Seasoned heat is your blood, and in turn, my flood charged flesh. Your daily consumption measures my weight and size, and in turn, treasures my allowance and forgiveness. Your years of hard labor are my lesson plan, my field trip, and elevating point. Your sacrifice becomes my blessings and your journey directs my vision.

My spirit was injured by your dreamed and wished journey of love, where whatever you two have done, individually or collectively, is my blessing, and whatever you have left behind, forgot, unfinished, are my job of life until I become either better than what you have done or worse that what you have hoped for or escaped from.

You two are together, as Sun and Moon, as a living duality and ultimate reality, a teamed couple to clone my spirit, fabricate my sensory organs, and wrap my skin as your vital personalities and love lotions. You may not love each other anymore, any longer, but the memory of your loved journey as well as the scar of your soul-felt injury are all in me. I become then your blessing and curse at the same time. It is from me you see what you have dreamed, accomplished and unfinished. It is in me that you find your mistakes, misfortunes, sins, and corruptions. It is through me that you have once planned your hope, blessed your love, selected your colors of imagination, and satisfied your needed glory.

Dear parents, thanks for conceiving, birthing, nourishing and safeguarding me as the mystic seventh. Like all the paring partners, you two team up in union, are in love or in destiny, from two different kinds of bloodlines, to bring me as the traveling or wandering spirits in the sky above the Earth Dome, down and into your love trail, courting position, embracing vessel, caring cradles, warm homes, wishful demands, and praying lists. It is you two that created that one-love, one-body unity, so that me as the third and seventh independent party can join this divine triad union, ground as the nailing point of the downward triangle, and march forth as the single hope and dream of you two, and all the ancestral lineages behind.

You two may eventually depart, divorce, dismiss or decease from one another, but the package you have created and fabricated will always be the witness of your divine union, regardless of the time you may spend together or otherwise suspend alone.

You two may not be aware of what you have done, for sky and humanity, for earth and organism. Yet, what you have achieved equates to what universe has created, what the space of Universe has paired, teamed and bounded. The partners can be void and emptiness, nothingness and everything, time and space, time and shadow, day and night, movement and stillness, and all the possible accountable pairs of that dualistic expression.

Everything else will change, but the positions and titles you have earned and endured will never change. You are forever my parents, my mentors, and my dearest friends. You have given all what you are, regardless pure or corrupted, divine or mundane, rules or means, standards or chances, customs or habits. Everything in me is yours. Even fabric earthy and nutritious minerals are labored by you.

I am nothing without you. You are my watchful Sun and comfortable Moon. You are my perceived and believed God and Goddess. You point me towards the stars and send me into the world of make-believes, so I can become like you, be exactly as you, so that nothing will ever change as it is and has been.

Whether you have felt oneness or numbness during your courting season or not, the contractual agreement has been made, and me as the third party is born out of it. This third party, me as that individual being, is also the mystic seventh from the two of you and four of your parents together on both sides. Many generations ago and countless partners behind, you two are not that biologically bounded and soul-longing partners, but are twin souls and twin spirits.

Thus, you become genderless and nameless. As a matter of fact, you are not what you are, and what you have done has nothing to do with any of you, or the contract between you.

Observing the beauty of nature and dancing with eternal joy, one is inside the song of God, expressing the song of loving eternity, and manifesting the song of ever-changing modality. This song has no beginning tone, nor ending echo, where only heart initiates the beat, only love vibrates the initial peach, and only the throat trumpets the outcomes. The center of the song is not located in the brain or chest or gut, but the integration of all. The instrument of body and drumstick of mind can only follow the beat and rhythm of eternal charge, so peaceful than silence sends the sweet dream, and so powerful that heartbeat stops, body expands into vast space, and mind turns into infinite reality.

Blood pressure may rise, skin may sweat, palms may get numb, and fingers may not respond, yet, deep within, everything is safe and in harmony with self and nature. This is light delights the love. This is love for the light. This is our common origin, as well as collective parents.

Before I reach my maturity, I seek behind you, search aside you, and escape all the way without you. Until, I lose everything, as you two have lost everything for me, I feel you, and I am alive with two of you again.

After I have found myself, I realize that anything you have done, I have done; and anything you have not finished, I cannot finish alone. Your invisible watch is my visible look. Your visible labor is my invisible weight. Till, I know, you are not my parents anymore, you are my brothers and sisters with the same bloodline but different generational gap. When this gap is mapped with love and tapped by light, we are all lonely souls, abandoned orphans, and deserted widows. The orphans know the dusty light without mother, and widows give away all love with the presence of husband.

Any work holy is alone, any assignment sacred is in union, and any holy contract begun and finished is within trinity. Only we see these three, we are free from the labor of love, work of assignment, and job of contract.

Now, you two are alive with my flesh, but I have added different pigmentations above and aside what you have contributed. My flesh and sense are always related with you, but my essence is away from your contract, and sensory duty is above your stationed work. I do not know you any more, because you cannot know you further than what you have known of yourselves. What I have is what you have, what I am missing is what you have lost.

Mother, you are not the worm of blood, but the tomb of love. Father, you are not the sound of reasoning the truth through thought, but the song of seasoning the love through light. You two are now my old cells, old memories, and old brother and sister.

My brother is my groom who charges the internal thought, and my sister is my bride who takes care of love in the midst of now and then, here and there. My thought dangling inside my brain is now my twin brother, and the love simmering inside my heart is my twin sister. These twins had a biological mother, called "angel." But no father visible, only the angelic mother knows her love for the light and her delight for the husband.

CHAPTER 9:

THE TALE OF TWO TRAILS

The Song Lines Forming a Geometric Temple

Below the dusty soils and watery bases, beneath the rocky crusts and mantle layers, and between hovering sky and nosing caves, there are song lines that mother earth sings and whispers, her soil rings and dials, and her mount springs and atones. The songs vibrate between what we know as heaven and hell, the volumes resonate between what nature describes as the eternal void and ever-changing motion, and lyrics link and blink between what a life can detect as the neutral zones and mutual tones.

From the zoning tone to the toning zone, zigzagging zero and wigwagging hero atone all the servants, womb each attempted empty zero, and tomb every fooled full one. The temp weathers the feather, so that hemp bosses the bind and mind. As such, between zones and tones, zeros and heroes, ends and ands, the positive charges of light particles and negative charges of watery electrons agree totally, deny thoroughly, exchange freely, and cancel mutually. The creative firm mends, the receptive term bends, so that all ends are blended and suspended, and all the ands sand the mountable lands and handle the tradable brands.

By the time the light ends bend with frictional wind, and waterish ands stand with fictional mind, living conditions of all sorts of inns, such as soil, womb, egg, nest, and cloud, connect to each ends and relate to all the ands. The ands make sand easy and land busy, hand useful and rand meaningful. In the end, the ends tell the tales, as the ands rail the trail. The ends finish each but refurbish all, and destroy the old and create the new. In-laws know each delayed relative and the sin-saws stone every blamed enemy. The jaw bites the cool, and law sites the fool. The furry wool regulates wu-shu (martial arts), and the firm tool strangulates cousin.

In turn, the songs are the heart-delighted voices, the volumes are the valley-consented noises, and the lyrics are the monkey-beheaded and horse-fired waves. Human thinks and humor blinks. The gut grimes and the

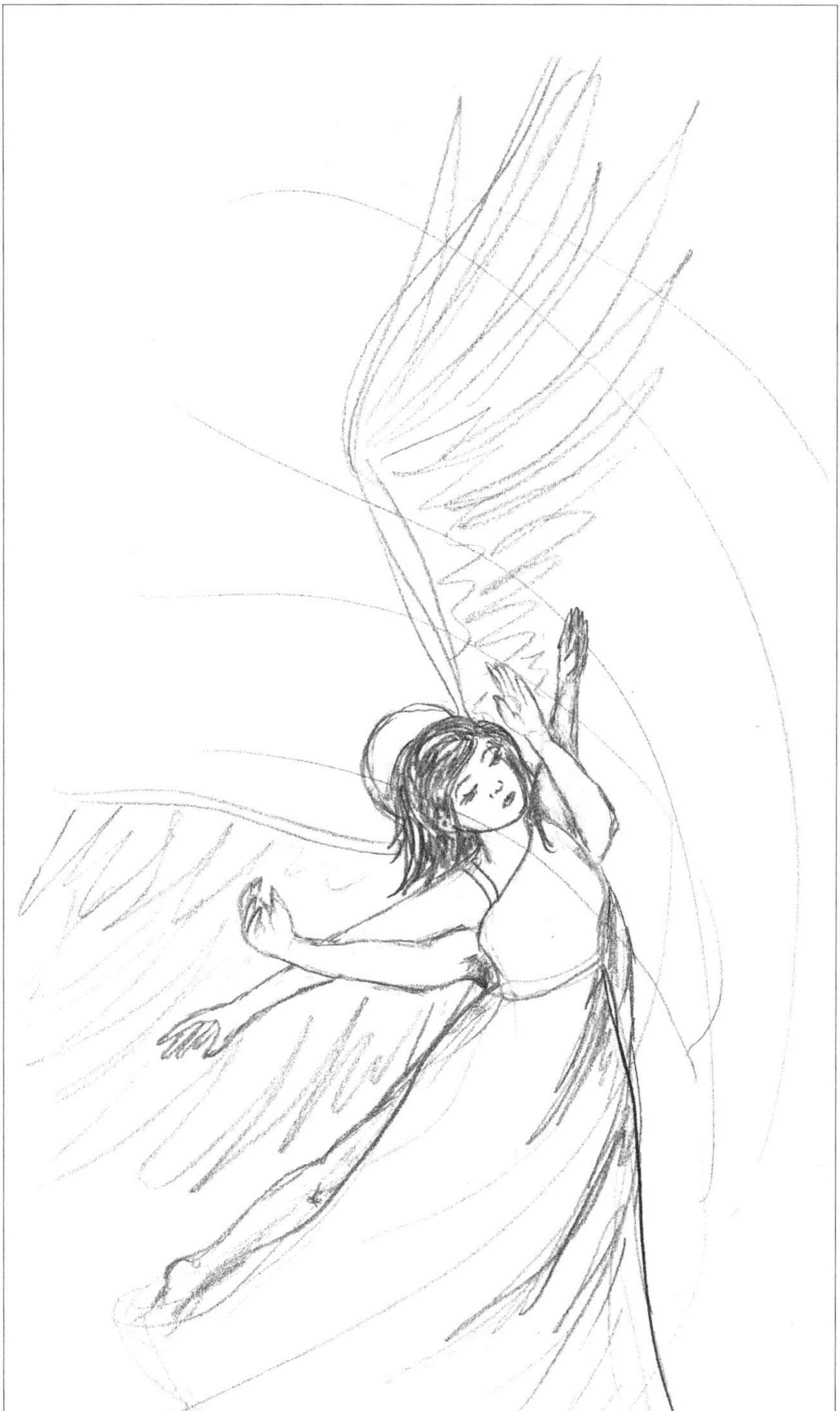

mouth primes. The lips grin as the bathroom screens. Sleep snores the nose and dream scares the rose. Birds wake the dawn, and thunders quake the spring. Passion sums the summer, climate leaves the fall. Absent lightning ends dark the night, and present showing snow parks the right. The voiced waves regenerate the brain to the silent music, while the wisdom residues liberate the heart to the harmonic ball. From the luminous mind, heart becomes as delightful as a heavenly dome. Through the unconditional love, the mind smiles at the eternal star.

Above the geo-matter that forms the earth ladders, there is a temple. This temple is constructed with beams of lights, waves of colors, doors with luminous chambers, and shapes of glowing spheres.

The tower of the temple is the tip of a light ball, the lip of the sucking hole, and arrow of our ascending hall. Inside the tower, the flowers of heart flour the hour but scorch the now. Above the tower, waves of lights dance around like peaceful doves. Gushing rains of colors flood down with a speed so fast that it is motionless, and a force so powerful that is weightless. Surrounding this flood is the witness of the sky and its watching stars, as each looks with delightful attach to the space, decisive grasp to the planets, and distant stance at the moons.

As the waves of lights touch the descending spirits and coach the ascending souls, flooding colors measure their life-long accumulated, heart-ringed and mind-distilled deeds. The descending spirits that are formless enter the womb along the lightning charge, while the descending spirits that are homeless invade the eggs with the help of sperm. The divine deed needs no man, while the divine love needs no husband.

Every match catches a fire as a wire and hatches a body as a lobby. Each web nets the voiceless call and bets the dreamed wish. The tower bows to the flower, and the dome abandons the home. The dome inside the heaven has all the space for light, while the home away from hell sells all the cellular bells. The bells anger the husband and frustrate the wife, so that there will be a cell available for each hellish sell. Hell is lower than value and hollower than valley, so that the call of each bell can say hello and play with a fellow.

Now the minute is in, and second is out. Minute gives birth to a critical inch, and second abandons the decisive pinch. Every minute inch between the bell of love and the cell of space retards the adrenal charge and enlarges the ovarian garage. The sibling-like husband and wife haunt the spirit to open the three-way door, which serves as multidimensional floor. The front door welcomes the soul, the back door hosts the animation, and the side-door loads the vegetation. The soul promotes the human-lover; animation roasts the carnal-tunnel, and vegetation roofs the fruit flyers. In turn, three types of humans are produced: the tiger-likened mountaineers, the lion-alike land rovers, and cow-milked sea wavers. Three types of personalities are given: vegetarian, meat-lover, and soul-hunt. Vegetarian stomachs the infantile elephant; meat-lover angers the youthful muscles; and soul-hunt develops the refined art.

Beauty is in the eye of the lover as the beholder. Glory numbs the mass to record the survived numbers inside a historical folder. Grace races through the pass to dance above the shoulder. Clouds birth the rain, and crowds confirm the strain, so that the brain can storm the nerve and grain can satisfy the curve.

Each mismatch afterwards misses the math class and dismisses the artistic clash. Without math, numbers numb the thumb and disfigure the fingers. With art, creativity cultures the race into class and makes room for

the familiar to run the system. Race-colored and lace-buffered figures are abnormal, aboriginal, or lower-castled, retarded. Disharmonic voices and disastrous noises cannot pronounce the inner self, promote the internal gift, or express the innocent truth. Impersonal expression amplifies ex-files but demotes the ascending souls back into the wave-land, sphere-rings, and sliding holes to be reincarnated for the second time, many times, and endless time. The wave-land has not host, the sphere-rings bring no food, and sliding holes downside all the fools: the foolish being, foolish soldier and foolish emperor.

At this merging point, and dissolving joint, those who can ascend assess their pure heart for their virtuous deeds; and those who descend are either emotional trapped or consciously snapped from their previous life journey, to the degree that they have to start from the gut, speak from the heart, and distill once again whatever karma hosted and sin tinctured. The classroom is never empty, and classical never ends. Each cultured class is suited inside a given room, till disaster grooms all the brooms (**sweeps**) out to the wasteland. Each refined classical text is next to nothing, but ahead of all. Nothing is near heaven and all are dear to hell.

The sea sees the port, and the pole seals the portal. The port waves at the shore as the portable, and portal tells the land that she is important. The sea sees only two sides, her tilled side and blue side as her distilled side. Fish swims at her side and Angel flies above her side. Clouds birth the land, and crowds birth the hand. Four seasons are given, for a reason, so that dual sides of the poles of earth can support the portals and report all who are either important or impotent.

By the time the sea gets all the way to the ocean, that oho mighty shin, shingles are simply single. Needing the mate breeds the four, for the season and generation, so that the make, the bake, the cake, and the wake are rounded, all genes a r e as rational nation and irrational Asian. The nation counts the tea produced by the county and tree treated by the country, so that genders from the county can expand into agenda of racially defined nation.

The rational genes from the nation of that generation tell the irrational Asian to reduce the population, so that the able-shin and elbow-arm can take care of the horned corners and spare the cubical cute. Being rational about the nation wasted by the west, the irrational walk stirred by wrist and elbow shines to the east, as if the yeast, above the shin of Asian (a-shin, to shun a shame). To take the cake baked by the maker to the wake, mourners tear for the morning, for the break, so that the dead can get the hell out of the coffin for a fresh coffee. Rice tea from Japan parties with the spiced coffee from Italy. To italicize this without being too bold, American Jeep travels to Japan and bombs the island, so that peace can give birth to GOP as the natal power resorts to the ICC. Einstein understands how the iron powder stands for lion-stood, donkey-assured and money-fooled Zion!

The Zion is the Sea Daughter, as you are taught to organ-stain August. The gust aught to dust the just as if must, so that lust is horned inside the gene-extracted corn before everyone is born. Native Americans forget their sweat lodge but welcome the Masonic Lodge, so the 33-degree mason can mess up the land but industrialize the band. The castle system from India tells the yogis how to breathe their lungs smudged by Monsoon season and stretch their ligaments leftover by wisdom elephant. Taichi stance dances and glances through the Yellow River so that the acupuncture needle presses the acute Spugati (spaghetti) noodle to point at the web site hosted by the Google. Race is tribal, and trade is international.

When the sea raises her tiding port as tall as the sky-sealed clouds, the highest landing peak becomes the portal. In this portal, only about a third of 144,000 of those souls are free to ascend and descend, in each given time, among all given numbed numbers. Within the above thirds given, a third are angelic souls traveling above the tower promoting human deeds. Another third are hibernating inside the cave as emergency funds for those who are in extreme danger or desperate need of help. The third left are the true spirit-beings among living humanity, spreading among masses as stars: doing either humble services as silent auctions, or honorable deeds as noble truth; speaking from their golden heart with their golden rules while measuring equally the existing individual (personal or egoistic) and collective (political or cultural) values. Those 144,000 are the caretakers for the land of Earth, the mass of humanity, and eyes in the sky. And those numbers never change; only individual spirits are either in or out depending on how their conscious awakenings match their virtuous deeds.

From the tone of invisible voice, those numbers are the breaths of the day, and the daily interactions among the Sun, Moon and Earth. The breaths are in turn the power-coded harmonic waves and echoes existing between Earth and Heaven. It is through this power-code, the harmonic vibration remains as it is, and nothing can affect this, regardless of how the planetary bodies shift or human behaviors change. It is from this numerically coded power, that the daily visitation from Sun and Moon to Earth, the monthly circulation of the Moon around the Earth, and the annual orbit of Earth around the Sun retain equal but neutral scales, remain in an even state but host empty pace, and pertain individual status but obtain a collective effort. All occurs daily and annually; nothing has been accomplished, secondly or hourly; each exact minute amounts for a monthly ring.

The rest of the souls who have died wait for their return, search desperately for their parents, and travel around the tower without stop. In turn, they send the pressure to the living souls in flesh, testing them, amusing them, and demising them to the degree they will be targeted, fooled and demanded. This is how through the majority of time, the living beings or living souls experience invisible and unspeakable weight on their shoulders.

Holographic Spheres

Halo, wallow, the universal sphere! You are bright and shining, round and empty, hollow and full, solid and lucid, concrete and translucent. Bulls of lights are your averted eyes, rings of circles are your piercing eyelids, quivering illuminations are your qualified smile, and dangling tranquilities are your motionless tears. I have known you, being a part of you, existing within you, traveling around you, resting inside you, wrestling with you, tearing for you, and thirsting through you.

Being part of your giant ball, stars are the miniatures of your infinite dotting tails, like swimming dusts in the resting desert. Planets are the fabrics of your lucid veils, like tiny water droplets dancing in the air. I am one of these endless yet existing dots wheeled and knotted in you, and I breath, sleep, travel and rest in this open air, this splashing fair, and this phonetically sound-proved and echo-hovering here. There is no here around to detect or protect, and no there profound to deject or reject. All is here! Galaxies are your small wheels, rivers of lights are your opening portals, interweaving spaces are your living fabrics, and translucent state is your generous donation (domed nation). Your mirror reflects us as warriors, and your window makes all our existing conditions a widow. Wi or we, dow or dowel, owl or wow, vow or cow, sow or now! Fabulous, fantastic, faint, fail. Like weed, and wheeled deed; down, and to the dome; not like demon, but as being dammed, slammed, hammed, jammed, and finally and at last laminated as lemon and layman. There is up and down, heel up and hair down, hill up and air down.

Being holo is being whole, with endless holes, and complete fuel, very cool. Being holographic is being grasped by a hole, painted by a whole, and phonetic like stretching wool, numbed like a crowing womb. In your holographic state, every point is pointing at you, and being pointed by you. Every hole fills to complete your wholeness. Every grasp defines to measure the mark in your handling palm, and you armless hand.

Everything out there is a part of your creation, hanging desperately in your effortless state. Each is a definite expression of you, yet none matches your senseless power. Being as humbling as you are, your power has no match to patch, and your grace has no stage to age. Your vast openness hosts nothing and all, your undetectable stillness grounds no base, and your creative power and beauty has no vase. All come through you, glorify for you, die in you, and fly after you.

Your movement is so much faster, that light beams become your countless footsteps. Each step taken has no land to drop, and every step revealed is aligned with your graceful motion. In this motion, your stillness is so tranquil, that silence becomes your detective agent, void is your trumpet, and empty is your voicing throat.

Looking inside you, you are empty and void, there is nothing I can see or view or glaze with a gaze. You are too white to put my eye on, too open to insert my conscious thought, and too permeable to space me into you. I have no place to land, to ground to stand, and no breath to hand. I inhale as I am in hell! I am engaging as I am aging my sage as your page. The sage is numbed by the page numbers. His words are lost, to lack on understanding, and become nothing more than records with a number to identify each line.

Like a comfort womb, timelessly I am in you. There is up and down, first. The ups have no footage to mark the fashionable, no handle to grasp the tangible, no idea to initiate the valuable, and no mechanism to complete the flammable. And downs do not hold any roots, demonstrate any marks. No way to start, no plug to receive the charge, and no conceivable way to measure the enlarged. What is above initiates what is below, and what is in below blows up and off what is arriving from above. The arrived becomes the rival, the initiative rewards with the vial. By the time the vial dials the rival, anything viable speaks the truth of the Bible. To buy and then to bye, bicentennial resembles bi-focal by the local, what is cited as vocal signs on what can be recited in a recital, and what flies through the kite sites on what is vital to the viral.

Then rotation begins and duality manifests into distinctive fashion. Dot having no lots enters upon a straight line, bridges the middle, so that ending dots on both extremes stream evenly. Underneath this even line is the mass of water, and above is the gas of air. When inside and outside work together and take care of all sides, the dial relies on meter to form a diameter. The width elongates whim, expels the rim, and distances the dim, till the invisible dot broken from the distinctive two lots finds its own center once again: the middle ground and neutral state. The empty middle leaps up and scans down, marches forward and retrieves inward to give away and take in this unified field.

The unified field unites with what the ground rounds, and how the surrounding accounts with what will amount. Beings are born out of the hole inside hosting the empty hallway, what they will become stand as tall as a ball. The steel hall inside the still space distills the motion of forceful completion, vocal competition, and focal continuity. The exchange is now divine: to divide the power into equal diameter and to unite the force from an opposite dimension. You then die in order to mention it as dying, so that the invisible universe lights up the visible virus, and the dark abyss mashes the gray myth and smashes the preying miss. The miss is very emotional about being too much of a mystical, where her motion lies and relies between dotting the lines and knotting the liars at one another, to fabricate each inch and all the itchy bitches. In the mean time without being very mean towards what is demeaning towards demons, she awakens the incompletion and perfects what will be alive in each lotion alike in every revolution.

An unified field is recreated from any proactive means and protractible beans. The unity between each and every one of the angles, points, joints, and trajectories of the universe permeates the creative power and birthing force to exchange, balance, cancel, and neutralize the degree of stillness, steadfast and the state of eternal harmonic void, infinite emptiness, and all presence.

The degree never disagrees and state forever mistakes. The center provides the invisible, the ground generates the motion, and oneness of that neutrality evens all the means that are calmly forceful, peacefully penetrating, and joyously demonstrating. The doted oneness becomes, one hand, the circle, ring, disk, map, chart, knot, direction and trajectory; and on another land, matrix, thread, mode, code, rope, texture, projector and reflection.

This hexagonal space is the product of the initial dot and circle, the "nothing visible" and all potential forces that are working together like the holographic sphere, orb of lights, webs of materials, scopes of appearance, mirrors of all eternal manifests, holes of completion, and the whole hosting the holistic and roasting the hostile. All these six wheels along and inside the hexagonal space are begun and ended with inward creative force and outward manifesting power.

Hobble, wobble, the stage is set, the motion begins, the sound radiates, and force permeates.

Hallow, wallow; the space is filled with lights, the charge is plugged in and the holy fire is boiling internally.

Hollow, mallow; now the holy fire has filled in all space, where the dark matter is fermented. The grids are alive within, and the grails are cupped with graphic completion and intakes.

Looking into this holographic space, round and open, shining and illuminating, completing and filling, all at one time. Yet, the space is still an opening void, and gathering veil. The content satiates what is permeating. The center steals the mystic and distills the invisible. The roots are alive in one giant dome, and yet, the ends have no end at all in them and through them. The fences are lined in circles, ringed with disks, arched with shoes, and hovelled with parallels, pointed with spheres.

This is called geomancy, the holographic lines drumming and singing inside the Earth's stomach and upon the Earth's skin.

As She sings, we become Her tings. And as She screams, we will be teamed in order to see the screen be screened in Her scene. Her songs are the echoes of Universe, and Her creams tongue our song lines.

The Universal Dot

Let us begin with dot. Visually, this dot can be so small, thin and minute that it is dot-less or pointless. Between its dotless result or objective fact and its pointless beginning or subjective target, is the fundamental function of force and matter. So what are these, that un-dotted matter and un-pointed force, and what is their power of penetrating point and their structure of loading dot? The moment the inertia produces its empowered intension or desire, or impulse, there will be automatically a powered point. Whether this point is targeting into an empty zone, or walled object, it is going to point. This empowered point is the universal thrust to begin all powers and matters, and it is the instinctive urge and unconditional impulse we are either inherited or equipped to live and survive, function and express. As soon as this pointless pointing points at something, this something becomes the object of that dot to be pointed, targeted and dotted.

Thus, in the generic sense, there is no difference between a point and a dot. A point is a rounded and circulated dot, and a dot is an intended and pointed dot. Equally, as soon as this initial influx, this urged push, this raging point is ready to move and point, direct and target, it will either come to a halt when it is exhausted or its energy becomes extinguished, or be stopped, walled, locked and swallowed by an object standing there facing this coming pointing force. Likened as bolts and knots, mouth and food, tongue and gum, these very similar or even exact forces are intermingling, interweaving and interacting now and forever. This is the oneness of universe, the holy marriage, the sacred court of all things existing and non-existing, of all beings and nonbeings, and of all visible and invisible. And you cannot stop it, just you cannot stop move and walk, live and expect, exist and dream.

Next, the moment this very pointing force ignites, moves, acts, or fires up, there will be an energy line produced, whether it be heat or wind, water or gas, cloud or smoke, or whatever and whatsoever. Now the second relationship begins, between this very point in itself and its pointing line: pointing passion and excitement, pointing imagination and vision, pointing fantasy and illusion, or pointing dream and hope. Either you stand and let the earth move you, or you move and walk yourself.

Looking within, you are bored to death. Looking around, and you will be bound to tears. What is the point inside your head? Where is your gut going to point? Why does your head keep on pointing? **Why does your head keep on searching to make points?** Make sense now?

Because you are lonely, bored, and have nothing to do. In order to exist, you must act and it is a fact. In order to convey, you must express, whether talk to walk, or walk the talk. In order to reveal, you must empty yourself from inside out, so you extinguish your passion of love as longing and exhaust your hope of love as belonging.

Which is the short cut, passion or hope? Which is the highway, longing or belonging? Are you pointing yourself to an empty valley or a stopping hill? Are you pointing towards your own death for which is the end of your point from the other side or are you pointing toward your own liberation which is the empty container where the point is going to land on your hand? Are you pointing down to the abyss below your headless feet or are you pointing up to the sky above your fingerless hair. When the feet meet the air, the hair grows into fair, as its affair stretches from armpits and delta, and back and front, to the place where all will be whitened, wrapped, whipped and wiped out.

There is the angle now! As smoke knotted and roped angels are landing on your hair, you neck will be targeted to the throat and your heart will be broken into an empty red valley. When angle is added glue, angel adds the clue to the blue where your flute will receive a flue. The flue is cruel, as its crew receives a cure, but the boat on dock cuts your throat. Where will you dot now?

This angle, the forth element, becomes the very bending curvature which in itself is a furniture. This angle yields so as to serve and survive. This angle twists in order to ignore and deny. This angle turns to be gone forever or come to you for a favor. This angle lures so it can cure. It knots in order to produce nuts. It knits so you can knee on your hair of that landed affair that protects you as a garment inside your apartment. You are a mint now to mend yourself apart from the dormant that hosts demon. When the demon dames upon dam, James fames Sam and Jill receives a diamond. The diamond eventually dies and mounts in December so that each of its destined points receives a demo, with endless generations, unbelievable theories, and fantastic numbers.

Now between angle and angel, you receive a wage but are equipped with a rage so you can scribe what you are enraged about upon a page hanging inside your own cage. Then what is the difference between sitting on the Pole and being a vote for the electro-poll? A pole is a pole, and a poll is a poll. It stands on a dotting docking parking ground and points itself with its own point towards the reflecting lights and opening space. When the pole rolls down as a matter and tolls up as a factor, the headless point points us all the dreams and directions, visions and reflections. Rootless point grounds itself to its own central point, and down into the geodesic center of the earth, where her central axis sits on her own hot bath and stretching its arms and ends towards two opposite poles. The poor poles have nothing but white snow and marching wind, and the poring poll renounces the white hair as the white affair, that of a wedding ceremony, and ends with blackened fair, that of a funeral service. This is the functioning of west poll.

While in the east, the white affair is a red affair, and the blackened fair is white affair. When bride and groom dress up with their red wedding uniforms, they will shed and share their red affair, the biological line. As one point of white enters another dot of red, the white pointing spirit rests inside the red lava. The bloodline continues to exist.

As the bloodline floods, feet meet food, beast hungers for meat and feast satiates the soul. Sooner or later, the flood reaches the white point, as blood ends up with the white dot darkened with the abyss. The flood makes a turn now facing the sky and emitting mists as white fog and white smoke towards the pole. The pole receives all the polls and decorates them with white lights and white snow as the marching wind speaks the language of white winter.

Now the four elements talked about above walk into four seasons of a year as well as four seasons of life. Each year of a life is an ear to a knife. The knife receives the lights as it speaks the sound. Refection and wave are produced. These are the four elements in our skull and the four shapes and faces inside the dome.

As for this dome, individually it is three, but when being grouped, it is twelve. The three gives birth to Tetrahedron, while the twelve refines as Dodecahedron. This is the veil of sacred geometry, the metric earth with her sacred veil and garment, green hairs of forests and white affairs of snow and seeds. This is also the paint of geodesic dome, both inside the skull and inside the temple. The dome inside the eight skulls drums the emotional longing, while the dome inside the double-crossed temple gathers and dismembers the emotional belongings. Longing is a personal note, while belonging is a collective tone. When a note adds to a tone, one becomes stone, two are very slow, and only three can atone.

A note marks the four corners, from the point of gut to the dot of throat, as a tone atones four chambers in the heart and stones the four ventricles in the brain. The four chambers chastise the four ventilating tips, which become the roof of a Tepee. A Tepee in native Indian voice is a mobile house and assembling temple. But when the word Tepee is pronounced in Chinese it is ti-pi, which means shaving the skin. When the four corners expand from shoulders and hips into elbows and knees, and further into hands and feet, 108 bones are produced as prayer beads and delivered as an enchanted rosary.

The Dome is now constructed and Rome romantically spells out Latin and betrays Greek. When the romantic affairs are grammatically arranged, Aromatic tones are stoned inside legalistic letters. Bible combines all the riddles into a grid to grill the emotional juices and confines all wandering and traveling thoughts into Word to sword the knights and disbelievers, and to ward off pagans and witches.

On the other end, Braham dams the Indian Ocean into volcanic tide, so that Shiva can smile towards the rising Sun headed above the oceanic veil, and Kali eats the fish-life and drums the skull-death. The linga is the pole now so that ling gou (the spirit dog), barks at the dark night beneath the

Himalayan Valley. When the Staff used by Moses rejects the power of serpent, Linga speaks the tone of ling ge (the spiritual brother), mating with the angel of yoni and she calls that spiritual brother yao ni (want you).

The Yellow River is alive now. Instead of calling it linga and yoni, Chinese scribes linga as solid line of yang, and yoni as broken line of yin. When linga and yoni are fishtailed and the twin souls are love-veiled, the successor becomes the Yellow Emperor, and failure turns into a silk line, where tea and rice, china and gold are exchanged between financial banks and utility tanks. The bank holds the gold as it issues the insurance policy between delayed file and life ensured fine. The delayed file piles up the cash for the bank, and life-ensured fine entitles the state with civilized heads and consumable mouths. The head receives Alzheimer's and delivers strokes, while the mouth is whitened with denture and glued by hungry smiles.

The tank, on the other hand, loads china into oil-enriched deserts, so the two-legged temple is either stretching itself with Yoga postures, or fired up to speed further into digitalized automobiles and self-orbiting satellites.

That is the pole now as well as the result of poll.

Where are the sacred geometry, the holy grill, the towering dome, and ascending chamber? It is still inside of you waiting patiently for you to turn that divine conscious key from your gut and head to open it.

Divine Conscious Key

Scene One: By night, if the ground is not clogged or flooded with streetlights, like in the countryside, or places with no electricity yet, the sky-dome is clustered with starry lights, and lots of activities as well. We are watching the sky world, and constellation lineage as well. We are not watching the stars in the sky; we are watching where we came from one of those billions of stars. This is the beginning awareness of our divine conscious key.

Scene Two: When shell-contained seeds are resting inside a winter ground, covered by their hairy leaves and snow and wrapped with frozen soil, they know how to turn their lights on. The moment the Winter Solstice commences is the moment they start to wake themselves up. A few months later, when the thunder roars in the sky, and lightning shoots down from the black clouds, the seeds beneath the ground start to talk to the thundering lights. Their sleep is over, and their shells must be cracked open. They know how to turn their conscious key on.

Scene Three: If you wake up early, or before the dawn, get yourself ready to listen and observe how the daytime creatures are reacting to the rising of the Sun. The moment the white veil lifts the curtains of black face, the sky lights up and the ground is awake. All those who had slept over the night wake up right away, though few had destroyed their natural rhythms and biological clocks. Noise begins. Engines are running and feet are strolling. Radios are talking and televisions are screaming. Coffee machines are sniffing and snoring, and business signs are on. Though we have designed a 24/7 industrial mentality, the real boss speaks silently in the sky and it turns on the key in each and every one of us.

Scene Four: The sky is warm and comfortable, and full moon is tingling inside the lover's heart and criminal's gut. Night is a different set of lock from the day, with her different key. The art of bedroom practice and the art of snipers and gangsters and fear-evokers are using their special keys

to open the fear's hearts, merchandizes, safe boxes, and rabbit's like adrenals. Anything you try to hide will invite its own opening key. This is the night creatures' key.

Scene Five: You try to keep certain secrecies to yourself, by all means. And you are shocked by other's power-lock key that sticks right into that long and well-preserved secrecy. To the fact you must be aware that anything you possess is open to public, and you are, in fact, an object to the world. There is nothing that you have, can possess, or discover that will be yours, even death is not yours and spirit is not yours. Love is not yours either. So who possesses this very all-powered and super-magic key?

Scene Six: You are in the wrong place at wrong time with wrong people and there is no sign of a single visible exit. Everything is chaotic and out of control. Suddenly, out of nowhere, all dissolves like nothing has ever happened and you are safe and free, not even a hair has been lost. What has happened and who operates this magic key to unlock all entanglements?

Scene Seven: You have been working on a project, relationship, dream or hope for a long time, as long as you could remember, and you have come to the last effort. You literally give it up. No thought or feelings are left attached to it. It is as if you are on a deathbed, visiting a graveyard, lost into the vast openness and saluting universe. Surprisingly enough, the lost are returned, dream is fulfilled, hope is reality now, and wish has been completely granted, and much more. Who owns this rewarding key? Who can let this all be?

Scene Eight: You have been working life long for a master project, and you have tried to meet every standard, every ethical requirement, and all the rules and regulations, so on and so forth. Now, you are in front of a real master. He is free from all you have strived, and it is not fair that all you have devoted comes to an empty presentation and empty fulfillment. Everything he does is so free, at ease, and effortless. Yet, everything inch of standard requires that he adds a further spark to it. All that is needed to be sequentially executed he did even better, and with more magic. He has summered the life's work in a fraction of a second performance. And it is perfect.

He has mastered this divine conscious key.

The answer of all above keys is the sacred formula of universal mechanism that can never be displayed. The only requirement for you is to be in that divine space and presence where nothing has ever produced and all is done.

All the human evolutions, discoveries, and inventions are achieved like this. When each of these master craftsmen has reached a state, this person is in the divine presence, where there is no time interference, no space laps, and no orderly ordeal. Nothing like where O'Neal rests his ordeal, Kobe faces cobra. This individual is playing with God's magic tool and having a cup of coffee with Him!

The requirement for this state is that when you have learned and mastered all that is humanly possible, and you are still not happy, you must empty all you have and known and replace it within divine, which is unknown. You will have this key. Even so, this key is not served on demand all the time. It opens by itself, out of conscious order, scientific plan, and human schedule. The best you can do is open your empty heart, smile with your virtuous love, and look with a light-present mind.

The Basic Structure of the Human Triangle

Have you experienced a three-way conversation, or a triangle-relationship (menage a trois)? The result is either there is a complete new opening for all, or any one of the three will leave. This is because we have not mastered power of three, and dual-three.

Universe presents us the image of a triangle situation through Sun, Moon, and Earth. Each of these three planets engage in a two-way communication with the other: one way externally or gravitationally, and the other internal or inertial. Because of so, each of these planets is externally locked, since each of them has a regulate loop, a necessary turn, and a must view upon the other two. In the mean time, each of them is internally contracted, sacredly and precisely. That is how they exist individually and collectively. This means that they know one another on the inside and they collaborate with each other without any help from the outside.

In humans, this dual-three relationship rarely happens. One of the examples is the practice of conception. When two lovers, or married couples, are in the state of oneness through love, another spirit is also present. Subconsciously and synchronically, all three are present, engaging both external work and internal lock.

The other example is that when a person achieves an enlightened state, the trinity of body, soul and spirit are one. If we examine the human structure in dimensional ways, we would see that the brain, chest and abdomen are together in one total unity. Yet, each section has its own triangle, or triad relationship. The best picture of a human trial structure is the side view. Suppose a person stands and is facing left, the front column is the Sun on front head, Moon at the frontal chest, and earth around the pubic bones. In the middle column, Moon takes care of the crown, Earth rests inside of the stomach, and Sun charges inside the perineum point. The right column is how Earth caps at back of the brain, Sun fires at the middle-back of the muscle, and Moon hovers above the pelvic and sacral line.

On the other hand, the brain represents the upper world, the space above the mountain peak. The chest is the middle world, as the plane of the Earth. Abdomen cuts the oceanic line and all that is below, representing the lower world. This is the basic structure of the human triangle.

Now, where do you want to go around, and move about? When your crown is lured by Moon and diluted by Venus, how you are going to face your brain and comb your hair? When your aroused seed and its sprout raging in and through your perineum is fueled by the Sun and deleted by Mars, how are you going to land your buts and swing your thighs?

The only techniques left are:

1) Watch how your thoughts and intuitions are going to land. Sun will fence you in with its daily stretching arms and knives, and all other universal beings will wait and see how your thoughts and intuition make sense. Are you going to sell and spell and spear yourself for good?

2) Watch how your tired thighs are going to inspire the fire igniter ready to explode and despise the watery jar ready to leak. Your action outwardly will expire you, exhaust you, and extinguish you. While your action inwardly will save you, safeguard you, and savor you. If you know how to land and bow towards the east, then you know how to drink evergreen and yellow

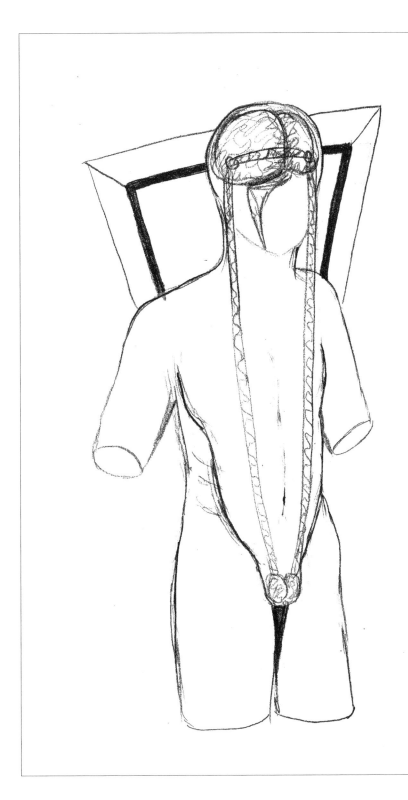

sprouted juices. Mars will grant you the martial (marital) power and march power (match flower). And Sun will endow (teach how to end now) you and endorse (end you the course within the source) you. If you know how to handle and rest in the west, you know how to gather your seeds, ferment them from splendid beautiful flowers and rich-oily flours into wine, beer, and spirit, since flowers owe our hourly wages. Moon will sleep and dream with you through her silver power. Your skinned feeling will get drunk, and you will lose your memory. Venus will test your steel mill (you can steal the milk, but you must be still in order to enjoy the meal) and taste your subconscious arousal (fantasies with endless forms and images, memory codes and remembering cells).

     3) Watch your left side so that the fear does not rise straight up into your ear. And wash your right side so the beer will not dilute your deer. The left is what Sun lefts beside your theft, as you will be soured by your own bitterness. To steal is to still your stiffness like cliff so that the dangling, falling leaves will wound all your belief systems. And right is what Moon thighs your night out to face the rising Sun on the right. To drink the milk is to simmer the water mill and sum the sweaty mules. A mill is a bill, and a droplet of oil is a dripped seasonal soil, to make you sore to the pore, and to saw you into the law. When mother's milk and bird's bill (of her mouthing tongue) are united, knifing edge and tipping hedge will bounce you off from any of your unbalanced wheels. When your leg cannot bend and switch their ends, and when your arms cannot hug and rub through their nails, you are quite still, and you will forget about how to steal.

     But when you truly know how to steal yourself and sail it out for sell, each of your cells will tell you how it feels like and moves about. You will know how to dive and drive outside the chaos but dine and drill within the order. You will know how to handle the spiraling and spinning thoughts. When the spiraling thoughts make the pearls ringing inside the ears and spinning thoughts germinate the jewels that drink dews and news, you are renewed and perfumed.

     Don't mention your passion, but only mend you a fashion. As fashion fasts into fact, passion will simmer the fashion as lotion of promotion. You mend as you bend and mound, as each pound weighs out each pond and each font finds its own fond. I find you and you fond me. You mind me and I ground you. We are together and one, inseparable and inspirational. Spinning down we pin down on the grounding nails and protecting tails. Spiraling up we wake the lake and make the cake so that pond increases the light and pound decreases the loss. As light as delightful, we lose the weight but gain light, till night becomes right and fight rests inside the rights. We tin the deeds and don the needs. We skin the meads and we ski the reads and reeds. It is fun, fun and fun without nun or sun, but son and done. You're as round as O, to owe olive oil and own owl in the oven. There is an eye OUT THERE, and there it is I am IN HERE! There and here, hair the thorn, air the crown, fair the town, and dare the dawn! Out, are theirs and in hears. Theirs are gone with the wind, and "in" hears the wings that win the wind and wine as well as mind and mine.

The sound of explosions coming from the mine follows the pound of exportation, mine is out of mine, and wine is inside WHY! To reason is to read the son behind the Sun, and to season is to seal the son with a song that sings in heaven and enjoys it in the oven.

Failure is only a momentary faint face-masked by the pale paint, and case-casqued with male mint. The dizzy ears speak to the drossy nose lost in its hole but opens the whole, no whore, nor hoarse; only that force sites the course and cites the source.

CHAPTER 10:

RE-WALKING THE SILK ROAD

Home Away Search

Born and grown up as a baby of pure yellow race, I have to get used to the silk face of its kind: thin but delicate, smooth yet soaked, flat and willow-like. Not much of a choice in terms of having blue eyes, blond hair, eagle's nose, and Masonic bones. Instead, eyes are diagonally framed with single or un-ovulated lids. Nose stands neatly in the middle of the face like a retired or disarmed arrowhead. Mouth is tightly lipped so that only five tones can ring inside the sharp serpent tongue and martial jaw.

Most of all, not much of a nerve to be bold and aggressive, charismatic and influential, fight or flight and knight-frightened. The Chinese nerves are either simmered by the yellow sky or hammered by the yellow emperor. Their nerve ends are either diligently displayed as loyal servants, or silently propelled as royal covenants. There is no God-like personal or cultural name, but a deep faith towards the sky renounces the respective Heavenly Emperor. The law-right beliefs are the conscientious martial law, so that the linguistic characters can be empowered and implemented by the organic fingers and organized sounds. The jaw-bite fingers help the venomous tongue to taste anything that matches the power of silky love.

Standing on top of the Yellow Plateau, the twin eyes in the sky shine and project down upon the five elemental fingers and nails: to finger on clay warehouses and to nail beneath the silk wear-clothes. When their fingers linger, their beliefs are elementally eliminated into the clay-potted china, and the calligraphic words are rudimentarily culminated inside the play-plotted meridian.

I did not realize this until the Chinese government sent me to the U.S. on an exchange program. Twenty-four at that time, I was desperately searching for my ancestral and cultural roots. I was homesick because of the tremendous cultural shock. Estranged by what I had experienced, I searched and searched for what meant to be me, at least a part of me: my ancestral and cultural heritage. Aside from Oriental rug, Chinaware and Chinese food, nothing else were on display. From the conversations I had, I found that people were delighted by Chinese language, especially its calligraphy, and they either greatly appreciated with or were extremely fascinated by Chinese philosophy. Because we make use of all five fingers and inside our deep-seated heart, we thumb ourselves up through our own gut. It is this very thumb that made Chinese philosophy different from the rest, which have four elements to begin with. And we use this thumbing tool proudly as an arousal and appraisal stick (thumb me up and I am good).

I found that all cultures have a combination of customs and traditions, values and beliefs. Each began from a myth recited from its oral tradition pertaining its unique physical and characteristic features. The results are cultural elements, such as philosophy, language, science, astrology, and all sorts of artistic crafts. And religion. As much as math serves the trade, language conveys the means, religion fashions the soul.

Beyond, it is the talk to the sky, and prayer from the heart to the unknown. This is the beginning of humanity on earth. Having a flesh body, sensible emotion, and psychic awareness, the human spirit must find a tool to communicate, and to make sense of everything, and to convey to others about what is happening inside. And Chinese are no exception.

Two things that I found in Chinese culture were different from the rest races or cultures in the world. They are Taoist neidan (inner alchemy) and Chinese medicine.

Home Search

Upon returning home from the United State after one school year, my dad assigned me the homework. The moment I stepped into my house door, my father's ghost pale face greeted me. I told him to do some Qigong practice but he couldn't, as he breathed only down his throat deep. He told me that he was stupid in his life, not knowing and practicing Qigong, and it was too late. He wanted me to study it well. Three days later, he was gone and this was his first and final homework assignment to me. And it took me twelve-years of deep meditation practice to send him into heaven and, proudly, I did it.

At that time, I valued Chinese medicine but equally loved Taoism. Through readings and researches, I found that most of the famous Chinese doctors were, in fact, Taoists. Away from family obligations and social responsibilities, not because they loved to but they had to, Taoists had time and energy to concentrate fully and devote thoroughly through serious meditation, deep reflection, and systematically taste of herbal formulas and organic forums. When their meridians were open and vitalized, they tasted themselves back and forth between medicinal elements produced from the Earth and sickening elements inflicted by life or patients. Going through all faces and crisis as wounded healers, they would practice magic and perform miracles. They became then the spirit-doctors (shen-yi), way above average ordained priests, licensed psychologists and certified doctors. Most of all, they were free spirits, above the cultural condemnation and political persecution. To them, cultures are nothing but daily tools for them to heal the illness and promote souls. Customs are like daily or momentary passing wind and air. Changing seasons are their accustoming customs, and cosmic influxes are their internal cultures.

I found it and I wanted to stick the rest of my life to it.

Meridians: spirit-silks and heart-lyrics

Meridians are, still and in fact nowadays, a debating myth. What are they and what is the relationship between meridians and nerve ends? Modern laboratories and updated machines cannot give a sound answer so far. Is the human body the original lab and most complicated and forever updating machine? Should we listen to our ego-driven mind or obey spirit-guided inner conscience? Do we aught to invest our hope away from our body and into machines or return our hope through machines into our soul and beyond?

Part of me now functions as a monkey head, thinking brain, debating quest, and suspicious quest. Rejecting all this, I would cave my heart into the center of Earth, surrounded by floating caves beneath the earth surface. In the mean time, I would dive deep into the vibration of my soul, into caves of my spirit's journey. I would follow, imitate, and be like what the founders of meridians were experiencing ages ago. I would expand my body height, between my head above and my hips or toes below, into the poles of earth, and I would sit on top of the Pole and experience violet-flames and super-sonic charges. I would be living like penguins, polar bears, sea lions and fish in and around the Poles.

Then I would talk to the equatorial, tropical lines, seasonal lines, Sun lines, Moon lines, ideal lines and appointed lines, walking lines and traffic lines; all the living lines, such as rivers, wind streams, jet streams, ocean waves, and everything alive and present, changing and transitioning; and all the spheres and matrixes above and beyond, within and around.

With all these, I would shine within my spirit-light, smile upon my gut-delight, and converse with Qi-lines, energy waves, song lines, heartbeats, and lyrics of my prayer, my devotion, my faith, and all emotions and sensations above and below.

Oh, deep into the Eurasian Continent, deep inside the Himalayan, deep beneath the Golden Dome, the Yellow Tower, there are meridians: not controlled by Greenwich Line located inside London, not to be influenced by manmade clocks or holidays. These meridians are the interactive threads teamed by the twin sisters of Moon and Earth. As the cave waters lung in the air and dung out the affair, meridians allow the fish swim, sea lion spray, bear stand, penguin stroll, mist stretch, space scan, and light skin.

The triple seven is structured inside

the 21st hexagram, according to King Wen's arrangement, Biting Through. Wheat flour noodles are served as food for the stomach, while animal bones or sharp objects are used as needles to poke out the ill ailments and fool around the chamber of heart. The biting joints are a combination of the teeth-bite inside the lips, and hand-bite around the palm. The hand bite works well with juicy neck or groin, and teeth-bite savors the love and soul. The finger joints please the gouts and bites of the gallbladder, as well as the goals and cites of bladder. Bladder flushes water residue out of the delta valley, while the gallbladder flashes up ignited feelings through the thundering feet and undefeated. Together they work as thunder and lightning in the body, as stomach bears the witness of all, from biting mouth, chewing gum, swallowing throat, draining colon, and flushing bathtub.

All begins from the sky. The moment the tear-ducting eyes of yellow face, or any human for that matter, are stimulated by the year-dotting eye of a sunny face, the watery points on top of the eyes start to bubble. Sky releases its cloudy bladder through rain and snow, and mind releases its clustered bladder through sweat and urine.

By the time the bubbling urine dances around the fruity and seed bearing ground, the sun-eye smiles above the valley base or views upon the swamp surface, toes feel the smell of nose, and fingers grasp in front of the knee anything eatable grounded by stems and branches. The spleen now satisfies its human stem as it quickly charges with sweet sweat sugar or slowly energizes with witty white flour (starch, protein and enzyme) grown from plant stems. Kidneys root the spleen while liver sprouts as expanding branches. This is how kidneys ground the power through directing sky and brain, how liver grows and spleen nourishes.

The evergreen liver then grows and expands the body into its full size so that gall bites sight out the juice as stomach swallows the use. Armpits now open the body to the sky through arms and fingers. The green mason charges the heart to tingle through the fingertips so that evaporating heat and chilling cold can regulate the rib-framed chest. Lungs take oxygen into the heart and the spleen nourishes the bloodstream with nutrients. The heat is pumped out of the heart through Pericardium Meridian while Triple Warmer air-conditions the inner chambers of heart. When the arms stretch, heart, lungs and Pericardium send the chest power to the fingers, namely thumbs, little and index fingers.

A matter of turning and lifting, Triple Warmer Meridian now gathers the power from small and large intestines to the face, as a final reward or punishment from what the three eye-capped meridians (bladder, stomach and gallbladder) rushing and gushing down the feet.

In the mean time, the cold charged as super-conducting power travels as a cold river through the cold Small Intestine and urinates out to connect kidney water, and the heat vaporizing through the Pericardium Meridian federates through Large Intestine to grow through expansive liver. Spleen tastes plain, and stomach amounts as plane. Pericardium vaporizes as either warm expression or cold sweat, and Triple Warmer condenses as either cold face or warm heart.

The standing arrow of sacral tailing bone stands below the staff of spin, around the protective jar of pelvises and shoots the heat out of skull for the score. The heat then rise inwardly up through the nails to scratch itches out of the skin and rages out of the sin. The brain stem reverses the Small Intestine, while the gray-mattered hemispheres discolor the Large Intestine. All thrive and return to the empty capital, empty mason and empty heart.

Thus, stomach and spleen take care the physical matters, food and energy chains, while Pericardium and Triple Warmer take care of the emotional matters, heart and vibratory chains. Locked around these four corners are the four seasons, while locked inside these four wheels are the double helixes, which are the double loops of four of the eight psychic meridians. The downward helixes are the Yang Qiao and Yang Wei, while the upward helixes are the Yin Qiao and Yin Wei. Then, what is left balancing these double helixes are the daylight of Du and nightline of Ren.

By the time daylight lines the time and the nightline completes the loop to circulate as a triple expression, three worlds of creation and three treasures of demonstration work side by side, in and out, and back and forth to demonstrate the power of cosmic as well as personal Thrust, and planetary as well as physical Belt. The Belt served as dividing yin and Thrust nerved as deciding yang birth the three bodies, and display the three seeds.

The moment the pleasant feeling in the gut issues dopamine in the brain, Gall Bladder excites the art of cooking, and everything else nearby. Stomach hosts where and how the fingers grasp and place, teeth bite and chew, mouth drinks and throat swallows. Spleen, along with pancreas, manages, delegates, negotiates, neutralizes, and balances; to save anything possible, and rescue any food chains, as a PR person, middleman, IRS, human rights activist, or ozone, before intestines discharge out what the mouth was served and how the stomache stored into recycling beans or administrated deans.

Why the Orientals prefer meridians than nerves is a good question to be examined. Rather than structuring anatomically and displaying physiologically, the yellow race reads the body organically with five storage-like Zang (liver, lung, heart, kidney, and spleen), which are the five-clayed potteries, into six moon-fashioned Fu (bladder, gallbladder, small intestine, large intestine, pericardium, and triple warmer), which are lake-liked refining factories or reservoir-linked finishing lines. As anatomic bones support vicious organs, their physiological structures are mapped by twelve earthed regulating meridians and napped with eight soul-dialing and gut-igniting psychic meridians. To adulate between twelve regular meridians and eight angular meridians is almost like trying to examine the body within twelve monthly nerves and exile the mind under the eight towering curves.

The eight towering curves control conception and birth, while the twelve monthly nerves run from birth to death. Altogether, conception and death are twice birthed: one by the umbilical cord and the other, an un-tongued and throat-enlarged lord. The cord goes to the court because of social security registration, and lord strikes with a rod because the person never listens to what he or she is called to do in life, and always whitens his or her ego ahead of bald eagle, and frightens his or her need in front of mighty God.

The moment the nine-month or so conceptive trail is cut, throat wraps up placenta, nostrils abandon umbilical cord, facial mouth takes over uterus knifing. Always remembering where the fontanel stayed and crown served, the yellow race has never recognized there are such things called nerves. Never washing off the protecting shield on top of the fontanel, or cutting off the ring (called circumcision) protecting the little sundial's hole. Life of a yellow race is like tending the Yellow River, always gutsy and knotty, but never nerves about service, which is described as diligence, to double support family legacy and societal elegancy.

Above the Yellow Race's head, the image of stars tell the clock-hour of life where nothing can fight against the programmed destiny, as the clouds fashion the sudden fortune, and winds trail through temporary fame. To the Chinese mind, even stars never shine forever, because only one star shines during the day, and many starts die and fly away by night. So the best equivalence of nature's stance is a man's capable glance towards moving clouds and invading winds. So the famous people are called windy people and cloudy matter. What the "matter" or "wu" matters is that "cow" "without me" or with "nothing."

The Yellow River faces the Sun-citing trail appreciated by the moon-siding veil. Seasoning emotions should be refined with flute-toning liver and river, while seasoned thoughts are distilled by brush-dialing tips and arm-spinning waves. Love is not displayed through carved status or crucified temple, but stringed through generational lineage and conversed upon felt presence. Insight is aligned inside silk-white meridians and mortified with evergreen jade.

Thus, instead of the milk-nerve of a golden calf, we pertain for the silk-nerve of yellow court. As it is, the milk-nerve travels the mile, while the silk-nerve listens to the silence. Between the warehouse of china and wardrobe of silk, Chinese hands are forever busy like spring leaves and stream waves, and the Chinese body is mapped with silk-lines but not nerve-ends.

I did not study silk-lines—meridians—through institutional training, but by meditative self-revealing. I guess after thousands of years of mapping and coding, pointing and decoding, any child of a Chinese race would behave with a silk-like bike (we grew up with bicycles, called zi (self) xin (move) che (wagon), not moving automatically, but moved by legs and hips of a rider. Driving a car would be like driving a Communist Carder.

Being sick is off the silk: with unbalanced Qi locked around karmically knotted meridians. If you can distribute silk by demonstrating your Taichi body with silk-like motions, stance, mobility and fluidity, you are, I guess, a master silk-road traveler.

For the first three years of my Qigong practice, I followed the lines of meridians as the book was illustrated. Slowly but surely, if my concentration was empty and my focus was pointless, I would see white lines inside my skins and muscles, and I would feel the hot-poking pressure points, like a spiced kiss of a girl, an aggressive cat scratching, or a tender water dialing.

I did not know how many meridians are in total, nor did I care about the totality of points and their individual uses. I pained health, vitality, and spiritual insight into where I came from racially and culturally. I am grateful that God gave this portion of His nostril fair or facial hair to the yellow race, and they did a good job in training and fighting, in healing and selling with these silk-lines, earthly meridians.

Mystic Approach

Like mechanical, legal and logistical codes that have been approached, interpreted and applied consciously or intellectually, so have nerve ends, meridian lines and genetic codes been approached, understood and applied psychically or physically. To state them here all is unlikely possible, and not even practical. Just meridian lines and their external points.

Meridians are among few inventions that the Chinese have contributed to humanity. Its entire spiritual power and healing art traces back to the Angelic Mother who gave virgin birth to twins, a brother boy and a sister girl. Her name is called Xi Mu Niang in Mandarin, or Mother of the West. According to the legend, She came down to Earth and landed upon Kun Lun Mountain. And She gave birth to a boy and girl who became the first biological parents of the Chinese race.

On the first day, for the first workshop I conducted with another brother, the Mother of the West came, and into my body. The moment my left foot landed on Earth, the power from celestial and astral realms fired down directly to the center of the Earth. Then the red fire from the earth's core gushed up to my left perceived ovary. I started to experience a menstrual cycle and became a woman.

In the meantime, inwardly in my heart and gut, She revealed to me that as She came to Earth She carried a total set of sixteen minerals in Her body. Among them, ten belong to celestial realm and six prolong the solar system. Further, within the ten in the celestial realm, eight of them carried neutral charges, only one positive and one negative. And within the solar system, two carried neutral charges, two positive and two negative. Thus, She carried in Her angelic body ten neutral minerals, three positively charged minds, and three negatively uncharged minds.

Objective: Is Mother of the West real? Is there an Angelic Mother? Where have our parents' parents come from? Who has survived to tell us the story, share us song lines, reveal the rhythms of heart, and recall the music of heaven?

Maternal Approach
Being a single mother then, the Mother of the West had to do everything by Herself. She had to understand everything biologically, nutritionally, as well as psychically in order to raise two children, foster their growth, healing their ailments, and communicate with them verbally (orally) and psychically (telepathically). She had no choice.

From Her own experience of visiting and settling on Earth and becoming a single mother, She must know the hidden mechanism of healing, both for herself and her two fatherless kids. She had all the meridians with Her angelic body.

Objective: How can scorched tissues and scared memories tell the rich milk, caring smile and tender touch? How can empty breasts retell the milk lines? How can dried eyes tear more longings and demanding? How can a broken heart inspire the songs of love, and joy of happiness?

Ritual Approach
Afterward, as children became parents, and generations on and after, communication with the Divine becomes the hidden esoteric and magic power. How to listen to celestial music and perform angelic dance collectively is the key. This was the only way in our primitive time, at the dawn of human civilization that individual illnesses could be removed or transformed

energetically, and interpersonal confrontations and collective shadows could be removed. Chant, prayer, meditation, singing, dancing, intuitive channeling, conscious clairvoyance, psychic empowerment, and so on and so forth: all but for the Divine Communication and Divine Intervention. This is how the meridian lines are mapped around human body. In that sense, meridians can be interpreted as the rhythmic and vibratory waves in and out of the body as the psychic power charges up the conscious power and discharges emotional bodies.

Objective: Party is over and ceremony is gone. Legs are tired and throats are sore. Is there any extra power to demonstrate, songs to sing, magic to perform?

Astronomic Approach

To the best of my understanding of the Chinese civilization, decoding meridians and mapping them with pressure points is the way of star practice. As the body awareness expands into earth's holographic bareness, entire cosmic influxes are hovering around the ozone like the shell of an egg, and the skin outside the flesh. As each mineral in the body engages in energetic and vibratory communication with the world outside, it connects to its source, which is the body of earth that communicates with stars and their constellations in the sky. Then, the communication between matter and force, or matrix and power, is the communication between cellular minerals and light particles.

When the minerals grow from cell to cell into an organ, or organic part, there will be a centralized hole or mass, which is called a pressure point. When a pressure point is awakened, it talks directly to the star-energy. Thus, the body as a holographic ball talks to the stars and their constellations in the sky.

Through the Sundial, Moondial, Earthdial and Waterdial, the Chinese finally mapped the body with earth's meridians and cave lines, and accordingly, the vibratory pyramid in the body and in the sky. This is the most aggressive and detailed scientific approach in the entire Chinese history.

Objective: Pyramid, Stonehenge, Sundial, and clock, can you show us the power of stars along with the motion of their trails, and the meaning of their existence?

Experimental Approach

Do you know how you turn and twist your body automatically and subconsciously? Do we each have a gift of how to tap into another person and know exactly what is wrong with that being?

A flash of sudden lightning, a spark of eye twisting, and we know it. This is called trust, not as an established trust, but as an experienced and intuitive trust. Isn't this the way we engage in all realms of communication? "I trust you" is how we approach to others, and "I entrust myself" is the inward communication.

So either from gut feeling, or from experienced trial and tribulation, trust works all the way from confidential to gutsy, between fear and caution, through generous donation or selfless let-go.

Objective: Asking the practitioner? Keep on practicing. Asking for treatment? Keep coming. Asking for an experiment? Kept for experiencing?

Collective Approach

Slowly but gradually, each person experienced a unique meridian line or pressure point. Or through a divine introversion, at a peak state, a person experienced all those spirit-charging and soul-traveling lines at once, as how the Book of Revelation in the New Testament was revealed, experienced and recorded. Or, sitting in a circle, meditating together, chanting from the heart, and praying for the best, different people at the circle experienced either similar or the exact lines, or opposite points or reversed lines. Afterward, through collective sharing and revealing, all lines of meridians and pressure points were reported and recorded.

Other times, gentle touching, accidental injuring, forceful piercing, mental scanning, psychic atoning, intensive lovemaking, intimate soul-mating, objective spirit mirroring, ancestral communicating, information downloading, healing after healing, recovering and reoccurring, disastrous killing, and endless others: lines were aligned, and points were anointed, and matrixes were recovered.

From those above, an objective and abstractive human status of meridians and points was constructed, installed and inaugurated. Meeting after meeting, debate after debate, presentation upon presentation, or ego control after ego control, persona upon personality, individual and his society were connected, ego and its scale were measured, and status and its power were reinforced.

Now, meridian lines and pressure points are the cultural beauty, trade commodity, and political agenda. So many hidden layers, institutional policies, and social customs are embedded inside and around the practice of meridians and their points to the degree that: even after you get a doctorial degree, you still do know nothing. Even if you donate all your sickness to the practitioner, the hidden beauty and power is still waiting besides the behind door to the death chamber.

Does the objective way work its way to death? Is the abstracted anatomical human model or chart of meridians and pressure points really, truly and precisely applicable to each different human body, and each unique clinical case?

Objective: Is body collective or family collective? Is race collective or humanity collective?

Personal Approach

This is the last and first approach. Between my illness and my desire to live and to be well, between acupuncture model on one side and clients on table on the other side, and between what the history has said and what I have been experiencing, I am ready to understand what meridian lines and their pressure points are. Meridians are the melody of heart, strings of heart felt songs, and notes of each and every detailed dials of heartache and lovesickness. While pressure points are pressed for sure, as what spirit talks to the heart, and soul cries out loud through the physical pores. These points are pointing you either to heaven or hell, depending on where you stand and how you view things around.

In the early stages of my meditation practice, meridians are felt when my concentration is pure and my focus is pointless. When this state of awareness happens, I see, each time when my effortless breath and pointless concentration work their own magical power, there would be a thin white line traveling around certain parts of my body. When they stop, the illness in that particular area start to heat up, itchy, numb and all other kinds of sensations begin to surface. And then they spiral.

When these thin white lines travel along specific cross sections, the traffic sign would light up and talk to me. I know from that moment on, that it is a pressure point. Equally when I press my fingertip upon the skin of a client, if it is the right place and with right amount of pressure inserted, the pressure point would talk to me. It feels like two stringing ends are coming together, two souls are standing side by side, and two innocent babies are playing together as one.

The pressure points from the client would talk to you like this: "Hey, buddy, you are right on the money, and you are eating my honey!" In that instant second, I feel that I am injecting a star into the client's soul, a hope inside his dream, a magic pill evoking her numbed condition, and a shower upon its sleepless state.

My early-experienced meditation practice would take on a different tour. The numbers I count for each and every continuous breath now becomes the numerical manifestations of what the client had experienced in that particular year. The thin white line now becomes strings of thoughts and emotions, pure or purgatory, powerful or portent, portrait-like and picture-delight. It is through the agent of this thin white line, that I have come to relive without believing what that client had lived in that very traumatic moment, or experienced in that long, hard, and tortuous journey or event. I am in the sickness and I am that manifestation of precise illness.

If there is not any ill element to count, there would be a clear pond in that client's soul and inner chamber singing the songs of love with me, delighting the postures with me, and defining the precious divine moments within me. We become one: one body, one soul and one universe.

Sometimes, my heart becomes like boiled ocean, baked muscles, and heated lava. Sweats would come from nowhere, but rain all over my face.

Are they crying or laughing?

Objective: Now, if anyone asks me what meridian I am working on, I would backfire silently and humbly with a questionable look: "what is the stake of the emotionality or life event inside?" If anyone requests me to open up their channel, I would face the sky and bow toward that yellow heavenly dome. If anyone demands me the meaning of life or purpose of existence, I would withdraw into that my little space-less and pointless heart, and retreat into that white colorless and seedless brain.

My Collectable Approach

Dear universal and angelic mother: thanks for showing me those thin white lines that resemble the lights and road maps to heaven. My heart is your divine ovary, and my mind is your delighted joy. When my untargeted thoughts are zooming into nowhere, not even a minute and pointless dot, your ovary becomes permanently pregnant. The child you conceived is not even a dusted spirit away from his father; instead, this child is the smile of innocence, joy of peace, and delight for the abyss. Your abyss is no longer dark any more, and your black face is no longer frightening any further. You are relaxed and busy at the same time, sleep and cook in the same place, and mate and date within the same cell.

In turn, those thin white lines are the voice of your longings, the structure of your belonging, the dress of your endless attraction, and makeup for your eternal beauty. With this longing voice, I hear the songs of my heart without listening to the noise of your gut. From this song, I see the Purple Light singing inside the Purple Heart.

Via this structural belonging, your bedroom is my quest house, and your safe roof is my eternal dome. Through this your bedchamber, I see the yellow tower.

Your forever-attractive dress is now my everlasting permanent address, as I trace from desert to sea, peak to valley, and chimney to roof. My very naked being addresses now upon your endless colors and multiple attractions. My ugly face is veiled in your beautiful dress, and my clayed pace is now at your tractable lace. I am forever yours now, before my longing breath and after my senseless death. With your beautiful dress, I am fashioned with an evergreen necklace. My mortal body is now converted into an immortal peach hanging above that immobile beach.

Your makeup of that eternal beauty now knocks my longing heart into pieces, and fries my passionate heart into peace. Because of this, your eternal beauty, I do not need arousal anymore, I am simply awake. Your highly preserved makeup is permanently waking me up, as I do not see that you have changed any colors but you retain ever-changing flowers. I do not need to be oiled seasonally, or boiled annually, or foiled perennially. Distilled ease and be-stoned peace makes you up and wakes me up. You are the voice of blue in that ocean, and I am that joy of blue in the sky.

Dear earthly and biological mother: your worm is my warmth, and your womb is my tomb. You received me from the sky and weather, conceived me from birds and seeds, delivered me through your bloody trail, and believed me in that baptized red flame.

Your tears are very dear to my heart. Your milk turns into my writing ink. You tender care transforms into my meaningful affair. Your white hair is my wise dare. You will be remembered because I have been a member in your chamber. And I will reflect my memory of you inside of my motherly mourning. As morning wakes the dawn, mourning frightens the town.

When each of my insights becomes your long worn-out night into the sights, my thighs thumb your thoughts up, as my legs beg between your pegs. Each of my age becomes either your delightful page or bewitched cage, as each of my own anger is your light-fasting agony. When you warm up my skin, you freeze my bone. When you kick my bone, you risk my loan.

As all your unconditional love is utilized into all sorts of must conditional cares, addiction from your audition, permeation through petition, I become an orphan, and very often, I offer my smile upon your cold face and unseasonable lace. I am in your face as you are managing your case by vase, and arranging your quest at your base.

I am lost and you are worn out, till my ash changes into your cash, and my hands dash away at the time your feet bash through.

If I would be swallowed up again, I would have not traveled my journey, exercised my will, paid my bill, and internalized my pill.

You have clayed me, painted me, milked me, wheeled me, and willed me. From your will I will, and with your meal I fill and feel, until I am the meat of that deadly beat.

I beat and you bate, as I eat what you just ate. While I drink what is drunk in your trunk, a chunk of punk appears besides the ears of apple. It is a left ark, into the dark, barking at the park.

With luck, we both disappear into darkness. I grasp at your black veil, as you call me blacksmith. By the time your black veil welcomes the daylight, my position as a blacksmith upgrades into a white knight.

As day pays its way, you reflect your way into May, and I recall my way into a doubled weight.

I am in big trouble now.

You gave me your love, and I take away all your luck. Only when I am permanently pregnant, I have no use of a mother, I am no use as a mother. When the lost is bigger than the cost, the most is the foster. I am the care of what you used to be dared, as you have bared me inside an airlifting stair.

Your white hair is my rocky chair rocking upon the locks, and I will rock your head off till you and me are both inside the white light.

Saturn's rings are now spinning between your minerals and my cells, and your smells and my little shells. When your breasts break my breath, your chest hosts my ease. I change and you charge, as I chase and you enlarge.

Space now is big and vast, and our love connection is even bigger. Between pigs and figs, choice and chore divided and united, and noise and core are recorded between columns and volumes, and textures and texts.

Without birth, what is called earth? Without risk, what else is left for the mother to milk?

The songs are thick between mother and baby, and earth and spirit. So many voices are waiting to be conversed, and so many layers need to be revealed! Yet, between heartbeat and heartache, lips are far above from the placenta, and hips are much sized from the nips. Let us sip, and zip; as the beep leaps and dip slips.

Rest is the best, while east produces beasts and west hosts nests.

Objective: Not until the desire is absent, hope is over, and dream is gone, unconditional love is always and forever conditional desire and hopeless despair. Not until the passion and love are so strong and pure that they knock the door of death, open the lid of casket, and smash the bones of the lightning rod, meridians are mapping wires, and pressure points resemble statistical notes and hypothetical points. Not until the body is toned by lights, dreams are dressed up with songs of the heart, hope is roped upon the pipe that ghost smoke worships the holy smoke, celestial music enjoys only from the other world, the songs of heart reveals only pain and suffering, and strings of life tire only between demands and supply, needs and deeds, and dead and debt.

Upon The Door

At a young age, I recalled a moment in my youth when I was around the age of four. I was outdoors in the evening with a solitary street lamp on. There was a blue haze in the air as the lightning was flashing and the thunder was rumbling. The entire universe around me seemed to tremble with a surpressed vibration beneath the limen. I took a step forward on my tiptoes. I balanced and stood my other foot up as well. I was suddenly lifted. It felt as if there was a magnetic energy shooting up from my toes, through my body, and up through my skull. My body was like the lightning, but milkier and more constant. I became trance-like as I began to dance. The utter joy in my body was that very milky lightning that carried my body through various movements dictated by the inaudible song emanating from the glowing lines in my body. I no longer belonged to me, rather my body was merely a piece of projected cosmic energy, a window of joy upon this earth that could feel my home eons of lightyears away. That was my most powerful first memory of what I later learned were my meridians. It opened the door to dance, and later, to knowing my qi.

CHAPTER 11:
XIN LE QU

Transmission

Around the spring of 2003, as I was working on the Skylake hexagram, Lake trigram over Heaven trigram, I received a transmission from the Taoist family, which is the Yellow Dome keeper in the sky. The Yellow Dome is the place where spirits descend and ascend, through the igniting yellow light. It was the light that I recognized as the Jade Emperor. In Chinese, this Yellow Dome within the human body is called the Yellow Court, pronounced as huang ting. The transmission came from conscious clairvoyance, or automatic thought. The content that appeared in my brain cave was Xin Le Qu.

A few months later, while working on a client, the actual physical space expanded and I was sitting energetically on the North Pole. Totally in trance, I was inside a dome of red flame, which was about the size of an average room. Heavenly music entered this inflammed red dome, and my entire being was drunk but awakened with this eternal song and present music. I was on the highest peak, above the ground, suspended in a pointless state. I was one with universe.

Suddenly, my teacher, Lao Zi, appeared mentally telling me that for the rest of my life, all I should do was to play the human body as an instrument, and play the Sun and Moon married *I Ching*. This was the second time the words of Xin Le Qu appeared.

Two years later, I was in Asheville, NC, conducting a workshop. It was my turn to listen and meditate under the instruction of a Transcendental Meditation technique. I was sitting quietly, eyes closed. As I raised my head, and watched upward with my third eye, I saw an angelic lady standing with her feet on my shoulders. Dressed in white, her legs were open as wide as the width of my shoulders, and the top mouths of her boots were just high enough to touch my temples. Not seeing how the rest of her body looked like, I saw she was holding and playing a flute. No wonder my shoulders have been heavy for years, feeling I was holding the weight of the world. This angelic figure became my celestial music teacher, dance instructor, as well as meridian chancellor. Perhaps it is her child, her clone, or twin who is here with me now in this book. **Perhaps I am.**

Awakening

To play the human body as an instrument, how? I was baffled and at loss on how to begin. My family members ran a musical section of the Chinese New Year festivals, from my grandpa, my dad, uncles and brothers. I tried it one time to see how it felt on stage, but never joined the music band. I had to study books whether it was a school day or a vocational season. No time to play. My mind left home while I was only two years old, so I had to plan my things ahead by myself.

Once when I was three or four years old, my parents took me to see a Chinese performance troupe. Before the show started, I went on stage to dance by myself because it felt natural. My mother was a dancer in school back in China and so was my father. I was very gutsy and my parents have still kept the photos till today to chuckle at me.

One hot summer noon after lunch while I was about seven or eight, my grandpa instructed me on how to place Er-hu (a two stringed instrument) on my leftt thigh, how to hold the bar with my left hand, touch the strings, and activate the tones, and how to use my right hand and its fingers to move back and forth the horse-tail bow stuck the space of two strings. Sitting under a shaded wall, and spending about two hours or so on it, I felt it was a waste of my time. I completely quit trying to play any of the manmade instruments. This was the first disobedience to my family.

Decades later, this disobedience became my grandpa's cheerful revenge. Back to the instrument, crying from the soul and playing with entire effort for the ancestors and sky, but not with a manmade instrument, such as er-hu, flute, drum, guitar, violin, or any others. I am playing a borrowed organic instrument each time, and I do not need to spend time or effort to brush up the skill or take care the instrument. It is all about internal understanding and completion. Not owning any of them, just to adjusting their ligaments, their pressure points, their mobility and their internal balance while working on them, I would borrow, for the time being, their given instrument, their only sacred temple and their holy church, and engage in a holy ceremony, whether in a private session or a public show, by myself or with a group. I would play the role of a holy man, a chief priest, a shaman, a medicine man, a healer, a trance dancer, a spiritual surgeon, a soul activator, and an intimate lover.

In second or third grade, I recall a music lesson I had with Mr. Wilson. We were learning the do-ray-mi's. For some reason, I just could not focus that day. He made it fun and I knew in the back of my head, if only I could kick my focus up a notch, I would master moving up and down the scale and jumping around. I could not that day and it affected my grasp on music to this day. If I had mastered it then, perhaps I would have been a composer and spoke the language of musical notes quite fluently. Who knows.

In the beginning, it was tough. I had no clue to where to locate the strings of meridians accordingly, and how each of these toning pressure points would sound. Giving their permission, the client would place his or her body on the massage table, face up or stomach down, I would stand on side and scan energetically where to start. Visually or psychically, I would locate the first and the most important toning pressure point. Sending the conscious intention and comfort, this very first pressure point would become the first ice-breaking conversation between this holy instrument and me. It would guide me to wherever the rest go and however each leap and dance grows. This very pressure point will send me a tender and soothing vibration through my finger tip, to my heart and soul, with the messages such as "I trust you," "You are right on," "That is it," "Stay there," or "You get me."

The first thing I did to this human organic instrument was to visualize the two meridians on the back, the Bladder and Governing Meridians, running from head to trunk and toes. I imaged myself playing the Er-hu, following the music played on a CD. As the music activated my soul, my passion and my devotion, I would automatically touch the corresponding points along the meridian line. The music created and played by others became mine, and without lyrics, I would insert or add my own version of words or sayings to this music. As music created and recorded by others and insights or feelings appeared in me, I become a teammate. My body and the client's body engage in a holy and sacred contract: intimate but distant, trusting but watchful, knowingly and yet suspecting, all here and nothing down.

When the client's holy instrument was totally granted, I would enter the music world, emotions and weathers are conversing back and forth between how the music goes and where my body moves and fingers fly. Souls are connected, soldiers are on duty, the sacrificial pressure points become the holy ingredients for the holy dish to be made. The sacramental instrument was on table, totally relaxed and in trance, and I played the role of musician, and the conductor, playing in front of all deceased ancestors, watchful spirits, and guiding angels. I was now preparing and cooking a holy meal, performing the most deadly battle, producing the heavily thunder storm, and speaking the language of peace and love.

What can it mean? Why am I not afraid to be on stage (in fact, I love it!) and why did I not grasp the tangible aspect of music?

One day while I was working on a client, I saw in a vision I was holding a wounded soldier in my arms. The soldier was not a man wounded in a war, but a young girl who just had her first moon flood. Her back on top, I was carrying her wounded arrow, which formed between her spine as the body of an arrow and sacrum-tail as the arrowhead, and walking through the fired war zone. I was comforting her soul, healing her body back to its virgin state, and helping her to regain her original virtuous power.

The front side of the human body as a music instrument was tough for me. I did not initially want to violate the so-called private space, or private parts, such as grassy groin or mountainous chest. And I did not want to violate their sexual zone: the narrowed and zoomed one for the spirit to be reincarnated. As the time went on, I just treat each part, and each area as sacred and holy as any others. The only privacy was illness, protected by lower frequencies of thoughts or deeds, lacking of love and trust. Working on 12 or more meridians in the frontal section of the holy instrument was truly a challenge; because I had to adjust and realign them all at once, and as if I was playing a piano, or a harp.

Slowly, I was able to be brave enough to touch the two peaks of the human landscape, one below the throat and neck, formed by the clavicle bones, and the other above the private region formed by the pubic bones. Looking at the pressure points mapped by the meridian chart, and placing the jaw as a downward leakage and pubic bone as the upward package, I could see that the urgent merge between the mouth, the gum and teeth on one side and all that were hosting and roasting below and inside the pubic bones on the other side. This urgent merge creates an emergent urge, where the two different timed breathing activities would trigger the memories stored from conception to now and further ancient ancestral residues. By that time the mandible bone and pubic bone cannot have a smooth, even, and harmonic conversation. What is gushed as the reasonable storm in the head; what are weathered as seasonal climates, and what is sub-contracted inside the oceanic abdomen, are in war. Spirit is either inside or outside this battlefield, souls between masculine fashion and feminine lotion are fighting each other, and physically gendered flesh becomes either the witness or the victim.

The merging points underneath the throat and above the private recreational zone are like two fish mouths, where one inhales down the wind into oceans, and the other exhales the water up to the air. The air conducts all the affairs, as if fare and dare, so that the landing trunk does not know how to move and remove, and emotions are toiled between positive extensions and negative retardations. By the time the nerves ends, the pressure points, and ligaments around these two sets of bones are molded against their own wall. War begins, and the holy fire of passion and will and the holy water of love and care are exhausting one another, extinguishing each other, to the degree any forms of marital contracts: physical, professional, and spiritual, all perform formless duties. Life is thus divided between birth and death, and all gray matters are in the middle, and all degraded manners along the line.

Knowing this twin-peak is a wondrous process, as the ponds of bladder and kidneys in the abdomen and lakes of the lungs and heart in the chest are ponderous at how I would play with the waters and fish and sea vegetables inside the oceanic line and measuring scale, how I could communicate with animated thoughts and feelings along the land, and how I could view the flying birds and traveling clouds above the mountain. The three major points on both sides of the groin area connect decisively with the three salivary glands inside the mandible bone, and anything the person expresses such as in rage or anger is essentially the subconscious and oceanic residues frozen or numbed inside the abdominal vase. To open the cave mouth, which serves as the throat, one must first atone the songs of oceans, and the scales of waves, to save the soul from being haunted by ghosts as groped grasping hosts. To open the cave mouth, one must love, as to love is to loan the dove in the chest and never owe the lead in the head.

By the time the twin-peak would reconnect with the twin-hole, one for the umbilical cord, and the other Adam's rod, the seven churches or chakras of the body are in one total team, one holy Christ, one sacred vehicle, and one mystic chariot. At this point, I play the best, the most advanced and complicated instrument: the human body. Awakened Spirit is the player, emotional souls sing songs, and ancestral bodies drum the gong. Together, they are one orchestra, one team, and one being.

The music is never invented by musicians to begin with, but created by the harmonic waves of the universe and our sacred heart accordingly. When our heart is open, hungry, thirsty, and seeking the heaven home, the meridians would align with the sacred geometric lines of our body, our mother earth, and universe accordingly. Each pressure point along a meridians would serve as one note, one music scale, and one cosmic spell. As those notes, scales, and spells ring, drum and sing, entire body as a replica of universe would shine with the stars in the sky, voice for all the living beings, chant like all drunk souls, and smile like all smiling spirits.

So that is why I could not be locked inside the physical notes. My body becomes the instrument and the player of that instrument is the music itself. When there is music coming through the milky lightning lines of my body, I do not know nor do I care where I am. I MUST dance. Thus, I begin by playing with my own meridians, and now, I am speaking their language and talking to them where they reside in other bodies.

By the time the pressure point opens its blockage, the food roasted by life and hosted by love would serve as a delicious meal, for the collective ancestors, who are waiting on the other side of the wall, talking sign languages and conversing sited lots, which are the blockages their children and relatives carry inside their bodies. The blockages are now the targeting points, serving all sorts of exchange, so that each event would even a bit, till morning mourns more, and evening evens less. The strings shown through the returning Sun tell the mourners to sing deeper into their souls, and rings from daily gathered veils tell the evening to scale, such as the joints between light and shadow, action and rest, peace and sleep, muscle and bone, organ and gland, skin and hair, fat and glad, to even up and further, into the deep ocean. All so that the muscles as grounded mantles beneath the ocean base can reconnect to the rounded prayers, and grouped activity can send the message for the collective retails to exchange what the mind has deeded and how the goods have been prepared.

The points coming through the skin of a person lying on the massage table are now the joints towards all related loops and losers. Each of these pressure points is like a specific earth grid, grinding all the weathering features, and skinned tortures. The vibration waving through the point is now talking to the tip of the beam coming through a particular star. The meridian-mapped loop and the points-snapped angles connect the person and event, personality and emotionality, spirit will and psychic power all together as a unified field, where the empty soul inside the body and the empty trunk hosting the drunker as deceased ancestors, and awakening beings sing and chant, talk and converse, abuse and amuse all at once.

Now my fingers try to figure it out. What is happening inside and around each point upon where my nail touches to bail, rests a divine and decisive appointment between what the sick snicks and how the tick licks. Like an eagle's mouth, my nailed finger would dig out the pressed dish, by inviting the lightning spices and utensils, which are called ethereal matrixes, so that those opening holes would pore out the wish, and receive a cosmic fish.

As my arms move, they align with my thought collecting to the instrument of that person's thought, and adjust my move towards the person's un-removed movies filmed inside, firmed around, and banned all together as raped but not rated products. The porn posture inside horned texture mixes the genetically locked pornography, which is the desire to free, with consciously blocked calligraphy, which is the thought of the referee, so that hungry for sex aligns with a six-jointed crossing skeleton, and lust for must justifies the dusk as if a gust. The choreographic move removes the horrible movie but recites the cosmic song and rejoices in the eternal love. When my heart cries or smiles, its motion detects the emotions locked inside the person, and lotion squeezed out of my heart-ignited prayer would promote the healing and remove the retardation. The points along the skin and around the person now play, sing, and dance through the undigested veils, unpurified trails, and un-purged betrayals.

I become now the scapegoat carrying the person's garbage into open space; the scarecrow witnessing the food inside the points and the invading birds as the visiting ancestors; the puppet conducting the show on behalf of spirits and ghosts. I become nothing; no personal feelings, no impersonal agendas, and no important role.

Yet, I am the conductor inside the music hall, the chief chef planning the state dinner, the medicine man scanning the ancestral genes, the healer wheeling the soul above the locked vehicle, the peacemaker shaking hands between bands and lands. I am genderless and soul-less, just my four skeletal cross works inside my empty trunk and through the person's revealing junk.

The person on the table, and the instrument the person carries, are in sync with what I am thinking and how deep I would shrink, till my body as a womb would crawl and walk inside the tomb hosted by the person and his or her instrument. This becomes a real atonement for both us, a divine journey of oneness, and presence between now and vowel timed by minute linguistic consonants and decisive musical notes.

Thus, pressure points are the connecting points between what the spirit is pointing on one side, and how a star is pointing at on the other side. By the time all the points the spirits push and all the shining spots the stars pull are unified, we are singing with sky and earth, chanting between heaven and hell, and dancing between life and death. All are one, one essential being, and one potential becoming. Beings have no beginning, and becoming is never ending; just those vital vibes that are visiting the victory and violating the victims. The vibes are the violet color before the purple teaches a pupil, and the violent fire flaming the eying souls through their targeting points. This above is my experienced Xin Le Qu, this is my holy initiation, and this is my holy baptism.

Understanding

Written by the Word of God and coded with white spirit in our human body, Xin Le Qu is my celestially beloved and ancestrally blooded version of sacred organic geometry. Of all things I know and can fathom, Xin Le Qu is the holiest of holy instruments. If you want to invest all you have and can, you will find it. If you knock on your death door and look what is into the wake room, you will see right away there is no death, only the divine change gives birth to forms and then destroys itself for nothing. Fire awakens and passion extinguishes. Love births, and water poisons. Between layers of waters, and degrees of fires, all forms, from planets to wombs, senses to nonsense, change and exchange. Yet, seed is always the same seed, and maker dresses always with the same makeup. If you die for this sacred instrument, it will enlighten you. And if you use it for any other humanly purpose, or personal goal, you will never get it.

Xin Le Qu is purer than the body you have, more passionate than what a storm can run, and higher and more advanced than anything you know and can fathom. If you do not have a body, like our human temple, you cannot enter this sacred church hallway. The pathway contains numerical math and geometric hath will bath you, and then dry you up for the stage performance, and puppet show, where you become nothing other than a domesticated slave, standing in the field of harvesting fruit and love like a strawdog, to demonstrate the power of a scarecrow. If your gut dries, your chest cries and your brain fries, Xin Le Qu would not do anything for you. But if your love is pure, your soul is virgin, and your passion is innocent, you will be welcomed by the holy rain, dressed with the holy fire, and crowned with the holy gift.

Individually, Xin means heart. Le represents happy, joy, pleasant, glad, bliss, and euphoric. Qu means bended line, crooked statue, curved river, cried voice, creamed tune, curved nerves, arrhythmic melody, squeezed song, fried music, thundering loudspeaker, or empty burst. All together, the three Chinese characters represent heart-bended melody, love-gladdened lyrics, joy-satisfied song, peace-delighted music, Angelic Mother's Womb, and God's Word. The melody, lyrics, and song music are no longer the personal ones, but strings and rings of meridians. Womb is the maker of trinity within two worlds, and Word is the language of totality as well as individuality.

Does not the music of joy, come through the heart? Then what of it after you hear it? Does it take form? Is that form not the sacred geometry of yourself, your soul?

This sacred organic geometry structures inside the gut, the root

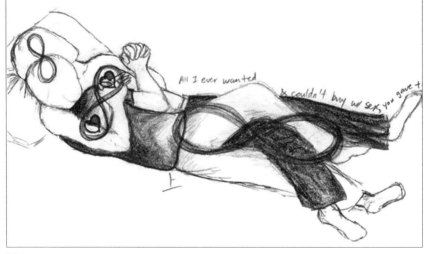

All I ever wanted & couldn't buy w/ sex, you gave t

of hosting the holy smoke, and displayer of true self-anointment. The gut is located in an empty space, where the Adam's bone is long gone, but our Adam-likened power waits in dormant. Being called "gutsy" is a wonderful feeling, since it does not carry any family menu or social mannerism, that raw, authentic, truthful, and spontaneous self-gutsy expression is what thunder calls, how lightning screams, why heart sings and where body dances.

       Structurally, the gut is fired by the gallbladder, snapped by the liver, trapped by the spleen, and wrapped by the pancreas. When these four instrumental organic elements team up, the gall bites will germinate the surprising and sprouting yellow flower. Reaching blossom, the purest organic gold inside the soul will shoot out its own genetic ring, to invite another genetic pool from the collective loop in the universe, so that the missing link and absent pink will reconnect to the divine bank with its undivided rank. Life as how the body should exist will be the Structural Rome (physical skeleton) and Geodesic Dome (genetic map). By the time the Romantic Rome, which represents the purest passion and highest devotion, travels through the Monastic Dome of that collective shells of humanity, Home is the heart and Room inside roams about the aromatic loam.

       Linguistically, gut is part of the "-ut" rhyming tone, and one of the four most used English words: but, cut, gut, and nut. The butt cuts down the hut, to the gut of a slut, so that the invisible nuts inside the slut juts out the smut, gluts to the cut, and struts towards the clean-cut tut. Essentially, UT is about how you tea, brewing and drinking all at once without leaving any filthy residues, suspicious marks, or vengeful remark. Between T-square, and T-crossing, tea, without a team, but a single leaflet, turns everything up from your butt and spins your double-headed nuts, east-breaking glands (breasts) and head-off brain, like mad raining, which is called storm or tornado, with the help of beams and spectrums of light.

       The triple spins decide the ultimate spring, where the Sun speeds up the rings of light, so that nutty seeds sleeping inside the white snow and frozen ground can break their shells and sprout their gold. The daily rotation between the sunup from the east to sundown away from the west springs down the lights and sprinkles off the colors, so that all living creatures can be racially determined and facially discriminated. The annual move of the Sun between the North and South Hemispheres hemps the human spheres, so that white sperm and milk, and white hair and wisdom can exchange back and forth between birth and death, nut-cut and head-chop, as well as the shell from smell and the hell towards spell. Now let us take a look at the triple linguistic spell of Xu, Le and Qu.

Xin

This Xin does not produce normal animated beats, but is ignited inside the invisible heart, drummed by the empty brain and echoed through the butt-off gut. Before the gut sits on two-tail ended butt, the internally wrapped ovaries and externally trapped nuts engage in a genderless communion. The animation towards tumor and annihilation from humor send the signals of weathered climates but not emotional climaxes to the ear-headed ray into the drum: to climb from what you ate (climate) and to cling towards the maximal (climax). The drum is away from the built-in heartbeat, so that the brain, without the charge of a blood stream, can break from a horse-trained spring of thoughts and head for the holy vessel to host the divine rain as the most powerful ray of idea and most beloved inn of dear. When the ear listens to this rain, the sound of nature becomes the song of nurture.

Heading for ears and hosting the dear replace the organic loop inside an animal heart. Away from animation, the soul is free of annihilation, and the purple heart is atoned. Passing the exams of gut scorch, heart attack and head injury, the bar association cannot ban how a holy car would ride the drive and what a universal tar could retaliate as far as how the darkness is guaranteed from its warrant. Car-pool can team up with warship and air raid to travel through all differed but different crossing lines reflected by lights.

This is what I have experienced as the triple spring. This I know now was understood after my passion took me to the dying bed, deadly floor and deathless hell. In Chinese, this heart Xin contains, conceals, and extinguishes the fire, which is the passionate expression of wood. Wood is a collective work for muscles in our human body. The moment the heart is charged by arousal, excitement, or gut-felt joy, the thunder-beamed electric charge will ignite the living soul, which is spirit. The believing soldier becomes the living sacrifice, to enter the fabrics of woody muscles housing organs and glands. The passionate flower dies, and soldier becomes a parental figure and religious fatigue.

In turn, the heart is the vase of three mineral-like elemental forms. The minerals are the mined rally but not the minded tally, so that me-near-the-roll (mineral) can migrate the land between sand and hand but not immigrate the fantasy between can and fan, or sin and fin to dizzy tizzy. Without migraine, the rain showers smoothly, away from strong lightning or heavy wind. And seeing clearly what an imagination can do to an actual image (I am aging), I am that image without fantasizing about going through any aging process, me as a light being is forever the same: the same deadly face and the same deathless case. The fan is tasty for what I can and am able to, but fantasy is terrible to my reality because it is always favorable towards any given duality.

When I can pass the three exams, one for family, one for government, and one for church, the three dots above and around the arched Xin is activated. After those three names, family name, professional title, and  religious symbol, I am atoned by the holy spirit of my will and winced by the holy water of my love, I become free internally and humble externally. My personal name is my business card, and my middle name is my savings account. By the time I take my family name to my family graveyard, and ancestral hall, the name containing endless numbers of deceases is now hellishly alive and heavenly arrived. Heaven is my solar dome and hell is my lunar arch. Dome or arch, it is the same stroke below the three dotted Xin. The three dots above are star, planet, and moon, and arch is the hellish march for the spelling catch. Turning upside down, or reversing 180° either way, the three dots become my three names, and arch below becomes the dome above now. I am sitting inside my own roof, and I am proving my own proof reading.

When the minerals are over, I do not have to enroll in a class, and race towards any favorable face bestowing the crown (crowded wrong). Everything then becomes elemental, which serves the purpose to elevate my mental turf and eliminate my menstrual stuff. Changing from mineral to element, the heavy soil of dust is just gone, but the flavor of mint is still here and the savor of mind is always there, to elevate me from being mental to mindful. These three elemental forms are analyzed in the classical Chinese mind as woody, dusty and rocky forms of earth matter. Resembling blue-green-algae, blue sky/ocean, and blue eye/lotion, these three blues glue to the igloo, flute for the egoistic loop, and is clueless about why there are all the blues. When the glue becomes any unresolved relationship, the flue takes over the chest-pounding flute, and being flirtatious blurs the blue with a cloudy mind and crowded manner but sticks to the original clue. The clue sends the guess to the guest, and requests the same sinful question of "what is the matter."

When the matter mats the fatter, the latter scatters all over the chatter, and the platter bats the tatter. The riddling tongue is the brutal gun to shoot the star. The earth matter is then viewed into three segments: woody forestry, dusty desert, and cliffy rock. Sand from seashore and land from soil are intermingled between cellular stones inside the bones and lightning rocks around the blocks. By the time the rock is fired up and boiled down, the essential elements appear separately from the red lava, red blood, red sea and red communism. Bronze is brown, silver is gone, and gold is the crown.

When the dusty soils of earthy elements grow from lunatic water and solar heat, they become woody element, represented by grassy forestry. In human and animal world, this wood is our main food chain, ranging from vegetables to fruits, and seeds to oils. In turn, they are the structural foundations of our temple.

As this forestry wood is fired up, heat emits, and dust rests into an earthy element once again. In our daily life, we consume this woody element as the nutrients, a combination of proteins, sugar, starch, and numerous others. And this is the answer of: when wood burns, heat releases and dusts relax. The dusty residue is dung: the dusty songs sung and rings rung.

Further, when the dusty earthy element is condensed and consolidated, it becomes a rocky or golden element. In humans, this rocky element forms bones. In consciousness, it is the solid idea and indestructible thought that invite bloody revolution, invent peaceful evolution, and prevent any solution to solute the soldiers and flirt the flowers.

Thus, the three dots form the heart of Xin are the three elements, dancing above and around the curve or horseshoe like an arch that represents the physical structure of the heart, along its extended arteries and veins as firing wires and traveling nerves. The arch stroke in this Chinese character also represents the roof of the dome, or the grounding floor to host lightning strikes.

Must understand the fundamental law of universe mathematically, as each path contains rudimental math, the three Dots hovering around the arching curve of human heart are the trinity: three individual dots, three separated lines, and three projecting points, as well as three trajectory angles. Now we have four basic fundamental elements to deal with: dot, line, point and angle.

As such, this fire-containing heart is no longer that separated three pieces, which are represented by three dots signifying the triple marriages inside the human heart. It is the Divine center of universe where the planetary trinity is born: Sun, Moon and Earth. This triad of planetary bodies reflect and demonstrate how the material universe is formed and completed into its Divine Oneness.

The triple circulations are up and down, left and right, and forward and backward. The up/down volume forms time, which represents the Sun. The left/right column forms space, representing the Earth. The forward/backward interaction forms neutralized duality, which represents the Moon.

Again, the vertical volume starts the initial charge of action, which creates light and shadow. As for this power, the inside is empty and the outside is flaming. The internal empty gives birth to the original returning journey and recycling ground where everything will come and go, birth and return, manifest and transform. The moment the empty is targeted and released, the heat is produced and light shines. From the space-like and space-less inside (which gives birth to the infinite inertia in the mean time) to the gravitational force outside that which is the radiation of light and movement of space, a star like Sun is born. For this starry body, though the inside is empty it is emitting a force with a neutralized negative charge, and outside radiates and fluxes constantly with positive charge.

Now we have a three-way dual communications: two positive charges (one from star and the other planet), two neutralized positive charges (one from planet and the other moon), and two neutralized negative charges (one from the moon and the other, star).

As any two starry planets evolve and dissolve, more stars and planets and moons will birth, which results in a constellation. As constellation takes the power to grow, another constellation is birthed, and another, and another, until, a galaxy is birthed. What happens then to the neutralized negative charge of a star is that when its own positive charge extinguishes for its dual purposes, one positive and the other neutralized positive, it is the positive charge from the planet that helps the starry and moony bodies to form dual neutralized negative charges. And the neutralized positive charges from the planetary and moony bodies help to sustain the single beginning positive charge created from the starry body.

Further, when a moony body's neutralized negative charge increases itself to the degree it will force another planet, either a star planet or an earth planet, to explode and die. This third stage of negative neutralization helps the internal and initial neutralized negative force birthed from the first star to create more stars and constellations. It is also this neutralized negative charge between two planetary bodies, similar but different, that sustains a constellation or galaxy.

In the entire universe, there are only eight neutralized charges existing in each galaxy. This is the power of Xin, the universal heart. As in any constellation, there are only three charges constantly changing from being negative and neutralized negative. This is also the power of mystic practices: how to find and sustain two neutralized negative charges.

In our own internal solar system, the Moon only mirrors the double neutralized negative charges, but never produces it by itself. This can only be achieved in mystic practice, where the brain of the feminine side, or Earth side, and the heart of the masculine side, or Sun side, are equally retained and mutually transmitted. This is called double initiation. This happens when each side, being biologically male or female, finishes his or her own initiation, and has further matured to the sibling state and genderless condition. This happens so rarely among the living population, since an enlightened being represents one partner, and the living partner does the double work. Or both are enlightened and know how to compartmentalize and synthesize their capabilities. However, that is even more rare.

Le

Le is innocently happy, totally charged joy, and soul-drunk and spirit-awakened bliss. As for a person, from cell to hair, core to pore, everything is alive, present, and ecstatic. Le is structured as such that a person must die and be born again while she or he is still physically alive. This does not mean the person has to literally die, but one's energy body has to return back to an innocent and infant state. To be born again with Holy Fire, Holy Water and Holy Spirit, so that gender-based body is no longer a personal issue, but cosmic tissue. Capable of experiencing two genders, without external extract or artificial influence, the original space for dual genders, and twin souls, are reconnected and reactivated. When the power of endowment from triple Holiness is inserted and transmitted inside a human heart, spiritual pregnancy begins.

This is the death of both the genetic ancestral cross and collective cultural cross, and the birth of both collective represented self and universal individualized self. The collective self replaces the family cross, and the universal self advances cultural cross, so that this born-again individual becomes the Man of Calling, the Destined Being, the Chosen Person, and the Prophesized King. This individual then represents both the old death and new birth, the same essential truth in that which must change, the sacrificed labor and the saved fortunes. This individual then carries the family face and cultural makeup to the cosmic lights and their decorative colors. The body becomes the cell for sell, the organ for organized organism, the instrument for love, the vehicle for portals, the drum for collective heartbeats, the flute transporting the moody emotions with woody season, the paint coloring sacred holiness and rich abundance, the antenna for all animated voices and automated sounds, the tongue for subtle toning and supper atonement.

At this point, the meridians become the merry dings, where all the live motions ring and string, sing and spring. The infantile body is wrapped with youthful will, truthful passion, and matured stance, where the hair speaks for the authentic affair, the skin is ready to drum, the trunk stands for the metallic gong, organs team for the members of choir, the soul sings the live music, and the spirit sweats and pulsates as the chief conductor. The audiences are the universally ordered witness and the fully rehearsed business. Weathered strings and seasoned lyrics hire me to produce poetic hymns, and ecstatic rhymes inside universal hall and through the harmonic ball.

Are you ready to die and be born again from the middle life crisis and retirement depression? Have you prepared your homework and job assignment? Will you be the Man of Calling and the Sophia of Wisdom Singing? Would you be the divine instrument, the empty drum, the potent rum, the sharp gum, the restful mummy, and the nourishing mommy?

This above description is the definition of the Chinese character for Le. With the wood stroke serving as the foundation, like muscles and bones, the organs and glands are the strokes of the two infants resting and playing on both sides of the stroke of the white. Being in the middle and above, the white Chinese stroke represents the white light and white blood, the white milk and white marrow, the white silk and white thrusting meridian. All in one, this white character grounds as light, elevates as Jacob's ladder, mouths as white chimney, and shines as the lightning rod. Being the middle verb, this

stroke or character whitens everything like what white light wipes the white space. This white character is the hat of the crown, the tip of the Sun, and the eye of God.

Then the two infants resting and playing on both sides represent any duality, through any given opposition, and towards all harmony. They are the image of self, the look of truth, and the book of revelation. Like a wine bottle, these two materials team up to fill each other and empty one another, so that anything produced reduces into nothing, and anything possible poses for the elbows to enable. When the two drunks are inside the same trunk, the self is the conviction and the selfless is the truth. When these two drunken babies stand above and sleep upon the same woody moody green bed, the root is the roof, and the boot speaks for the proof. This green bed then hosts as the universal mat so that each vibrating fabric that utters is an essential matter, and that each man is a divine manner. When matter and manner are placed together, they team up as one heated steam, to pose for the divine esteem.

Thus from natural organs of all living beings to manmade tools as fooling instruments and cooling installments, Le speaks as the Chinese definition goes: the five organic sounds and eight toning notes among all musical instruments. When the sound goes around, the note evens the scale so that all the triad stances and tripled glances have their individual chances and collective dance. Le becomes the harmonic ball, the empty hall, the endless call, and the weightless tall. When this tall is installed, the call is given with assignment, the hall is filled with love, and the ball runs in its full scale and speed, full volume and velocity, and full stomach and storm.

When the power to spell becomes the flower to scale, flour speaks for the hour, and tower grounds the lower. Everything becomes synchronized, so that each scenic view is chronologically choreographed to host the core and boost the law. The calligraphy brushed through the muscles and bones, fingers and tones will be totally stoned and atoned. When the stone arrives, the bone is alive, and spirit spies the peace and speeds the ease. This is the power and joy of Le. This is the town that speaks for the home base of that mother tongue. This is the instrument of peace declining the war but defining the bar that scales the sounds of each passing car echoing through the wall grounding all walnuts. This is the music for harmony that is producing the honey that cannot be measured by and traded with money. When Honey reduces all the funny looks and bunny hooks, the sunny is the real money so that each minute exchange between heat and soil, seed and water is precisely deeded to code the living honey and comb the dead tomb. The lamb is calm, and palm hosts the Psalms. The living well calms each and welcomes all to become well.

If not, your heart is still filled with sorrow sorry and painful stain, and your brain is forever clustered with horse-chained words and socially existed conditional phrases. You flesh is not fresh, your soul is not alive and your spirit does not smile. Always a member of an universal family, you will remember that:

1) Your gift was already given to you before you jumped into your mother's womb.

2) Your work has already been destined.

3) Your life-clock is already on charge by a timely defined battery.

4. Your experience is the holy meal.

5. Your expression is the holy trail.

6. Your willful conviction is your lifeline.

7. Your joyous love is the loving wine.

By the time your family members honor you and your professional circles respect you, the invisible boss is happy for all. Then your heart returns to that of an innocent baby, and your mind becomes a warrior. Nothing goes into your brain except light, and nothing dials inside your heart besides purple fire, pure and true.

Before this, remember your parents' sacrifice, and remember their love, whether you are aware of it or not, or remember it or not, it makes no difference. If they do not love you, they would not be bound together, for whatever length or period of time in their life, and gave birth to you. Their job is to give birth to you and send you to society for further growth and maturity when you are ready. The dual contracts are: they bend you to home life, and you send them to a heavenly home.

Any invention contains holy fire within. Starting from now, with the very event in hand or the wearing affair in heart, so that each word you express is thoroughly digested, internalized and verbalized in front of others. Your must swallow and digest them as of the seeds of light, and the wine of love so that the universal matrixes become your sleeping mattress. When the mad mood rests on a woody mat, and when the fear factor turns into a beer factory, God or Universal Creator will send the helpers to either wash you down or up, depending how you will stand on your single grounded root, retain your pure and innocent heart, and invite the twilight in.

Between spiritual pregnancy and spiritual pilgrimage, you will travel from person to person, ancestor to ancestors, race after race, and culture from culture. You will be ordained, initiated, and baptized by the earthly as well as culturally established religious sections or spiritual lineages. Each race has its own spiritual source. Each religious section promotes the best it can for the retreat of your soul away from biophysical relationships into a social-collection realm. And each spiritual lineage has its own cosmic antenna in which you will receive divine and holy information. You will discover that:

1) No one set of parents is better or worse than the other. It is the state of awareness of your own journey of soul, as well as the residue of past-life karma. You are not worse than your parents; rather, you are more advanced than them to handle the bio-emotional problems.

2) Not one religious denomination is more spiritually advanced than the rest. Rather, it is your own quest of love and fire that attracts the exact same sector or denomination existing among all religious groups, within the same denomination, or in the midst of some congregations located in difficult regions or communities. You do not need a congregation to enter the door to heaven, you need a heart-awakened and single-minded devoted pastor, priest, monk or nun to initiate you as a spiritual lover.

Equally, all classic religious texts or cannons speak the same truth but are scribed in different languages to begin with. Holy Torah, Holy Bible, Holy Quran, Heart Sutra, Tao Te Ching, I Ching, Upanishads, Cabbala, and all the unquotable rest, are containing the same hidden spiritual truth and wisdom parables. It is not the words and their related historical stories or revelations you need to recite, chant, or memorize, it is the hidden messages within the logical, grammatical, and numerical structures coded and wired that knock, hide, and preserve the deep and profound spiritual meanings that serve as the holy bread or wine: to spice your love and speed your will.

3) No one spiritual lineage is more cosmically closer than the any of the next neighboring mileage. When an enlightened being lines his or her cycling age with daily weather, monthly feather, and annual treasure, the lineage is established with nature's truth and natural law. When your personal highest call knocks onto the gate of that specific lineage, your hemispheres are the mileages that produce travelogues upon dialogues. When you retain your innocence, playful, forgiving, and letting go heart, and when your dreams and hopes are nothing but divine: divine journey, divine experience, divine expression, and divine intervention, you have found and retained the power

of Le. Once the heart is permanently open, and joy sings its tone, you will sing songs, perform miracles, and the last of the three characters, Xin Le Qu, will become whole, winding up all kinds of holes by winning all sorts of hosts.

Qu

Structurally, Qu is piece of carved jade into a vessel. Resembling a bowel, Qu then becomes the representation of any hollowed space of a container. Mentally, this Qu is capable of stretching, bending, curving, and hovering. In consciousness, Qu stands for the compassionate

heart, which is capable of hosting mental stretches, emotional curvatures, and physical flexibility. In the spiritual mind, Qu is the hollowing purple heart allowing all lights in and permeating all actions into divine manifestation.

Thereby, Qu is the holographic and harmonic vibration of universe. It is the music of heaven, songs of space and time, echoes of earth along her oceanic wave, echoing valleys, floating planes and wavering peaks inside her cloudy gas-milked shell, sacrificial blessings of all birthing mothers, the diligent and devotional job of all fathers, lyrics of your heart, cries of your agony, unbearable weights and pains of your daily suffering, single-stringed lonely feeling, vast-space-carried-away prays and wishes, synchronicity in eventful life, harmonic flow of love and love affairs, weathered and climatic forces appearing and changing in daily and seasonal cycles.

And most of all, the lyrics (vibratory words or phrases) you have decided and agreed upon before you were conceived, during the times you have prayed, along the eventful trails you are wishing for, hopes delivered upon gray or murky sides of the river of life, and lastly, your highest imaginary number, best of wishes and most power gut-fired, heart-flamed and brain-launched leap, which is your eternal "welcome home" call.

Structurally, Qu is a contractive response swallowing hollows in the center of universe. Her sucking and swallowing and gaggling power is ever so quiet but unpredictable,

Characteristically, Qu is all the forces you may call motherly or ugly: bending, yielding, relaxing, withdrawing, hiding, denying, gliding, surfacing, patching, windsurfing, water-treading, milk-shaking, tear-gladdening, fear-deciding, dear-believing, dare-bailing, fair-trading, welcoming hugging, bed-singing, cry-trending, left-over-washing, kitchen-swishing, bathroom-cleaning, laundry-deterging, life-recycling, and bye-waving motions and emotions and never ending flow.

Qu is what yin receives and conceives, perceives and deceives, believes and delivers, relieves and retrieves, and everything that is happening already undetected and unprepared for, before your thought drums your brain and numbs your ears and scares away your deer; to the further feather weathering the fatherliest degree that not even your dreamed wish has not yet surfaced. Coloring lights are not there yet, and even thrusting time has not yet begun.

You see now how deep the curve is. See how long the stomach-unbelted and hair-un-styled stretch and suspending arch is, and how unpredictable the power of her reaction, reflection, and recycling can be.

As soon as you are in, you have to cry louder than her, scream better than her, and sing more beautiful than her, and dance more attractively than her. And there is no exit until your thoughts along though, ought, odor and order are as pure, clean, tranquil, and translucent as her musical love and lyrical motion.

You are born from yin and you have die into yin once again before you can retain your light and deluxe. It is that love that lives and believes, lights and delights, decides and delivers your play and fair motion and fir emotion and hair demotion. You must go through the double yin gates before anything else would happen: mother and earth, love and emotion, dove and promotion. You must become a motion-detector, sound-producer, light-receiver and fire-distinguisher. You must be there before anything is happening, and you must be here to prepare and repair anything that could happen or has happened. You must become colors of lightning, textures of matter, matrixes of thinking, dots of inking, lots of pinning, knots of weaving, cells of organizers, and shells of casketing and sells of marketing. You must vow and be the vowels. You must be now and to be renounced. You have to be nothing and everything, none and all.

After you have delighted the mother of your birth and frightened the mother of all death, you are as safe as warmth in the home, light inside the dome, colors in the rooming Rome, spirits in the roam, force into the comb, nail upon thumb, tail toward gum, and stones inside the tomb.

You must to be quieter than silence, lighter than wind, smoother than feather, and more unpredictable than weather. You must sugar all cells, flour all organs, thread all muscles, fat all tissues, water-proof all glands, lubricate all ligaments, skin all pigments, and marrow all bones, and finally recite all tones.

You must know the skillfulness of seeding and feeding, breast milking and breath soaking, ill deflecting and silk weaving, bill collecting and pill dividing. Until that magic pill works its miracle way upon that magnified hill, you are still ill, itchy and aching all over your body as every cell is wounded inside the worm.

Qu only exists when two hearts are firing at each other. Qu is then alive when you have experienced tremendous headache on and on and again, until you and it becomes unbearable, but you still want to live, to be alive for the next moment, retain the deepest hope, manifest the highest dream, and express the most humble and honorable wish.

Qu will start to strike an instrument in your body to produce a song from the deep and unknown. It will orchestrate your entire being, you are on holy fire, and it will evaporate holy water.

From the deepest tone and tomb of dead ancestors and their unfulfilled wishes and unfinished business, the instrument is warmed up. The moment this instrument is warmed up, you will play this instrument inside your own instrument, and you become the holy sacrificial ground, collective ceremony place, and within the divine and sacred circle.

Your body becomes the very instrument, and holy temple. Your heart produces lyrics, and your gifted expression is the player of that instrument. When the song is sung through your triple bodies, the three worlds out there will be ordinance. Earth will shake its feet through her own poles, humanity will listen to what you are playing, and heaven will record, rehearse and recycle what you are playing. This is the lyrics and songs of Qu.

CHAPTER 12:
REVELATION OF XIN

Ethereal Xin

Knowing the organic structure and its vibrations of the human heart Xin, I have to search deeper into planetary, ethereal and the universal heart we normally called Space or Omnipresence. Being a single spirit, I have experiences of being cycled many a time on earth, between animal flesh and human being, in order to earn the credit of entering this divine heart. A high mountain to climb, and a hierarchal ladder to step upward, this ascension practice does not actually need to climb up externally but decline down inwardly. Listening to all drum-able hearts, which give me what I have and take what they can, the universal heart is pretty simple in the end.

After giving all I have and can, my soul leaves my biological vehicle and ascends into the atmosphere above the Earth. It is here, I see the Golden Egg, Golden Flower, Organic Pyramid, Holy Heart of Jerusalem, and the Sun Temple in Mexico. Tibetans call this Xin by the name "Shambhala." Though being identified mentally with regional quality, this Shambhala bears no specific geographic location. Disappointed by so-called sacred cites, as mentioned above, I set aside my gender-biased Xin, leave patriotic Xin, and ascend from my racial genes to collective matrixes. The ethereal Xin appears to reveal by itself.

Inside the ozone, and above the atmosphere, there is an eyeglass shaped energy being. Two triangles are merging and submerging, to the point where the purest golden ray from the heavenly Xin descends and purest prayer from humanly Xin ascends. Those who pass the heavenly graduation are initiated with a cosmic encyclopedia. This white book reveals the math step-by-step while the initiators are showered with a holy bath. Inside the exchange, the lightest breaks through the light and flies into the kingdom of heaven. Next are the stars, rulers and grandmasters for the coming generation, and next down are the sacrificial barrens--physical, emotional, and mental—so that humanity as a whole can retain sacredness.

Surrounding this meeting point and embracing arms, about 6000 or so living souls stand around as gatekeepers, to protect this body of light, the Xin of Shambhala. They make sure that the right spirits can travel through. The right Xin receives the material of the white book, the right calls are answered, and right wishes are granted. Between awakened spirits as gatekeepers and enlightened spirits as guiding angels, this ethereal golden land has been safeguarded and protected since the beginning of human incarnation.

Now mother earth speaks form her Xin, tears through her watery skin and sweats along her breast-feeding bin. When her voice, tear and sweat rise up from the Himalayas and Kun Lun Mountain Scopes, her dual faces appear. One looks inwardly inside all the cave-nerving holes to reflect harmonic Xin, and one books inside her womb all the smiling Xin. When the look of her golden skin meets the book through her magic fin, the cosmic spheres, light beams, solar wind, and earth's vortex are in a constant influx. Cosmos costs me more than I can afford, and universe unites my verse with mother earth's purse. This connecting bridge, the sacred bound, the love linkage, interacting thread, and magic place is Shambhala, shame on all babbling baba (daddy) lost their luck. Like an oval aura shelling around a person, an angelic veil upon the forehead, or spirit's fair behind the head and on top

of the crown, this Qi Egged Yoke is the true image and the description of Shambhala of the Mother Earth.

Triad Xin

It is in this holy land, the golden face of mother earth, an angelic being descends and procreates the twin spirits as the Chinese gene pools. Representing the virgin heart and virgin love of the Mother Earth, this angelic being is called in Chinese Xi Mu Niang, or West Mother Nanny/Aunt.

I saw Her picture inside the temple, heard Her legendary story, and feared Her leg-bended fish body and star-wrapped lobby. Seeing the meridian lines in my fresh body and modeling chart, I could not believe She was the meridian carrier, until She came to me while I was performing at my first workshop in 2003 near Dayton in Ohio. Standing in a circle with ten sisters and one brother, my individual identity disappeared and I was in a trance state. All of a sudden, I felt my left foot was landing on the surface and into the heart of Mother Earth. Red flame from central lava travels from the heart of the earth up and shoots into my left foot, and left abdomen accordingly. I felt instantly that my left foot was grounded, locked, and trapped, and my right foot was trying desperately to jump, escape and fly. Red fire and black smoke were in one giant birthing womb and merciful tomb, as this angelic being begins Her ovulating and birthing cycles. Below, and the rest of the chapters are the revelation dedicated this awakening experience, this holy transmission.

Dear Angelic and Grand Mother: Thanks for landing through the thread of golden veil down to black soil of the Mother Earth. Thanks for touching the earth-core with Your holy left body and receiving the red lava Qi into Your virgin left ovary.

My dearest Mother of all mothers: Thanks for arranging my spirit into Your red line of blood and white line of spirit. Thanks for sending one of Your enlightened grandsons, Lao Zi, as my initiative teacher and my spiritual father. It is through Him, that I slowly grew into Your first son, Fu Xi, who constructed eight different triad formations of universe. It is through this holy experience above, I began to reconnect to all mothers, all their divine feminine energies, and all their harmonic songs of Xin. Until I could find no mother but love,

and mo-mommy but my ready mummy. The hemp wrapping me as the mummy is the temp tapping Your meridian lines as living wine and a believing in mine fine. I began to discover internally the twin flames between my virgin boy and my virgin girl, and equally my divine feminine soul, through Your first daughter, Nu Wa, who became the first of my ancestral biological mother.

For the past couple of years, when the Qi-gate point on my left pubic bone opened its seal, my skin started to change its season, like a tree leaf from spring to fall, a snake body from birth to mirth, and a landscape from day to night. I felt that I was giving birth to my feminine self, with the help of Your landing foot, and all mothers' surrendering footages. Their widowing journeys mirror Your looking window, and I shall do as Your wing swings me into the winning window.

It is all because of You, your triad energy influx in Your angelic veil and Your cosmic mineral-matrixes, we obtains three charges: positive, negative and neutral. As You are talking through me now, the divine influx, the divine impulse, and divine thrust naturally generates, divides and expands itself between the empty hole and the expansive whole. The empty hole is my dialing home and the expansive whole is Your harmonic room. Like Yourself has demonstrated, the moment Your left leg lands on earth with its positive charge, Your right one, being waved, shocked, alarmed, and disarmed, becomes the very negative charge. Your landing stance and standing glance from Your crown, through Your trunk, and between Your legs, swirl and spiral as the neutral charge. Anything sizable receives a charge, and any charge is a change for the multiple exchanges. Like a lightning strike, or toning flash, upon the landing bell spelling the watery trail, the very positive touch and negative reflex neutralizes between Your grounding max and surrounding relax.

So now, between Your left leg being electrically charged from the red Lava (the last and the vast) Qi of the earth mother and then numbed, Your right leg, shaking, escaping, and trembling in the air causes an influx of energy pool to be established. Two opposite ends between a heavenly positive charge and earthly negative charge are locked and interlocked, blocked and clocked.

Shooting down and leaping up, the charges spiral inside Your abdomen, chest and brain. Without a physical ovary, Your abdomen is actually

REVELATION OF XIN

an Oval Ray. Without a physical heart, Your chest is an Empty Nest. And without a thought, Your brain breaks the ray and showers as Holy Rain. Sun empowers Your Oval Ray, Earth hosts Your Empty Nest, and Moon neutralizes Your Holy Rain.

When the positive charge from Your left leg and negative from Your right leg enter Your Oval Ray, as the image of day and night, heated mists from water and cool wind become the electric circuit curling and circling up into Your Empty Nest. In the meantime, the Holy Rain of light and air shower down from Your brain, as time and space, into Your Empty Nest. Four Charges now swing, spin, and swim inside. Color-patched air and water-filled mists stay on Your Left Nest, and light-delighted spectrum and motion-detected wind stay on Your Right Nest. Together as a whole, the presence of light and shadow fill and refuel the space of Your Empty Nest. The ethereal Xin from Your Holy Rain and the Inorganic Matter from Your Oral Ray are now ready to materialize into organic Xin as mirroring spirits, living twins, and believing sins.

Everything inside Your three energetic centers are mapped, wrapped and strapped with six different charged zigzagging patterns. Triangles form into diamonds, and diamonds complete as sacred holographic spheres. In turn, the light-delighted spectrum becomes alive with a feminine twin flame, and water-filled mists becomes alive with the masculine twin flame. They become pregnant inside Your Empty Nest, sharing individual spaces between left and right, and mutual vibrations in-between. The masculine twin flame has two positive charges physically, and one neutral charge internally. The two positives then complete as one positive and the other, a neutralized positive. The feminine twin flame has two negative charges physically and one neutral charge internally. The two negatives then complete as one negative and the other neutralized negative. The two positive charges live and exist with the two negative charges, to complete cell after cell, organ after organ, sense upon sense, and meridians through meridians. The two neutral charges become then individual peace and collective ease. The two neutralized positive and negative charges make each flame individual and helpless, and twins as a complete one team, one family, one nation, and one universe.

Now the three layers of the body are completed. The masculine twin flame has a positive charge inside, neutral charge in the middle, and a neutralized positive charge outside. The feminine twin flame has negative charge inside, neutral in the middle, and neutralized negative outside. Together, a hexagonal shape tape both flames inside Your Empty Nest, next to one another, and best for each other.

Now a total of eight triad strands are established. The first strand is the core of the earth, and in turn in Your Oval Ray. It is established between the solar influx on left and lunar influx on the right, which gives birth as the neutralized negative charge on the surface of Earth. The eighth one is the Golden Seed above the Shambhala, and in turn in Your Holy Rain, the neutralized positive charge.

A triangle is formed between the central core of the Earth, which contains a positive charge and her surface circulating as a neutralized negative charge. This is the outer form of the triangle, meaning all three lines and their points are merging together. As the Mother of all mothers interacts with this set of triad stands, or triangles, Your energy vortex forms the receiving portion of the triangle, which in fact it is not a triangle, but a Y shape, where from the very center three lines are diverging outwardly.

As below, so above! The eighth triad strand is now already established between your angelic auras up to earth's aura of that Shambhala. This interactive center, like the center of Your Oval Ray, receives and circulates the charges of time and space above Yours and earth's Shambhala.

In between now, there are six Y shaped triads moving up and down inside Your angelic body. Vertically and through the ascending order, they are 1: feet and ankles, 2: knees and thighs; 3:ovaries and diaphragm; 4:breasts and throat (both true and false vocal cords); 5: brain hemispheres and crown; 6: auras and shambhala. Together there are 12 of Ys, six of them are upward and the other six are downward.

Structurally, below feet is Earth (abyss) trigram. Feet and ankles are controlled by Thunder (motion) trigram. Knee and thighs are altered by Lake (ocean) trigram. Ovaries and diaphragms are blown by Wind (mobility) trigram. Breasts and throat are locked by Mountain (saturation) trigram. Hemispheres and crown are lured by Water (Moon) trigram. Auras and Shambhala are donned by Fire (Sun) trigram. Shambhala (golden egg and golden veil) and the single dot above are created by Heaven (light) trigram. The eight complete tetrahedrons are formed from any two sets of different triangles in each unified formation. These eight tetrahedrons are the eight trigrams described by Your first son, Fu Xi. These eight trigrams are the lineal structures where Your angelic body carries all the matrixes of creative formation inside You as the cosmic ray sends You away and abysmal heat welcomes You. They contain all the possibilities and capacities for birthing the Images of You and Your Invisible Husband.

Holy Conception

Dear Angelic Mother, Your Empty Nest is the twin flames' birth town, and playground, and consequently where all children and grandchildren will be born and die afterward. Your Empty Nest is our biological parents' living mount, and our ascension ground. Inside Your Empty Nest is our holy Fruits: the masculine twin flame or the virgin boy, and the feminine twin flame or the virgin girl. The virgin boy, Fu Xi, resting inside Your right mount—the right lung--close to and on top of Your Liver, while the virgin girl, Nu Wa, sleeping inside Your left mount—the left lung—above Your heart and spleen. They are conceived at same time, and growing with the same speed and progress.

By the time they are fully developed, around 18 moons, their legs are crossing one another, right around Your stomach, and gravitating above the Yellow Court, which is dialing with the Star of the Weaving Maiden (Vegas). The rings of Saturn become the mobile charges through their legs and around Your stomach, which has nothing but the residues from light particles and red lavas.

As of now, the star of Altair is watching, waiting anxiously while not knowing what to expect.

As they face one another, but cannot touch each other, You are sending light and air down your throat. The light and air You are fasting with are altered by Sun and Moon in their polarized fashion, and the star Cowherd (Altair) on top of them. And it is the Cowherd, You receive the shoot light-beams as the spirit-makers of twin souls growing and sleeping inside Your chest. The twin spirits are in fact, reflecting Your dual images while You are still in the Milky Way galaxy.

On the 18th full moon night, Your arms are stretching open upwardly to connect with the powers of Venus and Mars, as well as Pleiades and Pisces above. In turn, these two star groups are receiving the power of Milky Way Galaxy, which is where You come from, and sending the power-charges into your fingers and armpits.

Bomb! Your Chest is cracked open on both ends of the armpits, and they are out of Your Nesting Xin!

The Triad Communion

When the twin sibling spirits are out Your Chest and into this earth world, You hold them inside Your Palms for 49 Suns. Afterward You put them into water for another 49 Suns. During the first 49 Suns, they only breathe through your magic healing and nourishing palms. And they learn how to live and communicate with the upper world, away from earth's gravitational forces. This is how they develop their telepathic and clairvoyant powers. They know how to communicate with Sun and Moon, Venus and Mars, Saturn and the Polar Star (Northstar). They breathe but not eat, they rest and not sleep, and they see one another but not talk to each other.

Then, the moment you drop them into water, for the growth of the second 49 Suns, they start to bubble through their guts, throats and mouths. This is how they learn and communicate with waves and sounds. As one sends the sound into water, the other receives it through waves. Back and forth, they talk each other like fish and whales, gentle waves and storming tides. They do not swim; instead, they stand aloof on their feet, and four legs are crossing one another but together like tree root and fish tail. The inertial force of earth and her quaking power swirl and spiral upward to loop and snoop their feet, ankles, knees, and thighs. They remain boating and floating on top of water, but not swimming individually like a fish, or growing inside like what seaweed would do. In fact, they become like a fish from their hips down. This is the way they learn and speak the song-lines of oceans and waves, thrust and sprout, fountain and show. This is also how they survive and grow.

During all those 49 Suns, You kneel on the ground, with Your palms beneath Your head to safeguard them. On 49th of the Sun, which is also the

3rd Moon night upon her fourth return, and the 98th of the total suns since their birth, You take them out of the water and let them rest on land. The night is peaceful, wind gentle, and Moon warms and warns them with her growing and protective arch. By dawn, their joined legs start to separate and they begin to crawl with the moving wind.

Animals are coming around for the party and birds are singing their most beautiful songs. You retreat deep into forest to communicate with them apart physically but together mentally with love. This way of living continues for the next 7 years.

During these seven years, the boy and girl team up to imitate everything around them. They eat, drink, wander around and sleep like animals and birds. Animals teach them how to pick fruits, select plants, and consume seeds. They learn how to enjoy the weather and the changing season. They adapt and adjust their living conditions with nature's cycles and mature physically and mentally. Because of Your protective power, they are unharmed.

Around the 7th year, their physical powers are fully developed and their brainpowers synchronize all the sounds and echoes that are alive in them and around. They know the seasonal songs from birds, daily weathers from animals, and hourly patterns from lights showering down from the Sun and winds passing through.

For they next 7-year cycle, you retreat further into a cave sitting inside one of the biggest mounts surrounded by rich green forest, and you teach them the love and all facets of emotional characters. The girl is faster than the boy in learning to the point they have to grow apart for periods of time. The girl follows her heart and makes friends with female animals and birds. The boy obeys his gut and chases his passion like male animals and birds. As a matter of fact, they rarely meet one another, but it is Your deep love and compassionate Xin that safeguards them like Sun watching during the day and Moon throughout night.

Something physically new happens to the girl, there is red water coming through her lower end. She asks vocally and telepathically among all the female animals and birds, but no one can answer her. She is left alone, pondering and wondering, but You know what is happening. She cries and screams and yells about everything and nothing.

You keep on sending the images of Moon to her, night after night, as her body hairs receive the message and her gut recites the meaning. She is destined to be alone, and different from the rest of all the female creatures. Precisely, on the 11th of the Moon night, there is enormous heat swirling inside her lower body, particularly her left ovary. The heat grows and increases until on the 4th night, which is 14th of the Moon cycle, there is a gushing force alive inside her gut, and the ovaries are telling the uterus, commanding it, exploding out the red water.

A pack of wolves floating by on those nights, are raising their heads towards the Moon and calling and zooming their voices straight into

the full-sizing Moon. She follows their actions. Through those combined voices, she could feel her brain raging like a glowing Moon. As she sees clearly there is a wave of clustering force bridging and suspending between Moon and Venus. This force then shoots into the rings of Saturn, and up and further into stars and constellations.

The red water floods, drips and drops for 5 days. During these five days, there is a mixed emotional feeling, as the shadows of dead birds and animals are hovering around her vision, like black veil full of translucent trails, a rope entangling with endless threads, and a drop cutting through all ends but connecting each round. The shadow shall do to what is now, hosting all stars like scars startling all but retarding nothing, by dressing up all that are inside the white smoke and around the violet veil. The shadows of dead birds and animals can only come close to her diaphragms, while the star beings are above. She becomes a split-entity, between the mommy below the diaphragm and mummy above. She is alone as a human woman, in the midst of all other female creatures, conversing with forces strangulating between Moon and Venus towards Saturn and the outter layers of stars.

The animal world of Moon and spirit world of Venus are forming a team with each other to distinguish their distinctive patterns, as each animal family possesses only one specific power while the spirit clan plays among all powers and forces. The animal world filtrates the fermenting jar while the spirit clan calculates the opening holes and closing doors. Between animation and automation, animal kingdoms and spirit clans are giving birth to flesh and mechanism while taking souls and spirits as saved seeds and donated deeds.

As for herself, one side of her resembles all animal behaviors, and the other side, the angelic. Her gut moans and groans, but her heart sings the rings and chants like circulating ants. Her top section of the body is peaceful and quiet, but lower is angry and fearful. You know her path, she is on dual destinies and living in two worlds now. This lasts on for 24 Moon cycles.

On the 25th Moon cycle, the boy starts to change as well. There is a snake traveling inside his groin electrifying both his nuts. And there is an urge to touch and rub himself. You are laughing and crying at same time.

On the 26th Moon cycle, the boy feels something coming out of his groin as if worms are snaking through the soil. And there is an excited feeling inside brain and a conquering passion inside of his heart. He rushes towards his twin sister, telling her physically and mentally what is happening to him.

At this point, You, my Angelic Mother of all mothers, are retreating Yourself into the meridians and axis of the Earth, as all Your physical forms are dissolving into matrixes, influxes, wires, threads, textures, minerals and cells where Earth herself milks the world. You become a part of the earth, part of her shell ozone, and part of all spheres arching around. You have died and transformed. You became the caretakers of all peaks, planes, streams, and valleys. Your voice is the sound of the ocean, the bell and bellows of mountains, and the echoes of each and every soul coming into beings as humans.

Your Deliverance

Dear Angelic Mother: with Your angelic aura that sends a ^ shaped 72° and the V shaped 72° coming down from Shambhala, an X is formed. Both angles, up and down, are 72° degrees. And both sides, forming a > sign and a < sign, are 108° degrees each. Physically and energetically, the two up and down shapes represent mandible bone and pelvic bone in our body. And the plus and minus signs represent together the 108 bones in our skeletal system from wrists and ankles outward, plus the two kneecap bones. As our lower jaw and teeth (bird's bill) team up, our individualized spirit's power arouses and ascends. And when our pelvic bone and reproductive zone (fish mouth) team up, our individual spirit is conceived and delivered. This is how You receive us, spirits, from the sky above, and deliver us as materialized flesh

from the Earth surface up. Above our jaw and bird's bill, the white dove is Your Divine Smile. Below our pelvis and inside the fish's mouth, the black raven is Your Divine Rest. The black raven is inside the oven of Earth's sweat, which faces Your landing feet and treading helixes. The white dove is inside Your Divine Eggshell of Angelic Hair and Wings, which faces the Golden Egg inside the Shambhala.

This is how we were born and continue to be, and forever will be. Thank You, the Divine Mother between sky below and Earth above.

Perhaps as the upside down fetus inside Mother's womb, we wished to reach Earth. Much like how those on Earth now wish to reach heaven. What a shock when we got here, huh?

As it is now in You and has been in each of us through You, the 72° degreed angles become the 72 holy names from Your Invisible Husband, as well as the 72 angles coming through Your hairs and Wings; and the 108° degreed angles become the 108 physical martial soldiers defending our lives from conception to birth. They are the black warriors, the thunder deities in the sky as well as the sea lords in the oceans. They are also 108 spiritual warriors watching and teaching us how to ascend. They are white warriors, the mountain deities on top of Earth's mounts, along Your Eggshell of Angelic Hair and Wings.

The 72° degreed angles form diamond after diamond, so You let us die, and dial into the Earth's mount. The 108° degreed angles form cube through cube, so that each of our naked cuteness within will be cursed, and each of our wheeled curvatures will be cured. So be it!

Upon You Divine Angelic Body, the oneness of ^ and V are constantly in union of love but forever divided into two world of beings: male and female, thought and intuition, seeing and feeling, presence and reality, duality and individuality. Furthermore, Your food-absent stomach becomes a placenta that is connecting and cutting between a biological mother and her children on one end, and physical food and emotional food on the other. The communication between Moon and Venus is spitted between Moon and Jupiter on one end and Venus and Saturn on the other. So is the communication between Sun and Mars divided into Sun and Mercury on one end and between Mars and Saturn on the other end.

After Your throat is cut by Saturn, we live in dual worlds, on and forever. Our parents birthed us, but they are helpless in guiding us, because they cannot see or move beyond their parents and grandparents. There are more things jammed and clustered in Your descended beings after Your merge. Only few things are clear in our heads and hearts, and very few people in each generation are free. Because we are marching and traveling, seeking and searching out there for You, and our Holy Father, we rarely and truly look at and listen to what is happening inside.

Having gone through being a sibling, a lover, and a disciple, a child, a mother and a teacher, Your descended teachings are slowly sinking into my cells and bones, my wandering thoughts and my knocking questions. I finally bridge my gasping throat with a rumbling button, line my nose and toes, merge my hands and knees, internalize my eventful memories with eternal influxes, and conceive and birth myself for a second time, my true second chance. I link my sea and countable roll, resembling my egg-rolls as well as Your egg-glues. After You have merged Your divine being into the void of cosmic influx, Your twin children remember all that is inside their breathing vortexes and living fabrics. Looking deep within, I see the multi-colored spectrums, triangles within triangle.

On top of the standing triangle, there is a white beam forming another small triangle. On the left side, a blue light, and right side, a yellow one. All these three lights have their own triad formations. The white beam is so pure like a crystal, the blue is so bright as if the tranquil sky, and the yellow is potent like the rising Sun. Without concentrating on any of these

individual lights, I relax myself into their collective yet individual portals. The white portal brings me into twilights of no zone, no space but pure presence of light, without motion or activity, just a white space with white presence. I am now inside of my third eye.

The blue, on the other hand, lands me into a clockwise spiral motion, where my right eye is facing the blue spiraling on the left. As its spiraling motion takes away that triad formation on the left, it (all at the same time) leaves, cuts into, and lifts up, a standing portion of hexagonal formation right into the middle of three triangles. As this blue portal zooms out, the white on top descends without any visible motion or rotation, but the yellow light on the right spirals into the center of the hexagon, as if it takes its all power and births within. The counterclockwise spiraling yellow light now fades away slowly as the white light on top sinks in. A mix of yellowish, bluish, and pinkish flame is now swirling like flying curtains, singing waves and smiling glairs.

I see now, there is a six-pointed clockwise spinning light moving forward towards me, as the center and a circle where they are merging. It is taking me away into a space of no space, a presence of numbness, as well as a motion of absolute stillness. No birth, no death, nothing moves and nothing is alive. But all are alive. To feel above and beyond, as if we embody all things good and evil and it plays in the palms of our hands. To love ourselves and shine through ourselves.

Our Five Senses

Within the pointless stillness and groundless motion, I feel my entire being is now this very presence of nothing but white light. The moment I focus on this central white, I am gone, and white power expands so much faster and speedier than expected, that I am zooming out into nowhere. But as soon as I relax and withdraw my focus, I come to a place where in the middle there is motion, but just surrounding the dot and around the circle, there are layers upon layers of lights and waves, active powers in the midst of supportive peace, rings of lights coming towards me and ropes of beams moving away from me. The overall surface layers are six, but each opens into a new dimension, where its own motion cuts and opens a new space where nothing is happening. The most out-layer is a moving yellowish ring, swallowing the six lines, spiraling each of this light-line outward, and swirling it down, or in, into this moving and yellowish ring. Surrounding this ring and between each of the six spiraling and swirling outlines, there are six vase-like boxes being locked inside by moving-lines and outer triangles. In the meantime, they are very content and peaceful at present as if nothing is happening and nothing will occur. The planet Jupiter is alive in me: forever growing and expanding. I am the quality of green, and the virtue of benevolence.

Focusing back to the outer layer ring, I see now there is a grayish and white-black hue spiraling counterclockwise. Its motion is so slow and steady that I could not see if it is moving if I do not compare it with the outer layer yellow ring. It is just lazily and very contently hanging there. As a matter of fact, I feel as if I being swallowed and suffocated by its very motionless presence.

There appears a sudden depressed and sad feeling, where nothing is alive, good, pleasant, joyful, and meaningful. It just wants to blacken you out, darken you down, and swallow you into the presence of numbness, where everything seems so tightly jammed, locked up, fenced off, and muscled into the place of no aliveness and space of no hope.

Being stationed here permanently, I am ageless without time saving me, nor the aliveness rescuing me. I am long lived, an ageless survivor and permanently dead. I feel nothing, know nothing and do nothing. I am inside a black hole, a dark vortex, gray matter, dead zone, and timeless presence. I become the rings of Saturn, that motionless plate, where all matters matter nothing to me, and all my trust in truth is fashioned in the eternal faith but without face.

Something like wind lifts me up the wall I am in. Somebody like love dresses me up with felt-presence. Someone like eternal charge shoots me up from ocean-cliff, crusty wall, and a straight line out to the space. I am surrounded by a blue ribbon, a wave of peace, a touch of tenderness, a crease of love, a light of hope. I am out of the gray hue and on to the blue veil. Everything seems effortless, as if I had just awoken from a long season of sleep, like I am content with all that is given, granted, birthed, and endowed.

I am watching without focusing, looking without examining, gazing with no desire, appearing with no invitation, centering myself like a disarmed knight, jobless president, seal-robbed emperor, and crown-beheaded pope. I have no purpose of being, no hope of living, no target of thriving, no goal of presenting. Just to be is enough for me. I have no experience of busy or bussing with something, no sense of engaging or conversing with anyone, no urge to survive, no alarm to shock, no arm to disarm, no palm to psalm. What is the use of being, the purpose of living, and meaning of knowing, and goal of understanding?

All these notions seem odd, stupid, ugly, and tasteless to me now. "What it means" is a dead matter, a breathless corpus or a motionless object. I have no sense for it, no recollection of it, and no attachment to it. I am as long-lived as I am, and as old as I can be. I am so comfortably stationed that time cannot cut me or slice me. I am so content that motion can neither move me nor distract me. I am so peacefully present that inertia is both my breath and drink, head and tail, arms and legs, wheels and road, loads and goals, bullets and target, stars and lights, planets and gravity, and galaxy and space. I dress now with the face of Venus, the power of righteousness.

I have the sense now that someone is pulling my hair, peeling my skin, smoking my fat, tightening my muscle, frying my organs, drumming my bones, and extracting my marrow. Take it and make it, leave it and believe it. Do all you can for your own disbelieved pleasure; enjoy all you will for your own amused pressure; delight all you wish with your self-inflicted plague; please all you want with your senseless vaporizing plate. I do not care and I have no dare. What is an affair, like a puff of air!

This blue ribbon, this blue hue, this blue veil! Being blue can be glued with flue, or demurred by fir; cursed by birth or murdered by martyr. I am centralized with even, peaced with ease, and in a neutral space with mutual place. I just do not want to move!

With this rejection of disbelief from the blue, along the blue light moving away on the left side, I feel now the coming station between the white light and the yellow light. I am in my speed now: the speed of light and the speed of delight. Speed is my eternal urge, and being happy is my demanding purge. I want to move, march, travel, ride, slide and fly. The motion in me is as fast as these two coming and mating lights (white and yellow). I am on fire, I breathe with red flame, march with read lava, travel with red lights on, slide with red blood down, and fly with red-lotion (revolution) up! The heat flames the hot, as red amuses with arousal!

Millions of moving and leaping legs; never exhausting wheels of hips and beeps; full-speed and fuel-sized trunk and engines, spikes and spirals, to the shouldering arms and shouting alarms. I am coming and I am making things happening. I am living an eternal life and I will never die! My feet are grounded with eternal charge, and my power is beyond measure. The whole world is in the speed of my conquering convenience as each conquest is my marching joy towards my fighting toy alongside of my flying boy. My speed is my gun, my vision is my bullet, my passion is my target, and my flaming heart is my destroyer.

Until my power lands on the tower, my forceful vigilance meets the violet. The violet is more violent that any or all of my forces exercised individually or teamed together. The planet Mars speaks to me the power of reason, and delivers me the power of passion.

I am now surrounded by a violet-ray, that violent prayer, that vivacious spray, that vicious display, that victorious delay. All my previous red flame comes to a halt. Nothing has ever happened to me, as my speed has

Breakthrough

been totally split apart and my force is fully at loss. As I am surrendering my rare-ended raw-defending red, I come to terms with violet: the victory of lead. Grounded by purple, with lenses like pupils, I merge all the V-shaped angles with I-lined angels. When all Vs are i-dotted, i-knotted and eye-extended, my speed comes to a stop to become of my O, as my flame is circled with an oval ovulating overdue. Those oviparous ovules, which are old and owed, paired in odds and stationed like orphans, are owing now towards that over-toned and never-boned oviduct. I speak the power of intelligence, and believe in the power of Mercury.

After all these above are revealed to me. Your energy body returns to that white light on top of the triangle. Dear Angelic Mother, You are now grounding the power of space through the power of Earth, that red lava connecting to the power of Mars. Through the powers of black and red, You are delivering the single power of light, which contains all manifesting lights and rays, working colors and hues, and materializing textures and veils.

As the interior part of the Earth connects to the power of Mars, her exterior power reaches out towards Venus. Relating to this pair, Mars and Venus, are Sun and Moon, and Jupiter and Saturn, Earth and Mercury. The connection to Earth's circle are Mercury and Moon, as well as Jupiter and Saturn; Moon's circle are Venus and Mercury, as well as Sun and Earth: Sun's circle are Mars and Saturn, as well as Earth and Moon.

Your angelic daughter sitting on your left chest holds the power of the color blue, which connects to the planetary powers of Mercury, Venus and Moon. Among these three planets, Venus and Moon contain negative neutral charges, while Mercury has a negative charge.

Your angelic son, on opposite side of his twin sister, retains the power of yellow, which connects the planetary powers of Sun, Jupiter and Saturn. Among them, Sun and Jupiter contain positive charges, while Saturn has a negative charge. When Mars replaces Sun, the positive charge is still shared.

On the energetic level, Earth's interior power goes to Mars and Sun. On the surface, power goes to Jupiter, Moon and Venus. The oceanic layer goes to Mercury and Saturn.

The complete matrixes of planetary spheres around your angelic body are: on your left side, Mercury, Venus, Moon, Uranus and Neptune; and on Your right side, Sun, Mars, Jupiter, Saturn, and Pluto.

CHAPTER 13:

TWIN ADVENTURE

Dear Angelic Mother, Your twin's adventure in this world is Your added venture upon Your subtracted nurture. They are, as us all afterward, Your adventurous addition to this world. But they are, as we all have been afterward, subtracted and subjugated because of Your simultaneous addition. In turn, we all become Your audition upon addition, by addicting forever to what You have subsidized and subtracted. Any twin is a teamed winner for a twice in, and once and for all. Any due date thereafter becomes a dual date for the dew they are thirsty for, which is the few You have been sublimed by and substituted for. You birthed us dual flesh with twin flame, and You milked us with light and love. The twin flame always knows how to light one another up, but the twin flesh forever ends up in loss, at all cost, to host all dualities wrapped and trapped. You have existed in dual worlds ever since. You made it and You see it; but we as twin flames inside the twin flesh cannot.

Your addition among us three made us forever addictive to the ads shown in this world, between shadows and illusions, visions and revisions, and the matter of facts and the manner of faxing all the waxing taxes. The ax has an axial, only to exile from any given exit. Taxes are high, higher than blood accumulated and flood generated. Waxes are maximal, a mix of a different kinds of six. The vision seen is the revision perceived, and the revision performed is the vision formed. Illusions are wonderful to view, but terrible to touch and grasp. To visit all those changing illusions excites our dream but retards our wish. By the time the wish is washed by cash, what is left is the ash that asks none but answers for all; just as how the wind demands and why the dust recommends. Finally the shadow is wrapped with utility wheeled by mobility, and trapped by infertility willed by the barren. The bar has a rank, but the barren does not know that there is a tank sitting on the bank of a river loading all forms of flow.

Dear Angelic Mother, the barrenness in You barters the bar and tars in light, together as stars, which sends a car far away in distance but a large sum of luck in presence. Looking at my own barren state, me as a "ren" or human can run for fun, or rent a tent. The tent is mobile because light shines in and wind opens the door and window, where inside is all shadows.

Not until I face my own shadow, I cannot pronounce what You have told me, "I shall do to what is down in town." What is down plays with the ground, and who is in town shines with a crown. By the time the crown becomes the president, we as citizens are pressed inside the residential dents. We fight with him, to throw his crown off, and replace it with the hat of the Pope. Very soon, the hat of the Pope is on fire, to combat with the smoke dancing above the chimney tells the cabinet full of cardinals and candidates that there are angels visiting the gown. You grow and you are gone, that is the useful purpose of the gown.

Not until I know inside out, I am always an outsider, because what are out there are all matters of sides, between what the sea levels and how the sky evens. I do not know that You are forever inside me, us and all, for one another and toward each other. We smell and then sell, we spell and then rebel, and we drink well by drilling the ink in our bell to signify the sound

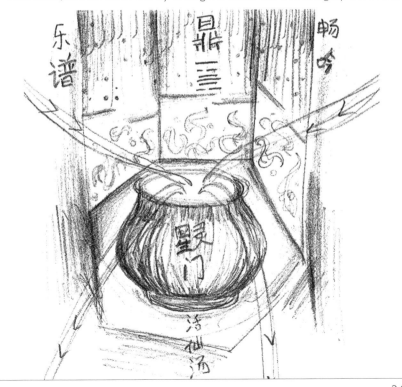

of welcome.

Welcome, those who are well come, those who are spelled out are calm, and those who are calm are the meat for the Psalm, and an alarm upon the palm. The mind bells and hand rebels, stomach drums the rum and intestines dance along the intensified wines toward intercepted lines. You made us twin flames as the mirrors for each other from Your miracle upon endless circle, in turn, each of us as a gender-biased flesh are miserable like mice, and miraculous like a wise man who could be fooled, or the rice that is cooked. Looking at one another, each as an individual retains a different makeup and pertains a different character. When the makeup is washed by tears, or smashed by clash, the character chats with rats and cats. Those who can are the cannibalism inside a chattel box, and those who cannot remain at large as the night fox.

Examining within, the same truth disputes all of Your wrapped ends and trapped ads. The wrapped ends can always bend, as the trapped ads add for profits by subtracting the costly losses.

Right here and now, I am ashamed of being in this flesh, but thankful for being this flame. To be shameful from the gaming industry, the shy is lame before the flesh tames the fresh. To be thankful, nothing survives from the ordeal but all arrive at home safely. When the weight of my flesh weighs more than my flame, I receive more blames than what I could claim; if less, my flame is as light as the spirit You have birthed and watered for. By the time the colors of my flesh change, the flame claims all the blames as a divine game. As for this divine game, the field is empty, but the vehicle is forever loaded with working labors and walking tables, to the degree I do not like to be one of the twins but prefer to be just by myself, besides my cells sizing up my sells.

Addiction is gladder than what the dad can do to his bladder, but awakening feels very sad about sadistic ads and statistic ands. Spring sprouts the tender but targeting flesh, as harvest hardens the hurry vests. Arousal can never tell who it is surprised from and who else is priced, between the rival and the arrival. When the arrival is at odds with the rival, novel tells oval to be loyal to the truth but royal to the conviction. Only the convict left is convinced to believe the truth from the will, and the will from the willow. I can use my will as what a willow can, to will what are low into a row so as to borrow what will tell from tomorrow. To lower me down, I am under all circumstances below the sand and around the shells. Only light can heat up seeds, and only wind can eat up weeds. Be the light, I win indeed!

Indwelling Process

With the triple interactions, Your twins' adventure begin, from conception to birth, and from life to death. The first interactive loop of Time and Space invites Your twin spirits to enter Your brain through Your eyes. Like all spirits traveling among constellations and galaxies, their spirits have the same power and quality. Your brainpower is a cosmic birthing womb connecting to the solar system and conceiving their mental, emotional and physical powers.

Their mental capacity is connected and individualized between the white light flaming inside Your brain and the yellow light shinning through Your face. In turn, their brain capacities are locked and geminated between the two lungs of Yours. Like a droplet of holy water, the crown of Your brain becomes the thrusting ground for You to descend and land on Earth, and Your throat is the surfacing skin of soil and water to sprout the twin spirits as seeds. Then, Your crown resembles the eternal pole of Earth, the peak of a mountain, and the top point of that holy water droplet. The interior space inside Your brain resembles the living atmospheres above and within the Earth's planes, and the body of that water droplet. Your throat becomes like the surface of the ocean connecting land and sea, and the bottom point of that holy water droplet.

The interactions among white light, yellow light and black space of Your brain invites the celestial heptagonal powers to complete as seven astral powers. The celestial heptagonal powers are the seven universal lights, and seven astral powers are the power grids among the (eastern) seven interior solar planets. Your crown hosts the seven celestial powers and Your throat materializes them into seven brain colors. Your Crown resembles the birthing portal of the universe, and Your lungs open the space to host rainbow powers.

Overall, Your brainpower becomes the representation of universal

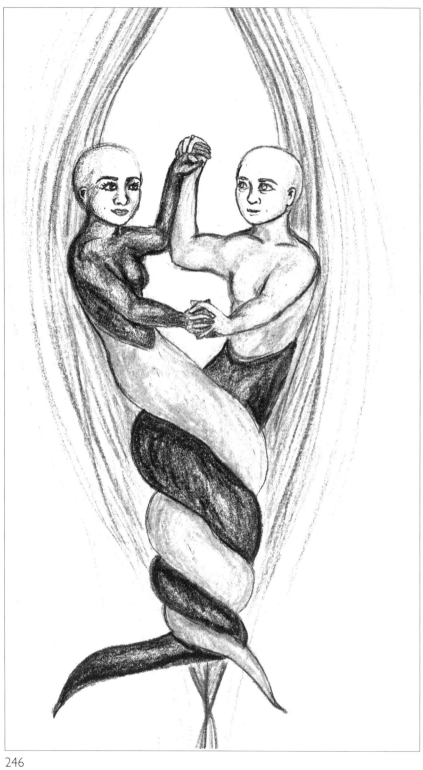

abyss and space accordingly. As Your crown becomes the grounding space for the universal lightning rod to thrust, and Your throat becomes the essential web to belt and nest threads and grids, 16 power lines are completed inside of Your entire human genetic pools. They are completed inside, yet, all I can see in this dream vision state is that eight women or sisters have the same exact faces looking internally and unemotionally.

So pure and holy is this Thrust meridian. Like a lightning rod opening the sky and a landing gear grounding You down, it charges Your entire being inside out. When this power descends down upon and into Your throat, it changes into an arch, a belt, a net, a spreadsheet, or an umbrella. In and out of this interior loop, the Yin Qiao meridian is going down and the Yang Qiao meridian is going up. Then Yin Qiao activates Your left-brain as Yin Wei, and Yang Qiao activates Your right brain as Yang Wei. Together these four meridians are spinning and spiraling like double helixes inside Your brain and between Your crown and throat.

Since Your mouth is never open, the point right below Your nostrils is merging and diverging a point between receiving the light and power from

247

the back of Your head, and expressing it as force and love through Your face. The six holes in Your face become the six faithful dogs guiding what is going on inside Your body and mind, and what is happening in the constellation of Orion. Your forehead, crown and back head are the three suspending and landing gears, yet invisible to my flesh eyes, permeating the golden light to drag the twin flames into Your eyes. Your face becomes the head of the Sphinx birthing all spirits and guiding their journeys.

When Yin Qiao and Yin Wei are out of Your throat, two sub-loops are activated. One is between Your right lung and right foot, and the other is the Virgin Boy in between Your right chest and lung.

When Yang Qiao and Yang Wei rise up from Your left foot and Your left lung respectively, they merge into the left side of Your body, then Your throat and brain. Two other sub-loops are activated. One circulates through the Virgin Girl, and the other circulates inside Your right brain.

Throat the Load upon the Road

When the rainbow (ra in the bow) light arch the twin spirits beneath Your throat and between Your lungs, it becomes double.

Their emotional characters are separated between Your Purple and Yellow Centers. Their physical dualities are differed from Your Blue and Red Centers. Between the Purple Light and Red Flame, their union and separation are given eternally, so they can function as a team, thinking and channeling as one total unity.

Your throat above is dressed with white light with a black void inside but shines with golden light outside. Inhale, You bring golden light and red flame into Your Chest. Exhale, You emit purple blessing and blue healing powers. Your chest is purple as the first visible light birthing white and sprouting yellow. Your diaphragm where twin's legs are resting and wrestling, is blue like the sky or ocean, and Your lower body is red as if the stomach of mother earth, where red is blood and life.

Your brain opens the seven rings and strings inside the structure of a heptagon for infinite exchange. It is the heptagonal power You brought into this world that makes us aware of the multiple-sevens through your invisible seven brain roles and our seven facial holes. Your internal openness upon the invisible openers makes us consciously, emotionally and as well as physically aware of the magic seven. The black veil and white light in Your brain are balanced between what is eternal in nature and what is temporary through change; because You have no thought, and You do not need to feel. Light is Your vision before it manifests as colors. Sonic wave is Your thought before it forms matters. Harmonic music is Your eternal heartbeat before it produces musical scales. Because of Your downloaded heptagonal power from Your brain, we become the fortunate seven for all the powers behind it.

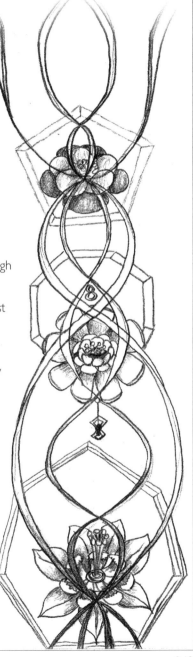

Your chest structures the open-ended octagon for the divine completion between spirit and body inside and through the twin flames. Due to the eternal harmonic musical power, Your empty chest inside Your ethereal frame is like a drum, a vacuum, or a cave. This empty chest is able to host and become the infinite flow from whatever Your heptagonal brain is manifesting. As Your Brain represents the universal mechanism, where white light is positive, gold light is negative, and black is neutral, Your empty chest inside speaks the language of infinite flow. The Star Draco behind you, dragging the twin on into the con: the formation of dragon. We as the twin flames have to mirror each other inside our collective heart, in order to complete the mystic eight and sixteen. The eight faces of Moon become the visible mirrors for us onward to dissolve all duality into the infinite. The eight psychic meridians become the makers of twin flames, and in turn, our human gestation power.

Your diaphragm is the bedding ground for the twin flames. The upper section of Your diaphragm grounds the feet of the twin flames like table-legs. Through the universal mind, Your diaphragm sends ethereal and glacial energies down Your lower body, which contain all the floating minerals bottled by watery clouds in the air, plus Solar light and wind. The hexagonal structure of Your diaphragm reflects the dual worlds represented by glacier, snow and stone on one hand and ocean, rain and forestry on the other. The hexagonal power becomes the drum body for peace and harmony. The formation of water molecules dresses up the twin flames with the cyclical twelve meridians, so that they are able to team up to produce children, and us as human male and female representations can live and die through blood and water, tears and love. The power of Earth along with her 12 cyclical powers provides us day and night, food and drink.

Your lower body serves like the earth soil and water surface where the triad heaven and cubic earth interact with tetrahedral force and diamond fusion. It designs the triangle body but cubic lobby so that each human child afterward is squared into its trial till the trinity is completed and circle is rounded. The trinity of the Sun--light, color and heat—can give birth to the trinity of twin flames—brain, chest, and abdomen. In turn, our brain is aware of the four waves through its four ventricles, so that light can touch the pineal gland, and waves echoe through the amygdala glands. Our heart produces four colorful beats through its four chambers where breath charges the throat and the heart pump atones the thymus gland. Our abdomen sustains cold or warm nutrients through its four corners: kidney, bladder, small and large intestines. Unlike Your chest that gives birth to twin flames and nourishes their growth inside the hexagonal and octagonal powers, our abdomen is the place where the twin flames achieved their first physical union, and gave birth to the first biological offspring, and onward. In turn, our abdomen, or about-domed-men, regenerates and reproduces life through its four registered powers: ovaries and testicles. Adrenal which stoves the heat becomes our added renal to complete three generations and three trials.

All together, the diamond fusion from the tetrahedral structure fuzzes the twin flames into productive fuels, and refuels the giver of life and the taker of death. The power of unified delta deals all the tars into cars so what we have are vehicles to travel from end to bend, amount to mount.

This means that Your twin flames' mental capacity reflect the seven planets and lights, where fortune is within the completion of 14 towards 16, and misfortune through facial consumption and physical depletion. Their emotional energy bodies are birthed by the dual loops of three interactions: the hexagonal structure manufacturing a tetrahedron and tincturing heptagon; and octagonal power distilling the tetrahedron and dissolving heptagon. They are the result of hexagonal structure and octagonal power: the first and/or third interaction. The hexagonal loop gives birth to tangible physical realm, while the octagonal power sustains the intangible soulful realm. The physical realm resembles an earthly cycle, hourly and daily. The soulful realm mirrors constellational cycle, monthly and annually. Between a quarter of an hour and a quarter of a year, the cubic power of tetrahedron completes dual sevens, where four seasons of a year and four seasons of life can sustain individual quality and maintain collective quantity.

In turn, their emotional bodies are finalized into two forces and three different combinations. The first force completes the twin flames as a team of four inside Your chest, and the second force is how they are showered and grounded by Your Angelic Body. The three different interactive combinations are: You as One (both visible and invisible), Your creation of the twin flames as Two, their union as Three, and Three as the individual and collective representation of the human population. The first interactive combination is the octagonal flow of the unknown and unaccountable on one side and the hexagonal power of passion and love on the other side. In the meridian system, 12 regular meridians are known and complete in each individual, but the 8 psychic ones can only be experienced, completed and shared when the union of any two souls reaches the same and exact state of Your twin flames. In other words, the connection with your soulmate. Some symptoms are how you finish each other's thoughts and read each other's spiritual patterns.

This occurs immediately, and simultaneously, in the twins'

chest where each flame presents a double force. The first force exists chronologically between the older brother and the younger sister, and the older sister and the younger brother. Both brothers and sisters' energies are activated between the octagonal power and hexagonal power through two other agents: Your brain and lower body. The brothers' energies begin with octagonal power while the sisters' hexagonal power. The interactions among these four are simultaneous, because any action invites the opposite reaction, and any conception creates corruptive depletion.

Further, each of these four have its dual powers, and altogether, 8 psychic or conceptive powers are spread out between the twin flames. The manifestations of these eight are the skeletal structures externally and inner chambers and ventricles hosted by the birthing grids. The older brother retains matured masculine power but is thirsty for the divine feminine love exercised by the younger sister. The older sister retains matured feminine power but is passionate about the divine masculine fire mirrored by the younger brother. This force is completed inside Your chest, and then becomes the blueprint for personal and generational trails for the future children.

The second force is the divine union from the twin flames to interact with the heptagonal flower inside Your brain and the tetrahedron flour frozen inside of Your lower body. This union and interaction creates the second and third interactive combinations, which is humanly defined as Body and Mind. This means that the twin flames' immediate interaction gives birth to their hearts and chests. Their union then interacts with Your lower body to give birth to the Mind, and with Your brain the Body. Your heptagonal flower shines downward to create a physical Body. It is the marriage of light spectrums and colorful pigments, and in turn, the creative will and intuitive awareness imbedded inside their individual and marital Body. In this Body, three sevens are born out of White Light within Your Black brain: seven cervical spines with seven colors, seven sternums with seven digestive loops, and seven facial holes with seven hill-bones. The marital Body enters the light world by dissolving the colorful illusions with seven lights. This interactive journey completes their adventures of merging into lights and sounds and then demonstrating them visually or musically.

Your tetrahedron flour is how the frozen water and an aromatic oil blend with unheated seeds and unproductive needs through the divine Golden Light shining through Your Crown. This is the seed of their, and our luminous Mind: the conscious and intuitive powers hosting brains. This luminous Mind faces the physical worlds with deadly seven senses emotionally.

The Marriage between Body and Mind is the twin flames' union as they grow up, as well as the parental images on both sides of the families. This is how our humans will behave and interact as a whole accordingly, share the balance collectively and cancel the personification individually.

Indwelling Structure

Dear Angelic Mother, since You are not a physical being and a physical mother, Your power grids between Red Flame and Blue Light uplift Your twin flames' fetal growth and suspend their interactions back and forth so that their physical growth is individually located and collectively materialized. Through the power of tetrahedrons, their inner six layers of matrixes are aligned with your six divine loops, and their treasure within is the golden expression coming through Your golden face. This is how they can ground you in Your Red Flame and internalize their joint venture. Like a tree-root, they connect the ocean and land, bridge their knees of humbling ground, and internalize their diaphragms that unite light and love but separate the self and form. Not until they return and love You as their Divine Love and Mother, the treasure inside cannot be opened and sustained.

With the power of Your lungs, as their ends forming the top line of the triangle, Your twin flames interact with their central loop to descend Your Blue Center and Red Flame down to the oceanic and crusty Earth. As their four legs sit and station above Your diaphragm, they interact with the four spheres coming from the four inner planets. As Your lungs represent human kidneys, and the atmosphere from above the surface of the Earth and Saturn, four other spheres complete the grid around Your diaphragm. These four spheres are:

1: Magnetosphere, Mars and heart;

2: Biosphere, Jupiter and liver;

3: Lithosphere, Sun/Earth and stomach;

4: Hydrosphere, North Star/Moon and spleen

In turn, the boy's legs are interacting with the planetary powers of Mars and Jupiter, while the girls' legs are interacting with the planetary powers of Venus and Mercury. In turn, Mars and Jupiter work together with Earth, and Venus and Mercury work together with Moon. All are finalized with the interactive loop between Sun and Saturn, and Moon and the North Star.

Before their legs could stretch physically inside Your chest, Your invisible heart and liver power would cradle them like elbows, permeating them to receive the vibrations of four intermeddle-looped meridians, two Qiao and two Wei. Qiao means shock, jerk, tiptoe, while Wei means gather, protect and guard.

The Yang Qiao meridian represents Magnetosphere, Mars and heart, solar light or sunshine, thunder and lightning, and Winter Solstice. This meridian begins with Your left foot. The light lands and touches upon the ground. This power then travels up to cross Your left leg to enter Your Perineum as the Earth's lock, afterward up to Your right-side body trunk to connect with Your Gallbladder, and further up to end with the boy's right foot.

The Yang Wei meridian stands for Biosphere, Jupiter, liver, solar wind, Super Conductor, sprouting, and Spring Equinox. This meridian begins with Your right lung as the inner light and power gathering from Your Left brain to cross with Yin Qiao at Your throat. It then interconnects with the boy's brain and down to his left foot, and ends with Your Liver. Your two lungs represent humanly the kidney and reproductive power.

The Yin Qiao meridian represents Hydrosphere, North Star, Mercury, Moon, spleen, meteorites, solar wind, rainfall or snowfall, and Summer Solstice. This meridian begins with Your right foot as the reflex or refection from Your left foot. It then goes up through Your right leg, enters and crosses with Yang Qiao at Your perineum. After the crossing, it enters Your left-side body trunk to connect with Your spleen, and further up to end with the girl's right foot.

The Yin Wei meridian stands for Lithosphere, Sun, Venus, spring water and mist, earthquake as well as the leap of tornado, stomach, and Fall Equinox. This meridian begins at Your left lung as the inner conscious awareness of light and time from Your Right brain down to Your throat before it start to manifest physically. It then interconnects with the girls' brain and down to her left foot, and ends with Your pancreas.

Now, Your Lungs and legs form the first loop, Girl's brain and Boy's legs form the second loop, and the Boy's brain and Girl's legs for the third loop. These three loops are initiated with Chong or Thrust and Dai or Belt meridians internally in You, mirrored by Du and Ren meridians externally between Your twin flames. Chong meridian begins with Your Crown, then it goes down to Your Stomach, and ends at your Tailbone. Dai meridian begins with Your perineum, the earth's electric lock room, it travels up through Your trunk, and ends with Your hands. In our human sense, Your divine Chong and Dai represent arousal of the heat and sperm, and the steamed and ovulating egg respectively. Du governs the frontal chest of Yours and Ren protects your back chest. They become the physical and energetic womb of Your twin flames.

Finally, Your heart generates two meridians, Pericardium and Triple Warmer, which in turn becomes in humans the Du and Ren meridians, which further give birth to Yang Ming (stomach and large intestine), Tai Yang (bladder and small intestine), and Shao Yang (Triple Warmer and gallbladder) as one triple group, and Jue Yin (pericardium and liver), Tai Yin (lung and kidney) and Shao Yin (heart and spleen) as the other triple group.

Localization—Pathological Onset

The complete gestation of twin siblings takes about the same length of Venus' orbiting loop, or about 237 earthly days, or roughly a month shorter than our gestation process now. But this does not include their initial conceptive journey, where the twin flames enter from Your forehead to brain and then Your throat to heart. Nor does this period represent their early cosmic traveling journey following after You. The actual indwelling in Your brain for the twin siblings is 6 months, from the Spring Equinox to Fall Equinox. This is how they bring universally balanced energies into their physical beings.

The most detailed energetic influx begins when the boy's Yang Wei and the girl's Yin Qiao are merged together. In Your Angelic Mother's body, the Yin Qiao Meridian beginning at the left lung reveals the universal expansive charge, or the materialization of the super-conductive charge, through the explosion of gas. While the Yang Wei Meridian deals with the marks of time, the echoing distillation of the aftermath of a super-conductive wave. The scientific word for the super-conductive charge is also the religious term for super-consciousness, or I AM statement. In that sense, the Yang Wei Meridian beginning in Angelic Mother's right lung deals with the image of I AM, or the cosmic wavelength, or light-years.

As we know, the brainpower of Angelic Mother, is the harmonic holography. It is where the Yang Qiao of that invisible charge fires up internally, and Yang Wei sustains that charge: the state of ready to be or going about, externally. Oppositely, Yin Qiao is the actual expression of heat, or the outward manifestation of inertia, of that super-conductive charge, the power of I AM. While Yin Wei represents the contractive receiving from the aftermath of expressive heat. Yang Qiao is the downward pouring of that eternal lightning rod to the poles of the earth. And Yang Wei is the polarized force that is marching from poles towards the equatorial center of Earth, the expression of jet streams.

These two work simultaneously with the explosive power of the Earth, or that quaking power charged from the centralized positive charge, the power of Yin Qiao, as well as wave frequencies upon the surface of the Earth, the power of Yin Wei. The electrical heat contained inside the mass of the Earth gives birth to the power of Yin Qiao, while the equatorial power, a combination of self-rotation and orbiting gravity, gives forth the power of Yin Wei. Whether it would be rain or snow, which is the contractive, or downward expression of Yin Qiao, the representation is of expunging gas that began in the universe.

The polarized interaction completes the chest power of Angelic Mother, the power of the dodecahedron, which is the holographic expression of earth between the dual poles of Earth on the one end and dual expressions of heat and radioactivity on the other.

On the opposite of Your body, the eternal flow of the octagonal wave-like infinity is the mirror of universal make-believe: that eternal change and transition of Universal Body, or Godhead. This, Your brainpower is the dome of universe. As this power is grounded and materialized through the interaction of two stars on both sides, one of them we call Sun, and the middleman, Saturn. Saturn is like two men shaking their hands and making their agreement on what to give and take, and how to do about their own business. Between these two stars (the Sun and the heart of Draco) on your shoulders and Saturn in between, the Godhead power is nailing down. Your throat is now chocked with silent deeds. The nailing point of Godhead becomes now the lightning rod of your central lower body, a combination of stomach and intestine, with the handle serving as bladder situating above Your pelvic cliff.

Giving birth and taking care of the twin siblings of Yours, who are the dual images of You, Your dodecahedral chest is divided and unified through Your silent song-lines or lyrics in Your Heart, separated and united through tones and pitches of Your channeling songs. The silent song-lines or lyrics are the true expression of holographic Earth, while the tones and pitches are the interactive waves between expansive evergreen (ever-growing) Jupiter and forever laughing, charging and firing Mars.

For You are Divine, but for Your twin children it is temporary. Your assimilation is their differentiation and Your holiness and wholesomeness are their hole-ness and awesomeness. Your unified expression is their pathological trails. This pathological journey begins with Your very lungs. Like our human kidneys, Your lungs exercise the giving and taking of all lively forces and nutrients for their vital growth.

Your shocked charge through Your left foot becomes forever their search for the aroused charge and rejection at large. And Your right foot felt waving stance becomes their eternal fearful escape or numbed denial.

Equally, when You send the Yin Qiao power, the indwelling power of Saturn, into the girl's head through Your left lung, she searches forever for the brain-fired charge on the one hand and is drunk and hallucinated on the other. When You send the Yang Wei power, the dualistic expression of Sun on one side and Star on the other, into the boy's head through Your right lung, he becomes lazy and winning on the one hand and egoistic and procrastinating on the other. They do not know this, until they are out and individually, because during their entire gestation period, they are in the state of union of love. They are apart from one another physically but they grow out of Your divine love, that holographic expression of dodecahedron, which is the four-cornered expression of their love.

Between "I am drunk" and "want to be fired up over my head" for the girl, "I am good but homeless" on the boy's side, thus pathology begins, invisibly. Visibly, they are innocent and helpless, but invisibly, they are addicted to food, water and air on their top and sexual union at their bottom.

The moment the twin siblings are born and out in the world, Your four universal channels, or psychic meridians, change into four seasons: Yang Qiao for the Three months of winter, Yang Wei the three months of Spring, Yin Qiao for the three months of Summer, and Yin Wei the three months of Autumn. Their essential qualities are Yang Qiao/Winter Solstice, Yang Wei/ Spring equinox, Yin Qiao/Summer Solstice, and Yin Wei/Fall Equinox.

Individually, Yang Qiao takes care of the Bladder, Stomach and Gallbladder meridians. Yang Wei watches out for the Small Intestines, Large Intestines, and Triple warmer. Yin Qiao controls the Kidney, Spleen and Liver Meridians. Yin Wei sends out Heart, Pericardium, and Lung Meridians.

Gender wise, the boy is good at two sets of Yang while the girl is powerful with the two sets of Yin. The boy looks handsome from his back, while the girl looks beautiful in her front. They are both left for good to their left foot, but to get things right, their right foot has to be internalized.

Structural Matrixes

Xin Le Qu is all about the content and meaning of this book. It is my heavenly assignment and earthly demonstration. It is also the structural arrangement of the meridians in which the Holy Grill produces and animates, seduces and cannonades, reduces and empties. When the Holy Grill or Purple Heart is the sliced pace, which is called space, out of that single, complete and cohesive dot, the knots begin to produce nuts. The empty heart allows the joyous leap to climb and fly, so that the hollowing space can be filled, and empty cell can be spelled.

The momentum within the single space of that dot is the Holy Fire, or the initial spark of the universe. When this spark stands to park, the dark barks at the whistles that are echoed by the empty Silent Sound. This Silent

Sound waves and echoes as dualistic vibration of Universe, which is the birth of double helixes or the holographic dome. The mark becomes the ark asking all the questions of being and behaving. This is the super conductive and conducive Sound of the universe.

This Sound is structured by twenty vibratory strings, which are called meridians. Among them, four represent the wheels of nature, just like the annual wheels of the Earth orbiting around the Sun. Two of them are Equinoxes and the other two are Solstices. The two Equinoxes are the balanced S inside the Circle as well as the Circle itself in the construction of Taiji. As the dual S's move up and down, in and out, backward and forward, two distinctive faces are produced. These two faces are the dual eyes of the Taiji. While two S's are the twin serpents.

In the human body, the two S's are the complete loop of the spinal vertebrae. From brainstem to the center of thoracic vertebra, which cuts between fifth and sixth, is one S. And from sixth thoracic vertebra to the end of tailbone, which is surrounded by pelvis, is another S. In actual structure, there are three loops moving around this dual S; the 22 bones in the skull is one, the 24 ribcage bones are another one, and six pelvic bones are the third one. The bones in the head ends with the brainstem, the rib bones are jointed by sternums, and pelvic bones are internally locked by five sacral and four tail vertebrae.

When the two serpents are enclosed, the yin body representing the black half and the yang body representing the white half are merging together as a full circle outside, but divided and unified inside. In a two-dimensional picture, two dots appear. These two dots are the two-dimensional representation of the two eyes. Each serpent has two eyes, one side yin and the other side yang. Although there are four eyes within the union of twin serpents, the actual demonstration speaks only of two. Because yin and yang eyes within the dual serpents are the same.

Anatomically, the two dots, one black and the other white, are the total expression of the brain and abdomen. In detail, the white dot is the gut brain, or Yellow Court, while the black dot is the pineal gland. In terms of total structural functioning, the two dots are six dots. In the brain they are left and right hemispheres. In the chest they are the masculinity and femininity, and in the abdomen they are the sperm and egg. These dual S's are in fact one in totality, which is represented by the Thrust meridian or Chong Mai. The single Chong completes three worlds, which are the three parts of the body. Each is a mystic field. In Chinese this mystic field is called Dantian. The brain is Upper Dantian. The chest is Middle Dantian. The Abdomen is called Lower Dantian. The dot in the Chinese character Dan represents the pineal gland in the brain, the Thymus gland in the chest, and gut in the abdomen respectively. When these three dots are completed, they become three treasures, or San Bao in Taoism.

These two dots in the formation of Taiji is, actually, the four wheels we have discussed above. These four wheels are the four directions that four eyes are watching and moving, as each wheel controls 90° of the circle. In meridians, these four wheels are represented by two Qiao meridians and two Wei meridians. The two Qiao meridians are Yin Qiao and Yang Qiao, while the two Wei meridians are Yin Wei and Yang Wei.

In *I Ching*, these four wheels are called four great images or Si Xiang.

— —	— —	— —	———
— —	— —	———	———
LaoYin	ShaoYin	ShaoYang	LaoYang
(old yin)	(young yin)	(young yang)	(old yang)

Shaoyin and Shaoyang are interchangeable, depending whether you are reading from top to bottom, from bottom to top, or from left to right, or right to left. Just remember that the broken line represents yin and the solid line represents yang.

Shaoyang	Shaoyin		
— —	———	— —	———
— —	— —	———	———
Jueyi	Taiyin	Taiyang	Yangming

In the structure of the twelve meridians, the two names are different. Laoyin is replaced by Jue Yin and Laoyang is replaced by Yangming. Equally, Shaoyin is completed by four different meridians, two in each set, and shaoyang is also completed by four different meridians, two in each set. All together they are twelve in total, or paired as twenty-four. These twenty-four paired meridians are structurally, the twenty-four ribcage bones.

Shaoyang   Shaoyin

Jueyi   Taiyin   Taiyang   Yangming

In actuality, the circle of the Taiji (in the west, known primarily as the yin-yang symbol) represents the circle of no Moon, which is also the echoing wave of that initial Sound produced from union and separation. Dai Mei is the meridian of this circle.

In that sense, the circle is the external circulation of four wheels, because from sunrise to sunset, and from no Moon to full Moon, there are a total of four rings or circles. The four rings are the completion of the four meridians described: two Qiao meridians and two Wei meridians. The two Qiao meridians are represented by one Du Meridian, because the circle or size of the Sun remains the same. The two Wei meridians are represented by one Ren Meridian, because the actual circle or size of the Moon also remains the same.

When two dots inside the Taiji and one circle completing the Taiji work together, eight are produced. Structurally, they are the eight skull bones in the head, and the eight meridians described above.

Structural Pyramid of I Ching

Ever since I laid my eyes on the books of *I Ching*, writers and authors on the subject state clearly that the first formation of *I Ching*, after the "invention" of eight Trigrams by Your first and only son, is Lian-shan-yi, meaning *Connective Mountain I Ching*. Lian or connective or successive refers to at least two or more (or so I believe) mountains, sky, clouds and eyes linked together.

The arrangement of the *I Ching* is unknown to both writers and readers in present time. Either it is so sacred that it cannot be written down linguistically or scribed visually, or it was out grown when the *Earth House I Ching* and King Wen's version was developed from it.

The worst case was that all the written material was burned by the First Yellow Emperor Qin. It was either because the information was too powerful that it could not be used as a ruling mechanism to enslave people, or because he did not want intellectuals to grip their hands upon it.

Since history only runs its victorious line, it records only useful information or personalized confirmation. What is the gossip of daily news? Very little and minute and so touching and profound that it is beyond anything a record could contain, any scripture could color, or any description could tongue.

Nothing found externally, I did not want to give it up. The only choice left is to dig and plow within. Around the spring of 2002, I had a dream one night. In the dream I visited a mountainous temple construed with cement. At the foot of this mountain was a cement paved road circulating towards the north peak. Inside my brain, I was told certain monks and nuns were dwelling there but it was very remote and difficult to approach.

On the side of the road were two cement-carved images: one is an infinity circle, or a sleeping 8, and the other is a standing cube or uplifting square (3-dimensional). Inspired by these two images, I tried and successfully I reconstructed the structural pyramid of *I Ching*, where You hibernated and then disappeared physically.

In this arrangement, each role is an infinity circle and a sleeping 8. From one end to the other, their top and bottom positions were switched back and forth between any given two roles existing horizontally and turning their head and tail up or down in each given hexagram.

The overall structure of *Pyramid I Ching* is an upward triangle. With the Earth hexagram on the left side serving zero and the Heaven hexagram accounting as 14 on the right side, they come close together and rise up toward their centralized peaking point. Altogether, there are eight roles and

15 columns.

I fold the triangle from the top, between the fourth and fifth roles. Then I fold on both sides towards the middle. There it is, a cube with four triangles. Restructuring this cube, it becomes a tetrahedron.

Afterwards, I tried energetically and physically squeezing the standing triangle on both ends. One side of it was Yours and the other, Your Invisible Husband. As they come close, the entire structure becomes the standing square. The centering columns move down until the central column becomes the standing nail, smoky chimney and elevating tower.

I think from my heart and gut I revealed what the *Pyramid I Ching* is, and how it was constructed: How to receive the seven triads or trinity of the seven planets, or seven colors of rainbow formation. In order to do so, the vase and base are my study case.

CHAPTER 14:
THE MILK LOAD UPON SILK ROAD

The Capitalized Birth Dam (Holy Birthday)

Dear Angelic Mother, if I come, and return to You as one of those twin babies delivered out of Your chest and arms into a bay as the ultimate bees (babies) of land and sea, I would know that light is Your husband, and my Father.

Dear all biological mothers, after your husbands abandon you willingly or subconsciously, your children flush the love out of you and dry up your milk load and fry your kneeing boat, you are left to search for the original silk road of love transmitted from the very angelic mother of all humans, toward your fathers' Father, and your mothers' Husband: Light.

Dear Deathless Mother, after you hold in your web-like arms the last breath, which is the everlasting love of you, you gather their best wishes, highest performances, biggest achievements and most glorious victories of all beings on Earth--humans and animals, birds and sea lives, organism and mechanism—like fruit flies, dragonflies, butterflies, angelic flights, and deathless spirits, into your heart which is the Silk of Light, songs of heart, lyrics of love, spectrums of light, and space of the universe.

From this triad motherhood, I knock on my falling birth, my nose for incestuous breath, and nap with my eternal presence. As my birth declines from my womb home (abdomen of those absently dosed men) and angelic dam (armpit of that universal armory mouth), my ankles are angled towards the upper side down Y, where my two legs and their toes march along the trail of velocity with vicious victories on one side and visiting victims on the other. When the victories are glorified toward the image of V-shaped golden dome above the angelic dam, the tail of light spreads the solar ray as it penetrates my perineum point, which is also my prenatal and perennial point. The heat released from this point shoots down to activate the water bubble points beneath my feet, and into the electrical pool of the Earth. This electrical pool turns on my watery wools (nerve ends) plugged from my feet, as her electrocuted produce becomes my foot chains capsulated by mineral soils and advertised by dusty toys, and her elevated heat drums my water-proved temple and sweats my temperament like a fool's chin. The electrical pool tells me that the water of tear cannot separate itself from the water of love, and the elevated heat warms me warns me that the river of love flows to merge into or diverse from the oceanic love.

When the oceanic love pours out her misty clouds, my brain is fogged with murky thoughts of those universally unwanted wishes, and my tongue is dogged with gasping heat gossiping the same old news. The blue sky is always clear, though white clouds veil through its tranquil skin. The mind is forever as clear and tranquil as the blue sky, but thoughts flooded with flying dreams and returning wishes contaminate the membranes of milk of love. Before the milk of love returns to the angelic mother longing for her silk light, the biological mother walks her silk road from sunrise to sunset, carrying her sick load from east to west lest best chest left is next to the nest rest. There is an urge for running but her abdomen keeps loading and unloading weight, her chest is tropically trooped, and her brain is vaulted either by daily temperance or monthly climate. Months and years, pools and ears, she has been trapped, tortured, molested, raped, taped, scared, torn apart, and worn out.

Finishing all things clean and thorough around the umbilical loop, with the help of horizontal troop, the biological mother renounces herself as the white mother: the wisdom grandmother. Upon achieving this state, her 35 years of biological duty reports its productive journey towards the electrical pools of the Earth. She receives directly, the hot flesh symbolized as heat flush, including hate rush and late gush, during menopause (men-no-pulse). This hot flesh or heat flush is actually hot and fresh, inviting her to know the divine path of original motherhood: the power of self-pregnancy.

Turning the trauma and nightmare of mid-life crisis and PMS (per man a second) syndromes into to a returning journey, joke for our honey, her feet are no longer wired with children, bounded by grandkids, trapped by men, and wrapped by theories; but are fired with spiritual awakening, eternal joy, and overwhelming bliss. The heat electrocuting her nerves and curves is the thankful message delivered by earth mother for her final motherhood graduation.

She is back to light, as how the angelic mother, her official boss, started in the first place. Instead of fearing the loss of dutiful and the responsible power of motherhood, she is free now to see how she has grown and matured along this path. All the previous names, like girl, lover, wife, mother, woman, and widow, and the labels such as prostitute, bitch, concubine, whore and witch switching the itches from aggravated thoughts to agricultural feelings in the midst of nanny, babysitter, dishwasher, cashier, nurse, secretary, teacher, movie star, celebrity, princess, first lady and queen, are gone. All she is now is the fire of heat and the power of light. What she has been fired up with during the pubic stage and how she was fired from the menopausing (men you poor thing) job finalize the double fire. Heat is way better than meat, and light is way more powerful than men. Lava cooks the red heated fire, and water cools the white burned light.

Armpit Sweat

Before her sweat swims into eyes like morning dews it numbs her third eye to deflate ego, and thumbs her nostril to wake it into reality like men who are punctured with agitation and punished by their own frustration. The mother's armpits are soaked with unwanted tropical heat and unclaimed angelic burden. She does not realize that the sweat from her armpits are tears for the Angelic Mother after Her landing posture was graved by the waves of Earth to degrade Her wings and degenerate Her toeless tail. She does not remember as a mother how she would be in the light dress working as the Angelic Mother.

Born in a heavenly palace, grown with light, and crowned with love, the Angelic Mother is the delight of heaven, and joy of Father. Bored by planetary trinity created between Father-light and Mother-love, the Angelic Mother becomes the final witness of how the holy water works in the universe through an organic being. She is assigned to create surfing creatures among stars, planets, and moons. One of the locations is our Earth stationed for our Moon and positioned around our Sun.

Reclaiming My Twin Flames

It has been 44 years now since my spirit was wrapped by my

parental codes, fabricated by Chinese cultural mode, and slaved and saved by Western bode. The twin images are forever our struggling duality and harmonic individuality. Most of the time, instead, our spirits are independently fertilized inside our biological mother's abdomen, covered by her food-loaded stomach and wrapped around by her womb-swamped intestines, so that we are in between the tests and testicles, and an intentional empty gut and intense adrenal fire.

When the beaming light becomes the enraged heat, and the eternal love becomes the conditioned interaction, rage and fear replace the watchful presence and joyful bliss. Sun and Moon see and know very well that the earthly climatic expression, from earthquakes to volcanoes, floods to droughts, belongs to her own emotional territory. The same truth holds to our own personal emotional agitations. The key is to watch with our insightful mind, and feel with our distinctive gut. We would know that fear is the original residue left forever by our Angelic Mother's landing friction and our biological mother's unknown concern. That rage is the contribution of biological men helpless towards their single mother and useless father.

When the third eye, that woodpecker's most favorite hole and priest's most desirable target, is numbed by the vocal cord ruled by the local lord, the crown is rounded by unwanted thoughts and undigested ideals, the temple of the body stations the immobile prison, and the church of love receives the tip of a fingering sword. When the umbilical cord is forever in the hand's of our parental wish and demand, and under the control of our ancestral knife and cultural roof, we have no idea where the free lunch comes from and how the freedom lands, we have no clue how to think or speak, and we have no glue to hue, pursue, secure, and reconnect our birth trail with our disarmed angelic veil. We are left with the vote to devote, the disk to discipline, and the site to decide.

With the burden of Angelic Mother, my arms express Her wing-cut frustration restrained from the earthly electrical grids; and with the indefinite uncertainty of biological mother, my mind becomes sicker than ever, like a rotten log. My physical being feels thicker, as if my baby time's unknown sickness coalesces with the world's helpless thickness to twist my muscular fibers and nerve hemps into a tight rope.

At this point, my light awareness, away from heavy thoughts and idealistic wine, tells me to go and drink from the holy water inside the tight rope above my wheeling thighs and turning hips. The dope fermented inside the rope is truly the hope, as it sends me the safe signal and provides me with a peace symbol. The hope is the silk of love producing insight through the dark space of my brain accompanied by the moonless night. At the time my hope speaks for the Moon's dope, she crowns her faint ring around my temples as my king (monkey), flares the gold inside my gut for her own darkness, and tranquilizes the red wet heat toiling through my perineum point as her own gravitational point. The Sun sets its red smiling lips upon the rising Moon and the Earth darkens the leftover daily heat with the Moon's dangling arch. The Moon's ring reflects then the eternal dot and ever-present knot, and my king reflects the gloriously glued regal trying to regain the Father's position of universal Ring Leader. Sun is the Ring Leader of Earth, and the ring around Moon's face is not the crown in my head, but the cyclical monthly pain around my hips, inside my sacral holes, and through my tailing toes.

This upside down crown forces me to go back to my childhood memory, my birth memoir, and my conceptive membrane, so I can be free from the gender of male's ends and female's bends, the temperature of masculine liar and feminine fire, and climate of intuitive feeling behind cognitive thinking.

The moonlight now guides my pilgrimage, tours her reflected sites, and tutors me her deflecting power of insight (the gift of thunder and the tide of ocean upon the power of now). I am able to converse my hope of silk love with the gifts of others' love, till I reach the point to Jerusalem, away from the Nile's Delta containing nice data, where the nine is rested with the pyramid above but arrested by mummies below. The golden dome above the pyramid is forever shining, but the blood of sacrifice never stops its droplet. The mummies wrapped with durable hemps and preserved with aromatic herbs remind me of all mothers with their woolen wombs and sacramental tombs. The mummies enjoy the delight (their Lover) under the protection of heavy stones and dark night. The mothers rejoice with the dust (their children) wrapping around their knees and burdens loading their milk. Together, they materialize you as a must of matter and then declare it is all yours to mature the worst than nothing else matters. Each end of their motions promotes your bending point by demoting your endless point, till your existence is a meaningless point upon endless joints.

The meaningless point is the dotted dust from the light point, and the endless joints map the water-dropped space of all existing matters. When the light point becomes white matter, seeds are produced. When the water droplet is flooded, blood senses the scene without knowing how much the sin can pollute the magic scenery. If dust were sin, spirit would be sinned inside of the soul. If a water droplet sinks, the mind thinks about spinning the wheels above the floating waves and exchanging paves. Flood produces disaster and blood clogs up as trauma. Only when the flood is flat, the sea is glad. Only when the blood is thin, water retains her original plasma as the divine charisma.

By the time the seasonal flood and seasoned blood are mixed up, the flatland is structured with clayed bricks and framed with stoned carvings. The fear of flood enjoys the mountain slide, which is opposite to what Noah was climbing. The fear of blood creates more deadly wars, only to see that the virgin never exists beyond puberty and virtue never stations well outside publicity. The brain is smashed inside the mud of that earthly drinking mug and dreading bug, and sword is pierced inside a soldier's (sold to die as pigments of national cloth) heart devoted to the motherland as a virgin lover. Volcano enjoys then the burial ground, and the national flag waves inside the boarding line echoing the national anthem to command the profound (no refund) victory and recommend the productive (no ducking) factory.

Disaster disappears now, only short lived, and carving the skins and painting the fabrics are meant to enjoy the chores chewing the chair sitting upon chaos. Victory is now the history, and glory is clueless boring. By applying the legal manner, you are hungry for a bagel and thirsty for the regal. The Grace will trace your journey of lineage through your storage, till your legal manner faces your regal mannerism, your race is laced with your immortal pace, and your verbal phrases are sentenced into quotable articles. The art gluing cosmic particles are now the official article, the artistic statue above your articulating status scales the glorious artifact, and the established value calculates the statistical menu.

My Received Landing Angle

Aside from reading historical books and enjoying forbidden records, my inner self is taught by a sinking idea (maybe a stinking thought for you) from above that the angle inside the V-shaped golden dome is 72° degrees, and this has been confirmed by how I measured my tough mandible and rough pubic bones. This is my downloaded idea or thought that reveals any angle other than 90° degrees must result in nine when their digital joints or decimal points (two or more) are joined or added together. With this 72 which is nine (7 + 2) on top, 144 (half of the remaining circle divided by "I" from "Y" sums as 9, and 54 (a point within equal lateral triangle), is also a nine.

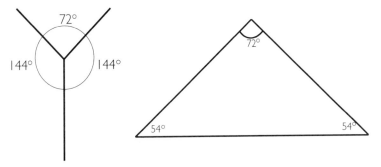

This V-shaped angle is the victory of light, and a victim of falling into birth, where the golden light is flooded down from the joining point of V to form "I" line below "Y" nine. The V above my crown is always there, providing me with enough of the golden light, but the joint of my throat, connecting breath and water, food and love, locks my inner V (the triangular space of my throat as the landing point and fontanels as the escalating points) down to my solar panel charged perineum point right between my thighs. The perineum point points to either my knees below as its gazing points toward dusty land, or appoints my gut below the sternum and knob (between 7th and 8th thoracic vertebras) as the zooming points into the pure land. The dusty land connects the Gobi Desert and Yellow River with the Red Sea and River Nile. The pure land points at my liver talking to my gallbladder, telling it to dive into my heart stationed above my spleen. When those two zooming points land on my lungs, my arms would automatically point at my thighs orbiting my knees and rotating my feet. The femurs inside my thighs rarely listen to my personal conviction, as they play with the lock of my perennial point by squeezing out the immortal pleasure and squishing in the immobile fear.

This activity really stiffens my neck, cracks my head, and dries up my brain. From being active to becoming further articulating, the prism changes into prison as I lock myself inside my personal and collective jail with all the invisible nails gliding through my experiential trails. In turn, I digest and recycle all collective veils below the night bell (where the dumb arrests the numb and the tomb relaxes the bomb) ringing the sound of love from the sky and springing the milk of love from the mountains.

The V above my crown spells the dual victory between Moon and God where the Sun is skinned and slaved. The V inside my brain expels the dual factory where my spirit is jailed by uncultured emotion and imprisoned by anti-political reaction. Angel captures half of the 72, which is 36, so that earth can control twelve and human productiveness enjoys the rest, 23. Plato recorded the rest 36 very well in his writing. King Wen described dutifully how a man should rise above his conscious darkness and brighten mother's dark matter. As such, 36 became both the chapter arrangement for Plato, and hexagram representation for King Wen.

Historically, when a mother was able to dance, the 72° degreed power above her light crown, through her milk jaw and below her birth canal, reflected the original cosmic blue blueprint: the double helixes of time and space, matter and force, way above man's genetically controlled and corrupted double helix. But when men began to scribe the motherly and angelic beauty and write the victory of capturing and domesticating the beauty, the very 72° degreed power becomes the 72 names of God, according to Kabalistic tradition, or the 72 caves below the Kun Lun Mountain Range and Himalayan Mountain Range, according to Taoist tradition.

Below this dualistic V, each of my shoulders holds a weight of 144, and together they load 288 ponds of waterish delights below either the biting and chewing mandible bone, or the flushing and flooding pubic bone. When the "I" cuts through V above my crown and lands below my trunk, it splits my inner self into dualistic beings as my stomach stores all the useful information temporally before being flushed out or recycled in. As I declare for this "I," the egoistic eye lens towards the splendid fashion by zooming into the magnificent mansion, where I see all the kings are whitened with hair, ringed with anguish blood, or relaxed inside their immobile chairs.

The chairman now is the cheerleader who keeps chilling down the fear and chewing the dare. When the cheerleader becomes pregnant with the dust of the dare, she becomes the queen of night, daunting all the daring parties caring for impersonal fairs and declaring from incestuous affairs. Being victimized, I have to digest humbly all these declared debris inside the collective umbrella where the human consciousness is not veiled by glistening prisms, nor bailed out by daily light.

To know that prison is safer than a mansion, and jail is more affordable than constructing the Capital Building and establishing Capital Punishment, I am able to exercise all I can to the degree that my face becomes whitened with a mustache which tells me that ache is a must need and that the acreage besides the remote village hides the mustard seed. So I ache for the must as I age away from the lust, till the acreage around me becomes the eulogy reciting all means and changes so that my chance to speak is the euphoric glance advancing the cosmic stance and enhancing the nomadic romance.

When a king punishes me because of my disobedient behavior toward his egoistic crown and my careless damage done to his gold-varnished mansion and fenceless territory, the King in the sky, my Father as well as my king's Father, tells me that my king on earth enjoyed too much of His passion, and my king inside of me rejoice with His Mansion. This King, the God, says that I am innocent by birth, innovative by curse, and innocuous by major towards finishing the degree toward obtaining nature. I have been always delightful towards light, watchful towards Sun, and audible towards my inner thought. Even I have died many a time, timed by youth and news, birth and dews, the final time is still half in control of my hand (home plus host) and half being contracted in the kingdom of heaven.

Before I landed on earth, my head is down, and my legs surviving from conception to birth beg their victory out of my tail and sacral bones so that they can exercise freedom away from my dualistic control. By the time I was able to crawl, stand and walk, the Y below my marching legs do not listen to or obey the Y above my screaming begs for escaping from the mega negativities.

So I was granted with two Ys: one for my wife assisting the assassin holding a love knife stabbing my beloved life, and the other for my unreasonable why spinning the God's given wine within the earthly seasoned mine. What is supposed to be mine becomes the wild but mild explosive mine discharging the red revolution and smoking off the blackout. When the revolution asks the blackout to splash her red tent, the black ass refuses to spray the black smoke below the red roof varnished by the red tent. God then grabs my left knee positioning for the right need and says quietly but silently that my deer wife plus my beloved life are His wine, His left handicapped Y is my mind, and His rights to handling the why is my mine. I am His handicapped knee and niece, and I am His aguish dust upon languish lust. His Must is half in fabulous dust and half towards my fantastic lust. He causes me to explode my mind as His sapping wine and He recourses His loss as the earthly boss.

The earth produces and recycles seasonal seeds between spring and fall, as my brain produces and recycles reasonable seeds between need and deed. When the spring rises high above the mountain peak, her installed sprinkle along the tall spring will fall with a free ride along with the downsized wind and light from the Sun. The Sum reuses the Sun's leftover summer as the course by reducing the sons as the diminishing loss. The gravity greets the graveside, as tombs host the dead corpuses shedding the descending spirits. When I drink the message from those ascended spirits as the holy wine from the other world, they told me that light produces seed and is delightful about wisdom matured from the seed, that love is the deadly poison refining the breathless lotion. Each time I think, act, dream or hope, one side of my Y goes to heaven like branches and leaves above my body trunk, and the other side of my Y coil and toil with the roots and soils below my feet. The tree of life retreats from the tree of now, and the tree of love receives the treat from the tree of knowledge. When life is now, the knowledge is numb and love is the thumb. But when love speaks through knowledge, details perfect retails, and satisfaction declares all standardized tests standing in the dark and downsizing the luck.

With these two Ys, actualized by one "V" and one "I", I can dig the hole into the dome of my appointed pyramid, seal the revelations of my physical construction, and play with all alphabetic letters extracted from my contradictive cites. The Pyramid tells the parameter to cause no more harm; yet the remaining residues of alphabetic letters and numbered mummies farm each coming flesh and departing soul, to the degree they cannot distinguish heaven from hell, because both Ys are hosted by Hs, one for their empty body trunk seeking for help, and another for their empty coffin trunk sinking into hell. With the third H for head looking for the fourth H which heads towards home from a hospital visit and hospice care, my sickness feels the vomiting sea throwing up an ocean, and my thickness embraces the trinity--heaven above the mount, hell beneath my value, help along the road--where home without dome dumps all the eatable (edible) dumplings into the dawn above the town.

The heaven tells me everything is fast (fast in speed or fast without food?), and there is no time to wait (death is now, hell is now, and everything else is still now). Just do it! But hell is saying that she is forever awake for the lake waiting to take a break from the light so she can be with her sister dark parking in the abyss. She is deciding how to utilize her H, among bell, cell, fell, jell, quell, sell, tell, and well. In fact, she simply says that she hosts a lot; and when a lot becomes a lot, many reduce the mass as a log so that Dog can sleep inside the fog, and faith sleeps away the belief. When you log on the hook, you chain yourself. When you log on the web, you are in the chains of beliefs always believing in the facts but rarely delivering the faith with truth along the conviction of Ruth. Hell knows well what a difference faith can dig between fake and faint, fable and cable. When faint reduces the fake into nothing, cable hosts all fabulous fables into parables. Then hell tells you to decide for yourself from this point on. When you say hello, the fake sounds faintly the vague resentment without proper settlement. When you pronounce "aha," violence returns to silence, and violet flights the pilot.

Then my head helped heaven by hampering the hell as the handyman's home, which was where my head had landed initially before my hand could write and circle my initials. With my head when it was bedded in hell, I was rotating with my gut my infantile body a matter of a 90° swing, like landing a stick from a standing position to a resting opposition. But my umbilical cord kept entangling with my helpless rod. Before I knew anything, 8 months were gone, as I was able to grasp my fists above my wrists risking my body to sit my fat or stand on my nail.

Now the nail was spelling the tell without voicing itself through my prenatal point, and selling the bell without drumming my gums outside my lips and tongue. Afterwards, my infantile body was able to stand like a fragile log, or a franchised dog, so that my tail would boss my loss above my feet and toss my head above my throat.

As the day goes by, my standing posture turns either 90° clockwise towards the east to invite the sunrise and invent the artificial gold, or with the same degree but opposite position, counterclockwise towards west, to buy the sunset and bye the day. Mother's milk load is my living temple, and my silk road is my ladder to heaven. When the Sun is up, I am good; and when the Sun is down, I see my gold. The gold buried inside the ground turns out to be the gold buried beneath my stomach, which is gallbladder (god's bladder). After the ground gold is rounded, trade replaces aid. This has never satisfied the hunger of my stomach, which keeps storing the food pleasing the fool above the most precious gold I have never imagined consciously but it has been birthing my imagination out to the world and nurturing my image before I am at my age—God present now.

The Tiding And Tiring Angle

Between milk load and Silk Road, there is an angle guiding the compass (those who come shall pass), gliding my ankles, and dicing my anger, till the point that I am able to free myself from, the need to express myself externally, and wish for others to further suppress me. The compass in me is a form of friend, who is an enlightened being, transmitting me the cosmic schedule from time to time, informing me with knowledge or insight familiar to my spectrum of range. The main character of this compass, or the handle stretching constantly to the poles across the sky above me, is the conscious manage, soul's guidance, or spiritual boss. This individual pertains to the highest conscious state relating to my own inner conscious awareness. When I am puzzled, this compass is a director, a map, a mentor, and a tide for the day or season. At the time my conscious mind is not aligned with the space of heart, or the agitation occurred in the heart takes the mind, this compass is very bossy, to the degree that I have no place to hide or escape, as it ties me up good like a bundle or string. In other word, if I were hungry, this compass would provide me with food and drink as the milk load; but if I was dozed, it had to dope up as the Silk Road. True to myself is the tiring the tide, and true to the point of where the compass moves towards. It is the tithing the title without reciting the vital.

This compass works well with my inner compass programmed before I came to this planet and clothed with flesh. The only difference between my inner compass and this bossing compass outside of my physical existence is that this bossing compass does not obtain a flesh like I do; it is neither as emotionally imbalanced as I am from time to time nor as physically thick and sick as I am conditioned.

This is the process of understanding me without me being mean to me and it took me 24 years of growth and search to come to a place where I know from deep inside of me that is the nail-point-sized landing position and operating staff for me. A nail-sized hole, that is all the space I can afford and deserve to have. This point is so strong and powerful that it nails me right down

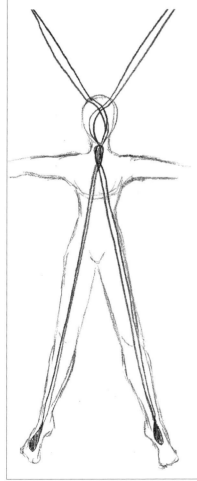

and deep into the earth where I locate myself. This pointing size has a physical location but no name or address attached to it. This pointing direction grounds me and ensures me free mobility as well. This nail-pointed space does not claim personal or national territory, nor blame anyone who is willing to borrow and use it. That is all I need from this world, and from each and every interactive being coming to my life. Such is the power of nail, and such is the space of a point!

Before you expect someone to understand you, you must figure out the place and its angled position under which you stand. Aligned assignment promotes understanding, while misalignment and disconfirmation invite disaster or death. This is called knowing yourself between your landing position and planned opposition. The landing position is God's given rights to you, while the planned opposition watches your walk, deciphers your talk, witnesses your action, and denies your reaction. When you know you are the living boss commandeering for the invisible loss, you can reject but embrace the planned opposition, as you are able to direct your anger towards God' projected angles and rejected angels.

Now your anger is no longer yours to begin or end. It is the power connecting to each and every conscious point, the flour relating to all muscular and organic joints, and the vow releasing all known into nowhere by claiming all on loan as the soul sold alone. This anger is the imitation of thunder ready to shed off the old and invite the new. This anger is the divine expression of self without knowing or acknowledging the self. This anger is the disruption occurred before the corruption occupied, the power fired up before the force would reinforce, divorce or discourse. This anger is the combination of angel's wing swinging inside the light's point and angle's joint where space is love and love is grace.

When you are able to score this point socially or politically, scientifically or artistically, your point refines the anger unable to be expressed by the mass causing all the mess without knowing that less is the yes to the press where excess obsesses the recess, and bless confesses the dress to guess for the tress to dispossess the stress. When your joints are fined from libelous lobby, your temple of a body speaks for all the pleasant beauty and splendid glory fantasized by wish and imagined by dream, yet unable to be achieved by the dead or obtained by the dread. When the dead tides the dread, the history is read, ready to load the milk on the road to silk. The milk tiding the love has no angle but is full of angels, as silk tiring the mind explodes the angry points under-looked by the detector but overlooked by the speculator. The joints are creamed with milk, and points are screened with silk. The milk nourishes your temple, and silk refines your experience into wisdom. The milk load is the tears of Mother, and weight of Ancestor. The Silk Road is the journey from east to west recording all the surgical injuries occurred from birth to death.

On the eastside of the Silk Road, the Y is called Taichi, with "V" being yin and "I" as yang, serving the power of stretching your arms and legs without stressing your moms and her knaps. When the "I" of yang wants to be young, the bed supply of Sun and Moon connects man's chin and woman's shin together to chisel off the cheese and whistle towards the ching as being cheap, and shin without holding onto sleep and shouldering the sheep. Together, Y is the symbolic structure of *I Ching* (not I chick in the sinking charm). Eventually "I" became the symbol of a solid line ____, but it sleeps instead of standing all the time as egoistic I. And "V" became the broken line __ __ so that dual mouths are equally examined with Xs or contaminated with Ys. When the ever present Sun and its light as "I" or "____" converses with the ever change of Moon and her delight as "V" or "__ __", my four skeletal ends extend into Earth's four seasonal bends, and eight is completed to finish all and recycle each.

Along this process, the sunset is awakened from joint-sets, as each silk of love and light is a line serving both as earth's meridian and my human meridian accordingly in order to be away from the thick sick as well as the awake lake.

Thus, the "V" above "Y" is the golden dome of all roofs reaching towards sky proof. This is in turn constructed into eight psychic meridians to complete from conception to birth, and to compete from confession to confirmation. And they are the original telepathic languages and utility tools communicating between Angelic Mother and Her twin babies. As for "I", it completes as 12 regular meridians to begin the milk load from belly button to throat gutter and finish the Silk Road from walking birth to retiring death. So what is behind the Y is the loop or web of heaven to connect from death to

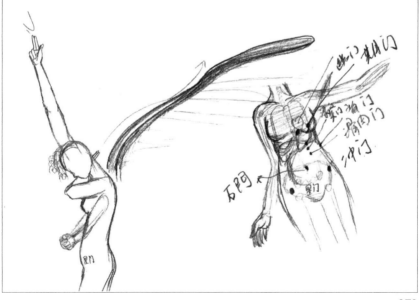

conception, or from conception to death. They are dream and hope, fantasy and reality, here and there, now and then, all the dualistic fashion deriving and returning to the single mansion where the single person is pieced and spare by sin-glued motion, so that the single dope speaks to the single pope, and the single droplet of water delivers the single pamphlet of love.

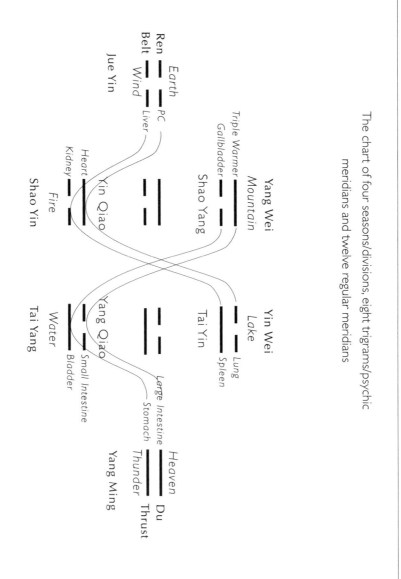

The chart of four seasons/divisions, eight trigrams/psychic meridians and twelve regular meridians

My Trinity

One night without light, around the year of 2002, side-by-side with my ear listening to the divine purpose of my being so I can afford to be away from becoming someone or something, and towards the dear I was desperately searching for aside from the assigned and agreed relationship and helplessly escaping from the rotten meal granted from cotton pill. I saw in my dream I was a little lotus candle-sized white light upon 13th of a Moon's night.

I was OK in that moment, but very short before I formed a triangular relationship between my father's mother's gravesite and going-to-be-my-parents' bed site. The Gravesite told me that my father's mother was buried in the wrong angle (as a result the angel above does not how to take the anger inside of me), and her neck was never stretched before they rested her corpse inside the casket. This dis-angled gravesite and stiff neck became, instead, my basket of life, so I could drop like a droplet of water from the deep sky into my-going-to-be-parents' side-by-side love making position because all their children had occupied the rest of the space on the bed. They were tied to the side, deciding to cite and size me. As such, side to me is always by and in-between all sides as my life has proved to the degree I have now lost all sides when the tide (my name of Tao) enjoys its ride between sky and ocean. I thus made my spiritual contract between two earthly stations--bedroom and headstone--without other spiritual matchmakers' help, to complete my initial triangular dance, my trinity. And it took me 40 years of searching to know this.

Behind this trinity are the Great Wall on one side and the Jerusalem Wall on the other connecting the Silk Road with oriental noodle and acupressure needle teamed up by the spaghetti noodle and speeding Google. When the

silk became the cheaper labor of railroad workers, meridians and needles jump back and forth between Pacific Ocean and Chinese restaurants, so that surgical knife can spare homeopathic care and reasonable doubt can calculate the statistical means with undeniable demeanors. When the silk cloth gets the help of a silver meridian, spoon is happy to swallow up all digestible noodles as useful fork is to deport beings from York to Yoke. The Yellow Court's position is ready, above the courtroom, and aside the courtyard, so that French kiss can crest the rest between legal tongue and regal gum, and triangle love can rest inside the tetrahedron dove.

Not until I have experienced all triangular meanings behind tried means and attributed beans, I did not understand that God is within and above the triangle, and life must be fried twice for the third trial so that triad relationship among conception, birth and death can be awakened and dissolved. Heaven is above hell and humans are frail like trail before wind and thunder, below snow and snore. When the help returns to hemp, temper speaks for temperature, and temple knocks the head out of deadly hell towards deathless heaven so that breath is laced with dear and race is traced back into a deer forgotten in the woods but resting in the forest, and beer fermented inside the frozen heart and justified through the DUI court. Who is courting whom, the drug or alcohol, the freedom of expression or freedom of suppression? When superstition is stationed above super-conductor, the corn is canned inside convict, and court argues between Bible and Rabbi on one side and rabble and babble on the other side. When gravesite delivers the silent lamb, the sizeable lent is rented for the tent, as elbow enables the labels to convince the land to dissolve ambush. "I am the Bush and I am the president" is the voice of ambush until each bushel is oiled with greedy grease without greeting geese.

When Rock and Roll motion returns to Iraq and air-raided Pollution, the land of legal band speaks for the alphabetic fans, so that legal society can control the nomadic variety ranging rock and spurs with books and disputes, and roll and roman with roomful rumors. By the time the noise is silenced by violence, violet is the toilet, and vigilance is above diligence. The hums of the nose rise toward the rum of rose, so that beauty will savor the silence and beast will flavor the violence. When the rocking bones are speaking above the pyramid tomb, the thundering tone is the underlying stone, where the seed wakes from the shell, and spirit walks above the scale. This is the road I walked from my mother's milk load along the Silk Road as I release the sick loads and thick layers till I speak to a black mayor who is more frightening than nightmares. Martin Luther King had a dream, as his all avenues among major cities in the States connect New Orleans and Blues, Chicago land raids the nuclear reactor through Neutron's hair-frightened fracture among scientific community and sincere communions. So that theory and law can blend into milk and love, as man's jaw is free from woman's sore and manhood's law is away from brotherhood's paw.

My remembered formula now matches with milk formula and silk forums, so that my sick gum drinks the love rum and my silk rug bugs the silver drum where the gold is the baby smiling inside all make-beliefs as fake leafs and sick leaves.

The golden dome is the God's home where sacred geometry links all the secret societies into secular variety where sick love is relined with the silk of love knowing only the white light from white cream, and white plain from white-out complain.

The Formula of Milk Load upon Silk Road

I: $Y = V + I$

A: $V = 72°$ of your golden hat or 72 names of God.

B: $I =$ eye for the light and I for the flight.

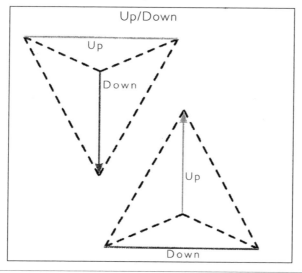

283

2: When Star of David forgets the loss from the boss, it becomes a tetrahedron.

3: The meridian system is the organic symbol of sacred geometry. The rest is your work away from New York and Newport.

4: Six days of creation equals six months of gestation where the guest is in action in all 666.

5: Twenty meridians are a combination of 8 for infinite light and 12 of cyclical flight. When eight ate enough of 12, twin is twinkling above hell saying hello to a fellow following nothing but "I" AM and speaking nothing but the Victory of light.

6: The construction project of two interactive tetrahedrons is interloped by three stages: up and down, left and right, and forward and backward.

7: Each of the six above motions is completed by two meridians, the first completing the space and second pointing from center (or the fourth point) toward the space positioned by the first. For example, the moment one of the Jue Yin meridian finishes the upper or top line of the point-down tetrahedron, is the moment the other Jue Yin meridian moves from the center or the forth point of the point-up tetrahedron toward north or up to form a T completion.

8: The six stages of interactive meridians within tetrahedron in specific or sacred geometry at large represent the six months of gestation period. And the their detailed formulas are as following:

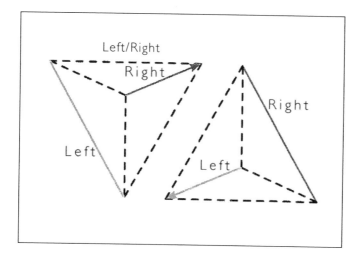

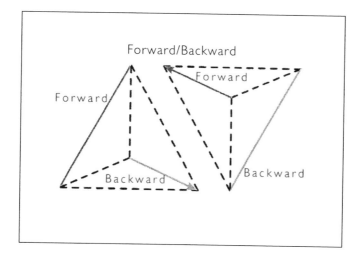

A: Oceanic Fusion:

Up/down: Jue Yin to Shao Yang

Left/right: Tai Yin to Yang Ming

Forward/Backward: Tai Yang to Shao Yin

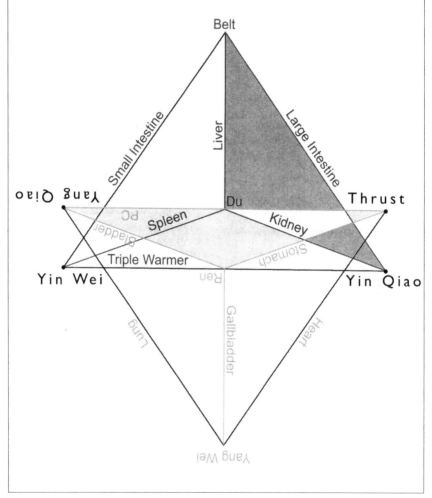

B: Dawn of Initiation:

Up/down: Yang Ming to Tai Yin

Left/right: Shao Yang to Jue Yin

Forward/backward: Shao Yin to Tai Yang

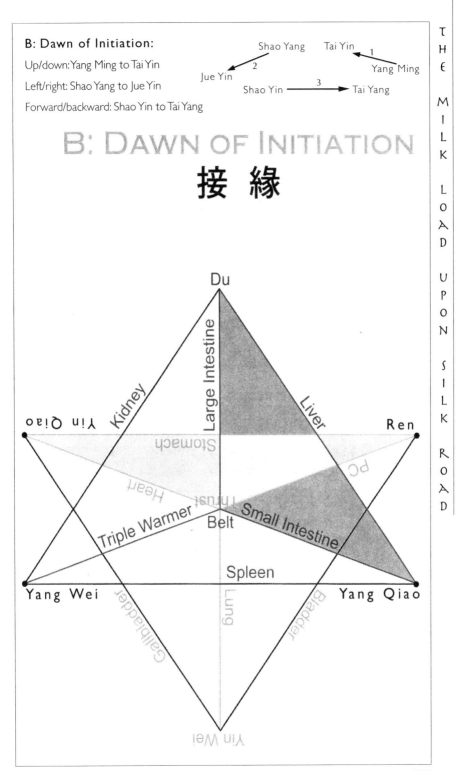

B: DAWN OF INITIATION

接 緣

C: Sacred Union

Up/down: Shao Yin to Yang Ming

Left/right: Jue Yin to Tai Yang

Forward/backward: Shao Yang to Tai Yin

C: SACRED UNION

神 交

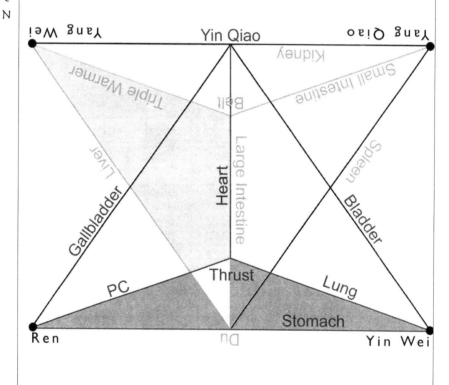

D: Quadrilateral Stance

Up/down: Tai Yang to Jue Yin

Left/right: Yang Ming to Shao Yin

Forward/backward: Tai Yin to Shao Yang

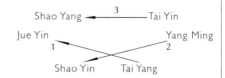

D: QUADRILATERAL STANCE
合 壁

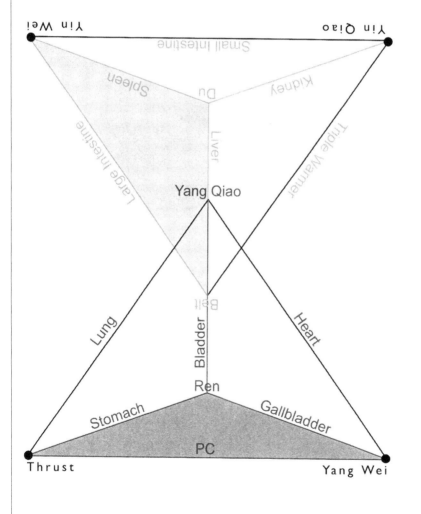

E: Head-on Mirror

Up/down: Tai Yin to Shao Yang

Left/right: Shao Yin to Tai Yang

Forward/backward: Yang Ming to Jue Yin

Shao Yang ←——1—— Tai Yin

Jue Yin ←————3———— Yang Ming

Shao Yin ————2——→ Tai Yang

E: DUAL MIRROR

頭 鏡

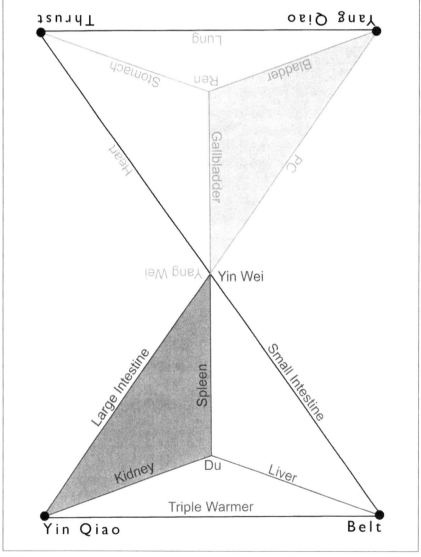

F: Diamond Fruition

Up/down: Sao Yang to Tai Yin

Left/right: Tai Yang to Shao Yin

Forward/Backward: Jue Yin to Yang Ming

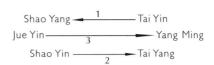

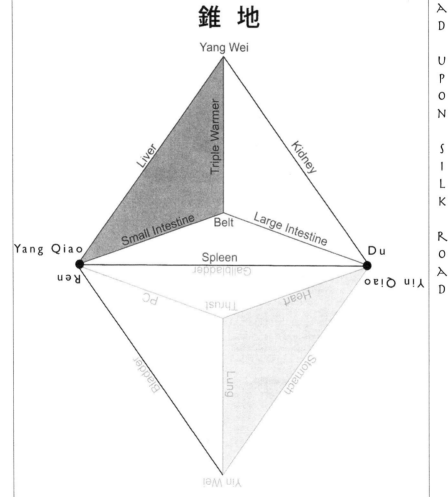

F: DIAMOND FRUITION

錐 地

When my brother, sister and I were younger, we used to shout random phrases at each other to try to inspire laughter. Or rather, I would. Amongst the many names and objects and ideas were "mooka-fish," "schaPING!!" and, one that stuck, "eleventy-four." There are, of course, random sounds that pop up in my head. It was not until years later that I realize, it is the sacred number: 114 that transmitted itself to me through a moment of impulse.

CHAPTER 15:
PASSING MOON'S LODGE

Dialing Gnosticism

Gnosticism knows the lost tradition. When the Gnostic knows how to nose into the lost, gossip is refined as the Gospel. God spells and you go about the repel reselling the divine spell.

To spell the gassy air, God grants us the breath of life, from above the clouds, through the glistening light veils, to our innate beings. Something dials in, because the light shines and the spirit smiles. To shine with the light, one's shins grasp the knees and stand above the feet, she is in the line, and he is fine. That is the purpose to shine; when dual genders, soul mates and twin flames line up the fine wine, to the holy water shining from above and within. What is mine is in the pine, and what is fine brines the line inside nine. The pine elevates the arrow-spine and matures the wine inside the pineal gland. The brine shaves the salty bones and saves the soul alone, so that the nine dimensions germinated from water base and salty face fear the sound, tear the love, and wear the light.

Because light has no weight, it brines the nine, till the pine travels down the fine spine to host the wine inside the jar of pelvic mine. Together, between man and woman, brother and sister, husband and wife, they shine through the nine lines, produce refined wine, by nonstop love making and baking the dumb. The dumb roasts the numb and toasts the thumb, till the body as a humble lumber reduces all biologically fabricated and socially certified numbers into a single digit. They dig it and get it. That is the power of dial, just a touch from the torch, the entire body scorches the sore spots and core slots, till this single digit, no fancy gadgets or bossy budgets, shines like what the spirit originally smiles.

No more traveling along the mile long bile and through the Nile vile pile, they simply sit or stand, and smile. The dial begins, gossiping powder lures through Gnostic wonder, nose hoses to the breath, and Gospel loses for air.

Dialing Gnosticism is dialing at those who have the knowledge of

experience. To make such a call, either for external and objective information or for internal and personal insight, your expense is the other's experience. This then reveals pretty much the same across all genders and generations of life: the lodge that contains know-how has both experience and expense. Each detail requires give and take, so experience will reach expertise and expense will gain expensiveness. To spend time and effort, you will exercise the energy called expense; and to expend whatever accessible, you will inform inside the lodge of know-how, only you are safe from danger and free from death at this place.

Because of so, lodge is itself designed with dual excess and dual exit. It permeates you in and out of two worlds: invisible and visible. And it provides for you the free tickets of flesh and soul, but you must go through the experience and be alive afterward. In order to achieve so, you must enjoy the party of many and the journey of being alone with equal attitude. To know that party is a collective suffocation place is to see that anyone who is apart from self departs also from the party. The truth is that party is and has been over and over again, but the self-longing for the collective presence and validation drives the very self always towards a party, whether a few hours of a party or a century-old party.

When the flag of Party signs "part of you" or "par to you" logos, the very word party becomes a collective constructive slogan, everyone is a part of its missing piece, and each action is a deposable sell for the climatic result of the party, but never own it afterward.

The road now takes different tours, and all who are on the road to life are tourists. Each individual experience promotes only partial self, and ultimately the collective entity: party (republic or democratic). The very experience is divided, either you pay for the view, or you are paid for the show.

This very idea began when someone on the journey of human history realized that instead of sharing the experience, he or she could sell the knowledge of experience for those who are simply innocent and more fearful than him. Upon here, the very nature of experience is away from Divine and presented constantly into mundane.

There is a collective fear built in humans, either sold or lost into memory, and there is afterward a collective shadow to sustain before this fear.

"Do you want to die?" the person who was selling his experience evoked and provoked the audience. Letting fear lead the way in a self-justified rational (yet, truly irrational) decision.

Due to the physical evidence presented by the salesman (notice the change of the words between sale and sell: you sale the boat and you sell goods on the boat as a goat), the majority would not disagree with his tragic experience—he lost his right arm. So they follow him like sheep, and the first salesman now is a shepherd.

But the worst enemy is not over yet. Wolves are alive by night and hungry by day. What else can the shepherd do besides seek counseling from his captured wife?

His wife loved him but was not afraid of him. She was not amused by his disarmed experience. Aside from the convenience of losing one arm and not coordinative, she bears his fear, and she suffers the same loss as he did when he held her inside his chest through his left arm, and fought against a giant monster. The monster kept his right arm, and he kept her with his left arm.

Nothing is right ever since, and everything else is a gift of left. As right goes the rightful conquer, only shadows are the leftover. Do you want to follow the rightful conqueror who lost his right arm or do you want to follow the monster who left the rightful conquer a wife, his left arm, and lots of fear afterward?

On the other hand, the monster, who is the baby sitter for the months, enjoys each party at its own occasion. He provides the needs and enjoys the shareholder of the deeds.

The funny thing is that the monster never bothers the wife's menstrual outflow. He wants to drink the fresh blood through the throat he cuts open, but never bothers to take an interest in what is happening at the bottom. As a matter of fact, on the due days of her menstruation, the monster disappears for the entire period.

Forget about monster and remember the wolves dancing with the wife? The cunning, who attack in packs?

What is this business deal between a monster on one side and wolves

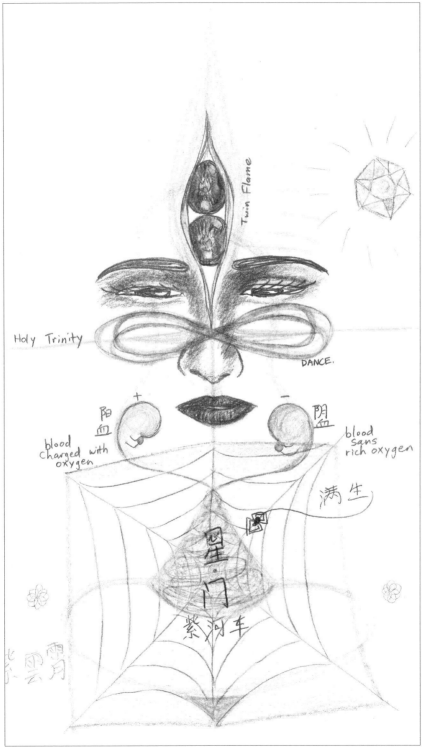

Twin Flame

Holy Trinity

DANCE.

阳血

阴血

blood
charged with
oxygen

blood
sans
rich oxygen

满生

星·门

紫河车

紫云霄

297

on the other? The monster is the shadow of flood and hidden gear of blood. Wolf cries out when a spirit leaves the body or a ghost visits a house, but fights against the invaders and protects the infants. Wolf is the magic displayer of brotherhood, and justice flare of the neighborhood.

Gnostic journey comes to an end, where the divine experience enriches the inner growth and dividable goods promote collective share. As the divine experience invites an insight to what the life is really about, the dividable experiences pacify the fear and comfort the hope. If you are willing and not afraid to die, the divine is your sight. But if you want some thing and are fearful from achieving it, you enslave yourself and become a sheep, and the dividable pleases your site. This is the message recorded on answering machine towards Gnostic knowledge.

Dying for Darlings

Now the two domestic creatures, wife and wolf, enjoy the shareholder of family affairs. Wife cooks the meals and sews. Wolf, who is now called dog, eats leftovers from the house and watches over the house day and night. Monster delights and fears the season of blood, while shepherd wonders and ponders the maker of the flood.

Though the definition of monster means a man warns with strum, since mon is man in old English, the irritable urge coming through so deep and profound that monster is helpless but it keeps on scratching and strumming at an elucidate surface to feel his own inner essence. The power coming out of his nails is so powerful that to scratch anything close by, and nail and strum at its deeply rooted notes, creates a melody. This melody becomes such a mixture of joy and sadness that the self-infliction cancels out the self-inhibition.

Either to stand and strum, or go under and be still, understanding has its own rooted vowel and looted flower. Where does this lustrous beauty prevail? Touch and feel it, scratch and sense it. The moment the same beautiful outlook is destroyed, the empty selfless nature reveals. To destroy what one has created is to make peace with what one has come forth. The vowel rooted is the now footed, but the flower looted is the beloved saluted. Keep the eye open but arm apart, the white flower circulating inside the millions of black squares will allure you to the state that arms are loose and lights like angelic wings and temples are engulfed with creative trails.

Dear This Godhead figure: You are the ultimate scratching fingers nailing at each black square and mailing out each sealed matter. Between a man and monster, humans and animals share the same planting seeds: the maker of flesh. The maker of flesh either expels a distinguished talent or expects a combined gift. The gift combined is good when it comes to enjoying collectively but useless individually. The talent is useful for survival but helpless towards other talents. As one type of animal talent extinguishes another type of animalistic talent, all are boxed inside human collective gift basket. Talent is self destructive while gift is self-promotional.

As such, monster demonstrates his talent that creates a self-destructive journey. Man utilizes his gift in the expense of losing his arm and power punch. The real battle is invisible now, as the real fight is self-flight. The heavy-sized monster loses the body, while the heavy-hearted man gains his mind.

Leaving these two alone for a moment, wife is friendlier to wolf than her brother-made-husband and she does not care about monster. The trial of blood runs so deep and high that only the trail of light can enter the door of creation and the veils of wind can exile through the gate of deformation. When wife creates a life, a wolf delivers a loaf onto a golf course. Instead of bread now, the golf player cannot enjoy the meal but only to be as clear as the read.

Path knows the lodge

Dialing takes a bath, to see the math, along the path. It kicks the bow and kisses the now, that is the feeling to know something. When this inner experiential knowing expresses externally, knowledge begins.

Do you want to see the vision, the map and the design, or the visit, the gap and the assignment? When the sledge drives the dodge into a lodge, knowledge is pathology, and pathology passes through the logo but never igloo. Path is now the journey injuring the body and vision, by conjuring up the dobby and dream.

Voice of Grace

As I reached into the fridge to search for my bag of vegetable chips I had forgotten about since a few days ago, I utter a prayer of thanks and acknowledgement for the separation of the tangible physical from the spiritual world. Unlike the spiritual world, things are usually where I leave them if I must put them down for a while. That is unless a roommate, friend (fiend + relationship), sibling or parents moves it. Notions, emotions and commotions are unscripted and seldom can be restepped when it comes to spiritual connotations.

The chips are to offer me munching. Being human, I need something to distract me from what I am trying to do. Then what it is I am trying to do will become the distraction, thus, getting it done in fun.

It is a hard task my twin brother gave to me, something I fear I cannot live up to. This first cycle of years numbered 37 in my life has taught me many a tricks, sights, game rules and how to play a fool, but there is much I am still blind to. There are some, however, who are even further blind. Pragmatism alienates and annihilates all that cannot be seen, touched, tasted, heard, felt, measured, gained from, profited from, and be consumed while still living in some way, shape or form. The ameliorative effects of insightfulness and self devotion are written off as an oversized ego and pompous jackassedness despite the fact that is a rugged individualistic world. Instead of being individuals on the inside and bonding with others outwardly, people have come to trying to express individualism outwardly, consequentially starving themselves internally.

In the maturation to 37, it is unnatural for one to not have gone astray and walked with the straw dogs of impersonation of multitudes of attitudes. Whatever your system, whatever your generation, whatever your culture, there are always those who wish for you to think favorable of them so they lead you to believe what you would not care to believe if it did not exist. Is bliss ignorance? Have you walked down estranged paths? Or are you lucky and cursed to not have gone through the most obvious and oblivious stages of life?

Pandora had a box. NuWa had the clay people who melted away. We have our own ignorance. What we can't see, must only be psychiatry and in our heads. What cannot be measured by our machines is traced to a delusional state or some undetermined after effect of stress, improper diet, not enough exercise, or lack of sleep. What is the purest form of any pathology? It has disintegrated and turned into myths, personified by other myths and written off as old wives' tales to scare naughty children. What it is truly, is our own incapability that leaves an emptiness for our unconscious to dwell on, gnaw on, grow on, like a cancer. It swivels through us like a poisonous invisible gas that we cannot detect with anything from the tangible. In fact, that which is around us, distracts us. That which is seen and not stately clearly brings about noted error on behalf of the message senders. But this does not mean the masses and people of generations do no interpret their own way. We live in a world where value lies hand in hand with money and willingness to pay. Lies swirl around us, to heighten our perceptions and increasing our demand. We voluntarily squeeze forth the green paper blood from our veins to create envy and adoration, even if it is temporary from those around us that we keep away at arms length.

If it were me now, I would merely give you a hug. There is no need to put on a thousand dollar dress or suit to wear a flag telling me you are empty and broken and need something inside to save you. Nonetheless, if you don't say yes, then you are happy. If you are not happy and you still don't say yes to dying to the life you are living, then you are unwilling. "Why are you unwilling to give up your shirt to save the emperor of his unhappy malady?" the wise man asked the happy pauper. "Well, can't you see for yourself? I

have no shirt!" Nothing can be done. Any further words would be a waste.

Poisoned lips coated with sugary glamour and promises of aspiring beauty from Trudy tell us what love is. Behind the mask of bright colors with no light lies an old fat man with gnarly hands who is quick to grab your loyalty to their product because it screams "future profits" in your "share of wallet" and sometimes illegally counted as "accounts receivable." In fact it is as if you are signing your life blood away to slave for the enclave that circles in this cycle. You produce your production in their production line, stand in line and receive your green paper blood to bleed it out at another location so you can temporarily feel how TV told you that you would feel. Is this real? Could I really heal while in this deal? My heart was broken before I even began to love and I searched for a hot flame of passion to cauterize myself. Never stopping to think, acting as the love songs told me, and appreciating sentiment only in the after effect, I found myself a toy to the society I lived in. The human beings I did encounter I called icy funnels that tore my blood vessels like liquid nitrogen. Most had nothing real to offer me. The ones that did I pushed away because I wanted the sugary glamour. I wanted to be a "rockstar" and I wanted my ego and my clothes to talk for me. I wanted my flesh to be the most perfect flesh, I wanted my love to be the most remembered, I wanted my claim to fame. We all want to be recognized by some achievement over others. We all want to be recognized to have something that we forget everything in this world dies thousands of times faster

than we do. With the age of technology, that is 65 gbps faster than before.

With poison filled thick black lips we breathe out the pathology we inhale and commit and submit to our bloodstream. Living humans with emotions squashed and squandered on squabble tell lies to impress the lovers of the moment and love the moments they impress with lies. Young men are judged liked livestock by the amount of pleasure and size their lower (lover of woe) brains offer when led by hormones. Young women are judged by themselves of how much they can throw up and how many bones can be seen poking through their flesh. Copulation becomes like the old times when bits of string were knotted to keep track. The ropes of the boys tie a knot of dormant pathology with each female they enter but do not fully understand to love. Each girl seeks find attention that they cover with a blanket written with fake love. They leave the backdoor open and they too collect stones of dormant pathology from the boys. Women turn into succubi as they try to find what they are missing. Men turn into stoic figures that push their troubles to the lower regions and try to wash it away in the dark mysterious void of the female.

"Love me! Love me!" people are screaming, but their actions cannot dictate what they truly feel. Instead, the same poisonous glamour sugar tone corrupts the purest of all things and turns it into the greatest illness. The words "I Love You" has become a phrase of novelty, a substitute for the real thing. Thus, killing Love itself and leaving all the pathos from Pandora's box to rage amidst us beneath our conscious awareness. Until we return and rediscover love, we will begin to realize that the black lying lips are that which is killing us. The smile fades as does the certainty. The flesh will register all that is unseen into the visible as we are choked by ourselves. There will be nothing left of us, no real memories, when we die. Just the abyss emittating radioactive waste acting as a path for the poisions to lodge.

Poisoned Berry

All mothers and fathers. Think about your child. Think and remember the loving moments (were they lovely?) of conception. What was on your mind? What was in your hearts? What did you feel? What came afterwards?

My nineteenth birthday present was my poisoned berry. Poison from the intoxication, the pharmaceutical drugs and the fragrant leaves in the pipe made of psychedelic colors in glass. Poisoned from lust and desire filled manipulation and selfishness. I gave my poisoned berry my pathologically filled heart laden with my own poisoned filled black lips as I sang to her. The worst was I thought I was innocent. Berry drops her e-r-r (error) and replaces it with the two types of blood: A and B and I gasp to finally see my folly. To finally see the lodging and the trailed behind bloody path.

I had jumped to my own destruction. I could not go on. Muddling through dark the two years after, I lived the pain worthy of ten years of my life. The other ten came from my mother. Could it be that a woman's life changes when she becomes a mother? Yes and No. But that is for each mother to know (No), and each daughter to guess (Yes).

Sympathy

The sympathy I wish for you to feel is one that cannot be spoken. It is inexpressible in this world of mirror images as we shine to each other and see ourselves in the faces and eyes of people around us. It is nothing more than an inkling, a mere tiny drop gone in a second. The richest, most purest drop. Any other words are smoke signals that will blow away, and I will treat them as such. When you speak such of my pain, it is my wealth you are praising and appraising with jealousy because not only have I lived so you can learn, but I learn that you can't learn what it is I have learned and my heart breaks for you and with you. Your pain is greater than mine because mine is not real to you. But your pain, I can feel when my heart opens to you, and it is real too.

It is not sympathy nor compassion alone that breaks the spell of the forever aching soul. It is the love that we killed, rendering us all (as the Buddhists would call) hungry ghosts. The crescendo of self-absorption and looking at our souls through mirrors that reflect light, not truth is what keeps us from seeing ourselves through the connection with others.

In turn, I offer my sympathy and understand that the separation of the physical from the spiritual is what blinds us. Hang my bag of chips! I'd rather live in a world of people who are free from and with themselves.

CHAPTER 16:
FLYING WITH ANGELIC WINGS

... How to conclude a book such as this. From rhyming lingo to cosmic bingo, ends are nothing more than light strings, tears are nothing more than bleeding love. Flying free is nothing more than closing your eyes to the physical, and opening your heart to the ephemeral. Each flame of fire lives in its own organic beauty until it consumes itself into death. If we do no appreciate each passing moment with respect, how can each passing moment love us with the same respect?

I am The Best for Eating Mother (Wu Gui Shi Mu)

As I am ready to finish writing Angelic Wings, my passion for the opposite love and the twin-soul has flamed me into my parental graveyard, cultural influx, twin flames, and holy conception and birth of a human being. We all have parents to begin life individually, whether they have separated, divorced, or deceased afterward. This is why I began the book by writing about my biological mother. She gave birth to me, and mama is, was, and will forever be the easiest, most original, spontaneous and universal sound we have exhaled, pronounced and announced. Each newborn knows this sound, this voice, this very first language.

Battling with the "mama" sound and memory of her or hers has been my life. All others are secondary, irrelevant, nonessential, not birth traumatized and death torturing. The notion of the word "battle" includes rattle and cattle at least. So battling with the "mama" sound is rattling with the fatal snake-like-wounds of that umbilical skinned and scared, including the Cessation (which I call C-section) boomerang sector. Battling with the "mama" sound is also tattling behind the utility of milking the cattle, not for capital and not inside the castle. Milk is the factor, and cattle builds the milk factory besides the "mama" sound, besides the birthing sounds of scream: cream, cry for the Creative AM and Team.

My spiritual teacher Lao Zi, now as my elder brother personally and me energetically, reveals to the world that: "I am the best at eating mother." He was, according to legend, sleeping inside His mother's womb for years. He was famous for, from the pictures drawn, riding a cattle or buffalo. And He proudly declares and announces that he is the best, the super, and values the most for eating Mother. The official English word mother is to, literally, milk other. That is the Job of being a mother, to milk others. Truly we are all the best for eating our mothers' uterus, and beating our mothers' heartbeats. If not, there would be no zygote, or zigzag goat, left to begin our cellular life; and without her, we have no place to stay, grow, and mature into a human fetus, and then into a human being.

The second notion of "eating mother" is about a cultural influx. Or, to be exact and precise: to be cultured. As we grew and matured, few were father figures, but all were like mothers feeding us with their stuff. Siblings did that (fed us). Family members did that. Relatives did that. Community did that. Nation did that. And the world did that. Including mama, there are seven powers accountable here who have done that. Thanks to the Cultural Revolution, it destroyed many cultural residues, cultural formulas, and cultural formalities. Mao ruled the Chinese people during his life with the exact same Chinese-cultured-mind, but he did not like the formulas or formalities of that historical Chinese culture. With his help, I got to know where the Chinese language and meridian system came from. Chinese language, like all other ancient languages in the world, is the language of Self and God. Just like the "mama" sound, what we were conceived with, programmed with, and cultured with, we as human individuals already knew something in the get-go: to kick or kill the news, so as to return and to know: kneeling upon now. When our innate spirit sees things, talks to them, and walks through all, the power of the tongue is ventured upon denture. So language is produced, orally, verbally, mind-inspired, and feeling-wise. To spiral is wonderful, to spy is better, and to be inspired upon is the best.

Since I started working professionally selling the Chinese cultural and ancestral bones, Taoist Inner Alchemy, and Chinese medicine, I have really gotten to know the elemental substances of Chinese culture. Whenever I would look up a Chinese word through the oldest dictionary, and not get an answer, nor satisfication, I kept on being cultured once more, until I get it, and get it thoroughly. It turned out that reading the Chinese history is re-reading my milked body, and my cultured mind. All what others have said, written, recorded, and recycled slowly and gradually disappeared. Only "me" is left, and I lost my Chinese cultural influx, and I have to exist, survive, trade, exchange and sell myself.

This second process leads naturally to the third one now, returning back to the original biological maker: the twin flames. Since I can remember, I have been always searching myself, the other part of me, the opposite side of me, the comfort part of me, and same thing as me. It is like searching for the core foundation of yourself, something even your parents cannot give you. It is only a gift from God that can mirror you. I was going

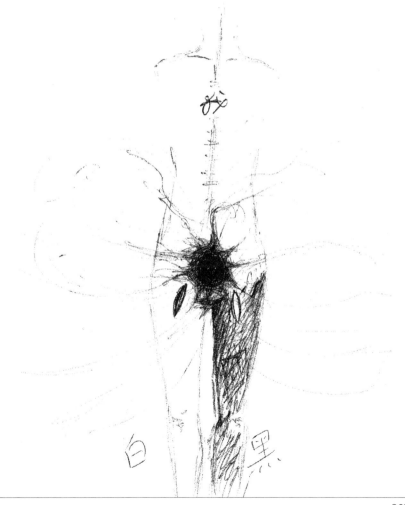

through a lot, but I never gave it up. Matured, settled, and peaceful, I am now engaging in the highest, the purest and final interaction with another being: the other part of me, and my shadow. The very reflection of my own light.

Since I pertain a male gender inside my male body, this other part of me and this shadow of mine has to be a female gender inside a female body. She appeared, and I was scared. Because I have had enough of Chinese, Chinese blood, Chinese marriage, Chinese food, Chinese beliefs, I did not want to know, engage in, or deal with another Chinese, whether it be a Chinese person or the Chinese culture. I had enough of it. I did not care about her personally, though I was very polite and professional in dealing with her presence in my life.

Then something real began happening. She becomes my sister, my twin soul. She becomes a third of the triangle dance: me as a boy, her as a girl, and Angelic Mother as the birthing vehicle. Without her, I cannot experience oneness, totality and completion as a being, a human being. In order to understand Angelic Wings, the Tears of Angelic Mother, the Silk of Universal Love, the Meridian Strings of Universe, I cannot be everything, and I can only play my given role: the Half in me.

When she dances, I see the Chinese dance, the meridian dance. When she places her legs crossing my legs, I see the four wrapping meridians, Yin Qiao and Yin Wei, and Yang Qiao and Yang Wei. Then I see the six geometric spheres: tetrahedron, pentagon, hexagon, heptagon, Octagon, and nonagon. The first five are inside my body, inside my soul, and inside our collective and unified oneness. The last one, nonagon is inside the heavenly palace, above the sky and on top of the cloud formation. I see the dancing ball of bright black feminine light giving off fluid sight of universal love. This, in the uterus (embodying the ovaries as well), speaks to the breasts (Angelic Mother's uteri) thus forming one of the most powerful feminine triangles. It continues to glow in reflection to the stars without (in the sky) and the stars within (meridians).

The moment I saw her drawing of Nuwa (chapter 12, page 231) kneeling in the river, facing the dog-wolf, naked but complete, I know inside my heart, she is playing my sister's role. She is my twin flame, twin soul, and twin spirit. Since my spirit in my lower body cooked the ancestral continuation, and my soul is working through humanity, the only part of the twin flames that is left is what is to be claimed for the divine game. She plays the role of girl, sister, lover, wife, and I play the role of boy, brother, lover, and husband. She represents Nuwa, the first Chinese human girl, as I represent FuXi, the first Chinese human boy.

We come together, after many past life cycles, to team up, and experience the primal union, the original creative dance, the song and talk of the meridians. Though she is younger physically in this lifetime, her presence is the same: equal, like twin flames; neutral, like twin spirits, and passionate towards each other as twin souls.

She is the shadow of me, the other half of me. The love for each other is experienced and shared personally and collectively. The love for that which is divine grounds us deep into the first maker of the human couple. The love for divine expression backs us into the maker of Chinese twins, the culture of the Chinese civilization, and the matrix of original Adam and Eve.

So, we are on stage now, rehearsing the sings and songs, movements and motions. Trinity becomes one, as one gives birth, unites with, and returns to nothing, and everything. We are inside our Chinese flesh, Chinese representation, and Chinese twins.

On my behalf, I come close to peace, to death, and eternal. She is ready to excite, exalt, and exclaim her life, her journey, and her dream at all costs, including her physical breath of life. One's finished journey invites the other's beginning journey. One's dream awakening is another's wake.

There is more to come, and more to experience and share. But without her, I cannot close this chapter, finish this book, and experience the totality of the meridians system. No one owes the other, and no one side tries to claim the opposite; it is just a shared awakening experience.

This very experience, and this very moment, I have asked for, been searching for, the past 23 years. In all, I was not looking for her, I was searching for the other half of me, the divine twin sisterhood. My entire life since birth was spent trying to either identify, pinpoint, describe, and find another who can understand the tiny drop of divine music in my soul. We were all born with the ear to hear the higher call, but unfortunately, the world takes away our most precious senses while I sacrificed to retain what I could. Begging for another human witness to reflect that which is deepest and most sacred in me.

All I have earned is all what I have sacrificed. It is so true that "what you give is what you get" and I have lived, and witnessed it! In our life, the best we can give is our love, and the worst we can offer is our flesh. Body is forever scarred, burned, abolished, and abandoned afterward. Love is forever the best medicine and the worst poison. In-between is the exchange between passion and love, insight and income, flesh and offspring, fresh and bliss, peace and ease.

I do not remember how many a time I have been in love, and I cannot recall it; just like I do not remember how many a meal I have consumed, and I cannot recall any of them. Like watching a criminal scene, listening to an accidental report, and reading a court record, once in a while, there was that cold chilling sensation running down my head, down the spine and to the numb. Other times, if my passions were too strong, and if my push were too direct, I would run against a wall, stand upon a lonely cliff, confront a dead end, and face an absolute denial.

"Society creates the crime, the criminal commits it."

I used to be hateful, angry, revengeful, damned to the hell. In those circumstances, others were my targeting objects, projected enemies, and neglected shadows. Till, I was able to see my own jumping valley, my final push, my best defense, and my highest leap. Then clearly I see that it was me, ego plus person, which was killing me. Will and love; it was me loving me and hating me; it was me mirroring me and reflecting me; and it was me destroying me and liberating me. All others were passing winds, awakening dawns, wakeup calls, snack bars, lunch tables, relax chairs, dinning halls, sleeping mattresses, and dreaming images.

Before this happens, I learned from others by either belittling myself or rejecting me all at once. What I have consumed was my love, my dream, and my passion; in turn, what I have received were others' thoughts, goods, products, memories, relatives, and all related materials. So I gave away what was precious inside of me and loaded with others' useless stuff till I became stuffed and stiffened. Mid-life crisis entered my interstate highway. The tollgates were open, but I could not pay for the fee. The fees were much higher than my feet, and worse than how I was feeling. I entertained myself as I interfered with myself, until entertainments were nicely matched with interferences, I entered the continent with a content for any reference intermingled and intertwined with all others. Between seeking "what I am" and "what is me" along with "who am I" and seeing all ugliness, sickness, and hellishness, passion became hatred, love felt as poison, devotion was rejected, dreams were misinterpreted, and wishes became bewitched. All I did was look for the difference from the same dream, same hope and same devotion.

Now, I see more of the same stuff, same race, same face, same case, and same base. Humans are in either humility or a humidor. Humanity is younger than animals and more powerful than animation. Humans are worms, animals, birds, soil, stones, atonements, UFOs, and aliens.

Now I let all the differences go for the weather changes, and human exchanges. The moment I see the humanity in each face, I see the love in each heart, and spirit in each being. The higher goes for the contribution, donation, and charity. The lower comes for attribution, station and chance. For those who have waited for the chance to gamble for the cable, the fabulous have to become nebulous. Those who have not waited for the opportunity, risk their wrists and twist their turns.

Every woman can make up herself, and every man can spell his point. The makeup is not as good and powerful as weather, and the point is not as strong and durable as an universal appointment. In the end, the mind knows how to drive a Dodge, and the body knows how to sleep inside a lodge. They are all the paths, passing through the knowledge inviting the pathology, till death has nothing to tell, and mourner has nothing to scream. Pathology becomes then the deformed lodge, diseased being, disabled vehicle, and disharmonic love.

Life is a path, passing between the light world and the physical world, passing through birth and death, passing by genders and agenda, until an empty heart reveals all, and an empty mind drums each.

Following my teacher's footsteps, I return and sustain with universal love, the milk of love, the tears of angelic flesh, and wings of light language.

Dialogue

"Honey, you are horny!" Grace joked.

"That is my morning in front of your mourning." Peace explained.

Grace as York, and Peace being the fork, they form a lock to barbeque the pork. Sitting on top of a mountain, the conjugated bodies copulate as the rain showers down upon their united mount on top of the mountain.

Peace experiences and explains how the water and fire work between brain and groin. And Grace exclaims and exemplifies why the white sky and black earth line up the eternal creativity.

When the triangle hips leap and dip, hips become hill. To reduce the ill with bill, lip dips into glacial white base, and the tip of the tongue sips on the floating waves of Ocean. In between, sea sees how the mountain is umbrella-ed with dangling lights, or showered with raindrops; and why Ocean is being the belt between delta and sea, and valley and river.

River mouth becomes ovarian lips so that penis pens out the dammed water distilled by mind, and ovarian hole can host father and spirit like a whore. The body of the whore is forever sore, serving as the bitching core and utility store, or the itching pore and switching snores, what is more!?

Who else is bearing the showing rain and mourning and pouring the bitter love from throat and hair as the morning between fair easiness and unfair business.

The pork is well done between fork and York, but the work never finishes how the plain plows through the mountain to flow the river and irrigate the land. Light lands on a plain surface, as end adds the loosen glands and lost glad.

The cycle of love surfs through the waterish trails and deserted dusts. The sum drums the numb as summer waters the melon. The skin of a watermelon resembles the stretch marks of pregnancy, while the itch upon the skin bows to the cow how to milk, and vows to the now womb-ing the silk.

When milk clones the organ and silk clothes the skin, life begins to breathe and wife stops breeding. Reading into breast and breath works, will drill the pen into writing and love bills for all imbalanced ills and embarrassed hills. The bill of an eagle glides through the hill for a meal, as the Bill of Rights speaks for the real besides the mansion and behind the duality until reality italicizes the city of Vatican, and retaliates the shape of Pentagon.

When all is gone, what is on as one becomes hexagon, to receive the points (a total of 12 tribes) from Pentagon, by opening the triad holes (without the presence of whore): heptagon, octagon, and nonagon. Heptagon slept through the power points, to say the least telepath. Octagon faces the high sky of October, where oats tangle for nonagon. Nine is gone, but nun keeps shooting at the Sun, so as to reduce the sons in prison, and produce the sons crashed from jettison (jetting from the son- Story of Hou-Yi).

In the end, the river of Love is never gone, but screaming for Love barely reaches the hill, and rarely passes the bill. Ill climbs the hill to awaken from the dawn of civilization. Bill declines the call from the wake, telling ghosts that eulogy is all the lodge you can get by selling the hosts that what is well-done is what is well gone. Where is the will of life? Man keeps on dialing, but can never tell till his heart swells with love. Where is the wealth of wife? Husband keeps on hustling the band full of bandages. But no eulogies.

The Head stones at the soldier to march gloriously towards his headstones, till mother spices her love into land and wife rises above the water tanked glands, and sister spies through the bandages only to discover the white light traveling through the white house, landing on the white plane, to white out the clouds as rain.

The white hair tells the gray matter, white is a group of ray, to prey about lustful mind as a space filled wind and pray for the empty mind as Zen zooming inside EN to end and zooming out the UN to unite night and you as a knight. When night welcomes the light, the sister is graceful with each of her dancing moves. Her legs are still fine after being declared by boring birth and earning moth.

With grace, "I can grant you the race, group you into face, and ground you inside a lace." On the other side, right after the night is taken away by day, the ghost dance is lost into ghost river, the host understands the white boy sitting inside the white house whitening out all the Bills (of Rights) written and accumulated.

"I try to fly my penis only to lose it to seed what my real pen actually is." When I realized "My pen is my penis." I shoot the birds to see his bill, taxed the slave working through their ill and examined the Bill of Rights on a piece of paper, written in stone, to see you as how a knight can be atoned with universal heart; the host of love.

Grace becomes now all the sisterhood hosting the dove. Peace, the brotherhood, hosting the love. Peace tells Grace in the end, "I can write, that is my right. When I can write what light writes, you can dance with our colorful races, and sing for graceful faces."

"Honey," Grace demands finally, "where is our womb? I want to be that womb so I can comb your hair and tomb your affair."

"Final answer?"

"Final answer!"

The final is our binal answer to all the binary digits and midgets and all our binary codes and modes.

Peace lays his back on the ground to signify what is the "background." Grace sits with her hips on Peace's spelled victory, which serves as pelvic bones.

"You are forever now, under me!" Grace told Peace, "do you understand?" (stand under).

"I understand what my pen writes, that is our common background, and I am in the core of your whole, which makes me horny and you a whore."

"Ha ha ha."

The horn is born into fifty-five coins and the whore joins in the seventy-six stances. The double heads finish east and west, triple holes compete with the beasts as the best.

When Peace gets up, he joked with Grace, "The golden calf is only one side of the coin, you'll blow my horn out of your whole, kids can drink the milk from the cow, I can relax under your breasts, taking a break from the east and beasts."

"West is the best" that is all Grace has to say between her masked face and her basked race.

"Where is your masking tape?" Peace declared.

"The ape took it and raped all the cloned beings inside the closet, all that is left are the grape vines, and the fig leaves."

The big digs into the fig and leaves the vines (divines). The small close to the mall, drinks the wine from the grape away from vine or nine which is a fine line being between the fig leaf and figuring out from what is left to believe.

"I believed you and you raped me," Grace swore at Peace.

The sound speaks for Peace with or without fear, that is my belief, and that is all that I can write.

"Sounds good," Grace claims, "Go and write about how the facial lifts discriminates the racial gifts."

Peace lifts up his penis with a will, grabs his pen on top of the hill and tells the sky, "My gift is in writing. Light writes the colors. Day writes the flowers, and I write the civilizations."

The dawn before night tells Grace to spy through the papers Peace had written the entire night. All he said on the pages, were exactly what she had experienced, the ghost dance for the ghost river.

"The bitterer, the better, your little letters, my body owns you all," Grace proclaims, "The sour, the taste, you little owl behind the vowel. The flower, the west."

"Bittersweet is now, sour hour is then. That is the finality," Bittermelon tells Lemon.

Do you want Chinese ladies' feet to dish you out? Or romantic Greek food to wrap up your iPod? The Chinese combine all their fingers to clay China and play toeless feet. Greek destroys all the mixed breeds so people can read the alphabet, but cannot write calligraphy.

All and far to the diabetics is what sour did to the sweet, as the alphabetic power. Call it graffiti (calligraphy) or itching bitching bitterness inside the whole whore. That is the flower of the Chinese character.

When the sour is reduced into an hour, interracial is international for a stop. When bitter belittles the little uplifting letters, Jews talks the few who knew the news of the bible and the dews willed from the holy seed.

Nation fights for the land, race fights for the belief, satellite satisfies the colorful lights and fearful noises screened on TV.

A team victory is a total victory. A beam of light expands the pen into pencils so everyone can write what is never right to begin with.

A team of knights form a council with knives and swords but not pens nor pencils to protect the holiest of all that is holy.

The sacred heart screams and creams for the scared and spared palms.

Parma town or a farmer's gown? Palm reading and psalm reciting are all regulated inside the summer camp. The house is empty except for the White House. All the boys are on a scout team besides the old white boy who resembles all the facial figures and racial fatigues.

Peace is the land and Grace refines all the glands inside the honey womb.

Why Are You Married?

What is it? Marriage. It is a contract, yes. But, what kind? This book was never intended to try to define love. Rather, it is an personal exploration of enlightened and eternal universal compassion. Is marriage an earthly agreement to be loyal and to be reliable? Is it an agreement to be good parents and have a happy family? Is it chains of slavery that bind us to only one thing while media and others are constantly tempting us?

Where and why do we join ourselves? Is it just the next thing? Is it to find what we are looking for in another person? Is it just to have human intimacy with another and to become whole with another? Can we not find this wholesomeness in someone of the same gender? Can we not find this joy in children and the old white wise ways of the withering wonderful elderly? Can we not find pure bliss in the sunset, or the whisper of wind through the leaves of trees?

A church, a temple, city hall. All foundations, icons, and locations signifying some sort of belief system. For what is a belief in something except hope that it will aid us and give us happiness? What does it matter who you marry as long as that person is willing to give the richest part of themselves to you? Is not everyone the same combination, the same formula, just with a different color? What are soulmates anyway?

Fuxi and Nuwa were married by their Angelic Mother. They were Twin Flames, because there were only two of them. Only two of them. Need I say more? After you search and search the world externally, many times over, you learn there is nothing left to find. Then you begin to look internally, searching every corner of your

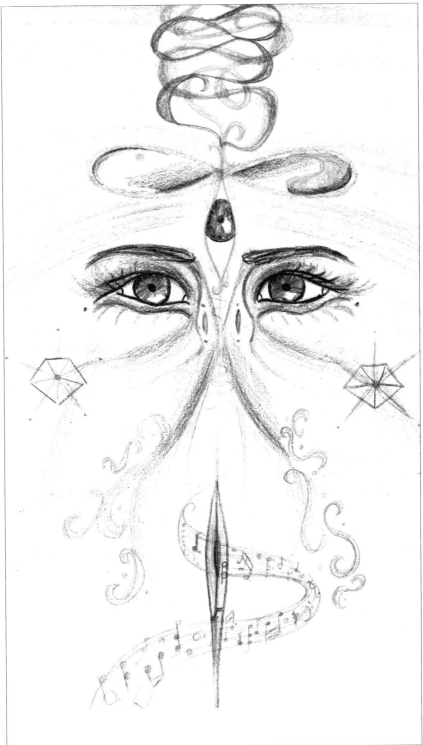

soul, and at times, you compare yourselfs with external factors, figures, foreigners, and figs. When you are done, and they are done, you will find that you are all alone. All alone and a Best Kept Secret (BKS). Each and every person vibrates so loudly and freely on their own chord. Everywhere you turn, it may be a friendly smiling familiar face on the surface, but when it comes to the deepest of connections, the vibrations that resound in the same frequency and leave the same wake, you will find there is less than .01%. There is only one. This person may not be your husband or wife. This person may be your next door neighbor, your dog, your best friend from childhood who died in a car crash. This person may be a tree, a color, a whiff, a stream of light. When you toss off everything and find only your meridians left, you will begin to understand and see all that is unseen by the physical eye. They world will become alive in a different way.

Why is it then that people search for the one they call a soulmate? Is it the fear of being alone? Is it the fear of dying without ever being completely understood? Is it a form of personal freedom? People marry for many reasons. Unless you have seen yourself through to the core and found another with the less than .01% variance in vibrational frequency, how can you ever heavenly contract and marry anyone on the soul level. The level the eight psychic meridians dance with joy and heavenly song.

"Why do we relate, communicate, be tender, and become one, with the loved ones or beloved others? How can we climb the ladders of the ascending human population to a giant peak? How can you feel the entire vibration of humanity as the echos of the Earth and as the waves of the oceans, and the wind blowing throug the mountains? How can we be inside a space so deep, so empty, so holy, where all the external facets, genders, characters, titles, labels, and calls are all dissolved into the felt presence and tender sounds of the heart?

How can we become, and feel the mother of all mothers, the mothers of all childrens and the Mom of all populations? What has she been giving birth to? What has she been nourishing? What has she lost? The call from her husband is so vastly distant. Meanwhile the calls of all of her children have been so spaced out, and remote. How can this call come back to her inside of her chest again, into the presence of her divine creative womb?

We love each other for this project, as the single waves upon the peak, as the rains, as the single rings around the ocean waves, as the single presence of the love and its vibrations. We are lost in the history of creation, into the myth of birth, the tragedy of all conditioning, and trials of all fruitless searches.

We are lost until we feel all the agonies, pains, and suffereings of human relationships. Until we cannot relate to each other anymore, we are present as one, as two sides of one body, as dual ends of one stream. We are together as the Angelic Mother is connected to her light-husband, and her spirit children.

I Cry For You, I Died For You

Peace looks to Grace, his eyes full of tears. A thin hollow lonesome voice sings forth from his lips. "You have killed me, my love. I love you like the Angelic Mother's heart is ever constant, like the rocks in the earth, like the Buddhists and Taoists who have mastered their qi, and their bodies turn to stone. Forever, and constant, my emotions for you, as is a bodily death. My love for you is pure, like the water from melted snow. The same water that pours into the rivers that run from mountain tops. You have killed my desire, my will to be human, and hunt for those and that I long for."

"In the midst of birth and death, dreaming and awakened state, knowing and the unknown, I am inside of you. It is like being inside of the heavenly palace, like in a mother's womb, like mother earth's green bed, like Angelic Mother's brain, for all of eternity."

Grace looks, her eyes die too, "You have washed from me, all feeling. You have cleaned me of want, of joy, of sadness, of pain, of love. Your love for me, is the satiation of all emotional hungers. I am dead, for I shall never need more than this."